Two Plus Two

Two Plus Two

Couples and Their Couple Friendships

GEOFFREY L. GREIF
KATHLEEN HOLTZ DEAL

Routledge
Taylor & Francis Group
New York   London

Routledge
Taylor & Francis Group
711 Third Avenue
New York, NY 10017

Routledge
Taylor & Francis Group
27 Church Road
Hove, East Sussex BN3 2FA

© 2012 by Taylor & Francis Group, LLC
Routledge is an imprint of Taylor & Francis Group, an Informa business

Printed in the United States of America on acid-free paper
Version Date: 20111003

International Standard Book Number: 978-0-415-87927-9 (Paperback)

Library of Congress Cataloging-in-Publication Data

Greif, Geoffrey L.
  Two plus two : couples and their couple friendships / Geoffrey L. Greif, Kathleen Holtz Deal.
    p. cm.
  Includes bibliographical references and index.
  ISBN 978-0-415-87927-9 (pbk. : alk. paper)
  1. Friendship. 2. Man-woman relationships. 3. Married people. 4. Couples. I. Deal, Kathleen Holtz. II. Title.

BF575.F66G736 2012
155.6'45--dc23   2011028348

Visit the Taylor & Francis Web site at
http://www.taylorandfrancis.com

and the Routledge Web site at
http://www.routledgementalhealth.com

Contents

Preface

We bring to this book on couple friendships more than 75 years of experience as partners in marriage—Geoff to Maureen for more than 35 years and Kathy to Dave for more than 40 years. In our own lives we have come to appreciate the importance that couple friendships hold for us. We each have close couple friends born of individual friendships that have morphed into couple friendships as well as couple friends each couple has met from moving into new neighborhoods, attending church or synagogue, or meeting couples through our children. We have traveled with other couples, sometimes just as a foursome and other times in larger groups of friends. We have celebrated joyous occasions with our couple friends and shared tears with them when life's turns have been difficult or sad.

We (Kathy and Geoff) value the friendships that we have with our couple friends. These friendships enable us to spend time with our spouses while also socializing with others. We learn from our friends how they handle children, aging parents, and work conflicts. We learn from our friends the many ways they show affection for each other. We witness how they live their lives and nourish each other. From our friends we see more options for how we can live our lives. These "two-plus-two" relationships are no small gifts. While we all have individual friendships, those friendships do not allow us to collectively, as a couple, hear and experience others. Individual friendships can be more self-centered experiences. Although they hold enormous value, they are different than what happens when one couple shares an experience with another couple. In the sharing, the partners in a couple experience not only the other couple but also each other.

Despite the enormous benefits that we derive, being with another couple requires negotiation. How do we weigh time with just our spouse versus time with another couple? How do we still have time for our individual friends and for ourselves? How do we decide whether we want to pursue a friendship with a couple we recently met? What happens if we like one member of the couple and not the other? What happens if we think we are being dropped by the other couple because we weren't invited to a Christening or a Bar Mitzvah? What if one spouse wants to discuss a private matter with the couple and the other just wants to go out with a couple and have fun? And, finally, how open are we to making new couple friends versus trying to maintain the ones that we have?

These questions help us to frame the book. As we consider our own experiences with couples, we bring our personal perspectives to the findings of the research presented. For example, we have come to see that partners in couples are not always on the same page when it comes to their interest in socializing with other couples. Some people tend to be introverts and others extroverts. They bring that style of interaction to their couple friendships. When two extroverts are together, they may tend to frequently look for other couples, a style of orientation to friendships that we call *Seekers*. Two introverts may be more content hanging out alone and may only consider one or two couples as friends. They may be very content in their relationship being together and alone. We call them *Nesters* as they are content staying in their home (or nest). People in the middle, or people who have different friendship tendencies from each other, may compromise and take a middle position on making friendships. We call them *Keepers*. They have a fair number of friends, often a full social life with family, and are not actively seeking others but would not shy away from them. This categorization got traction with many couples that we interviewed for the book. By the completion of our research, we were asking couples where they saw themselves, and most could easily see themselves in these descriptions.

We also asked couples what they did with their couple friends. While we heard about specific activities, we also learned that many people use couple friends to have a good time and a smaller number see these friendships as a venue for sharing emotions. In fact, those couples that were the most interested in making friends (*Seekers*) were also the most interested in going out with friends to have a good time. More on this later!

As we introduce you to the couples (both married and partnered) in this book, we have taken a bit of a literary license by sprucing up some of their quotes and removing unneeded words to make the passages easier to read. We have not changed the intent of what is said.

In the chapters that follow, we hope that an understanding of friendships in general, and couple friendships in particular, will help readers to derive the most from the relationships that they have. While we possess strong convictions that drive how we each have managed our own couple friendships, we do not think any one way works for all couples. Our emphasis is on presenting options to consider through the words of those we interviewed and the literature on friendships and on couples. Our own suggestions are also included in the final chapter. If couples who read the book end up with a clearer appreciation of how friendships can operate, we will have achieved our goal in writing the book.

Authors

Geoffrey L. Greif, DSW, LCSW-C, is a professor at the University of Maryland School of Social Work. He is the author of books and articles related to family issues and men and women's relationships. A previous book of his, *Buddy System: Understanding Male Friendships* (Oxford University Press), was published in 2009. In 2010, he received the University of Maryland Board of Regents faculty award for teaching.

Kathleen Holtz Deal, PhD, LCSW, is an associate professor at the University of Maryland School of Social Work. She is the author of articles and book chapters related to supervision and professional development. In 2011, she received the award as outstanding teacher at the University of Maryland Baltimore campus.

1

Two Plus Two
Couples and Their Couple Friendships

Tracy is a pediatric surgeon and her husband, John, is a stay-at-home dad with their 2-year-old son, Jeff. By any standard, she is highly successful. She is one of a few females in a traditionally male branch of medicine. John balances a part-time job that requires international travel with his child rearing responsibilities in this couple with reversed roles. Very much in love with each other, they want to add to their family. Getting pregnant a second time was difficult for them but, after a recent round of *in vitro* fertilization, twins are on the way. Tracy works long hours, sleeps little, and crams Jeff into her awake time at home. Tracy and John were once self-described party animals with a wide circle of friends and family to keep them company on their jaunts. That was before residency and parenthood brought their socializing to an inevitable end. That was also before they moved to Chicago to pursue her career.

They had couples friends in their hometown, friends of long standing that each had brought into the marriage. Tracy admits she and John are not socially adventurous now—they tend to stick within their own circle. They don't interact easily with others, in part because of their rare living arrangement of a working mom and stay-at-home dad. They had hoped Jeff would be the conduit to new couple friends but that has not happened, due perhaps to their reverse child care and work arrangement. It is difficult for John to make friends with stay-at-home moms. Tracy recently met another female surgeon at the hospital, but she is married to a man in his 20s, someone to whom Tracy, in her 30s, cannot relate. While she does not believe her marriage is suffering because they are couples-challenged, she would like to use the little free time she and John have to socialize with each other as well as with another couple, preferably one like them—with children. She misses the magic of couple friendships they had when they were first married and living in another city. Other couples were fun to be with, and Tracy and John often found themselves going to events or activities they would not have chosen on their own. These other couples helped Tracy and John enjoy each other more, too. But in a new city, such friends are hard to find.

Michael and Abby live in a small college town where he is a professor and she is a museum volunteer. Now in their late 50s, they have been married 20 years after having been fixed up by a matchmaker service before such services went online. Looking for another couple to befriend, with whom they could go to dinner or the movies, they advertised on craigslist. What they got were invitations to swing. They removed their ad.

Greg is the manager of a large home improvement store, and Sally is an elementary school teacher. Both are in their 40s. He works long hours, often on weekends. They've been married 3 years, and both have teenage children from previous marriages. Sally and her first husband enjoyed friendships with other couples they met through his job as a police officer, but these friendships ended with their divorce. She'd like to develop some new couple friendships with Greg. He's less interested in spending time with other couples, and his weekend work hours make it hard to find couples who can accommodate their schedule.

FRIENDSHIPS WITH OTHER COUPLES—GETTING STARTED

What do Tracy and John, Michael and Abby, and Greg and Sally have in common? They are all interested, to varying degrees, in the prospect of making friends with other couples. Tracy and John are desperately seeking other couples—they are new to town and want to construct a friend-filled life like they had in their hometown. Michael and Abby, though childless, are in a similar boat but in a much smaller environment. Their odds of finding a couple where they both like both partners are slim. Sally and Greg are in a different predicament—she is in the hunt and he is not. What these three couples also have in common is that they all find this process is difficult and demanding at worst and highly fulfilling at best.

THE IMPORTANCE OF COUPLE FRIENDSHIPS

People with friends live longer, healthier, and happier lives.[1] Friends keep us on our toes, socially engaged, and mentally active. They teach us how to play bridge, shoot a basketball, and cook a new dish. They point us in the direction of the next Oscar-nominated movie, Pulitzer Prize–winning book, and the best wine for the value. We place sports bets with friends, watch how they raise their children, and travel with them to near and far places.

Friends monitor our health[2] and can be the portals to better health care. Many of us have friendships where psychotherapy, exercise, annual checkups, weight watching, and smoking cessation are encouraged. We drive friends to the doctors and nurse them with chicken soup, pep talks, telephone calls, e-mails, and home visits. These are the fruit that individual friendships bear.

Couples who get along happily with each other benefit from their relationship. Linda Waite, a sociologist, and Maggie Gallagher, Director of the Marriage Program at the Institute of American Values, write, "Overall, the portrait of marriage that emerges from two generations of increasingly sophisticated empirical research on actual husbands and wives is [that] ... a good marriage enlarges and enriches the lives of both men and women."[3] According to the U.S. Department of Health and Human Service's Web site for the Healthy Marriage Initiative, those men who are happily married, as compared to those unhappily married, are physically and emotionally healthier and live longer. Women who are happily married are also physically and emotionally healthier than those who are not happily married.[4]

Spouses (partners) often consider each other friends and sometimes each other's best friend. Equality between partners can be an important ingredient in building a solid relationship.[5] Marriage Enrichment groups often teach the importance of friendship, according to Lauri Przybyzs, Coordinator of Marriage and Family Life for the Catholic Archdiocese of Baltimore. Many of the Marriage Enrichment Web sites support this as they encourage partners to be friends with each other so a spouse will not seek friendship outside of a marriage. Research suggests that if one does not have a best friend, the spousal relationship becomes even more important to one's well-being.[6] Friendship between partners is also recognized as a key ingredient in marital happiness, according to psychologist John Gottman,[7] whose thinking we will discuss shortly.

Further, couples who share friends (which include individuals or family members) tend to be happier.[8] These couples get to be together with friends and family and engage in enjoyable and meaningful activities. They are more fully integrated into their social network if friendships are shared and this may reinforce their own relationship.

So here we have the benefits of individual friendships, the benefits of being happily married to a person who is also a friend, and the benefits of sharing friends. This book will explore how friendships work between couple friends and how we believe a better understanding of these friendships leads to a happier marriage or partner relationship. We believe couples may not only derive great enjoyment from their friendships with other couples but they are likely to appreciate each other more. Their marriage or relationship will be strengthened by couple friendships. Tracy and John, while not unhappy, would be happier, she says, if they had couple friends.

We maintain a focus on partnerships as well as marriages because partnerships are becoming an increasing part of the couple landscape. According to a recent Pew Report, 39% of those polled believed marriage was becoming obsolete, up from 28% 30 years ago. In addition, a higher percentage of adults (48%) are now not married, whereas in 1960 28% were not married. Finally, cohabitation has been on the rise, particularly among those under 50, 44% of whom indicated they have cohabitated, nearly twice the percent as in 1990.[9] In our sample, nearly one quarter of those interviewed are not married.

Friendship with another couple is "value added." As we will discuss in the next chapters, with the help of the voices of many couples, well-functioning couple friendships make a marriage more fulfilling and exciting because of the following reasons:

1. Each partner is comfortable with the couple friendship, and the nourishment and fun that arises from that friendship make partners more attractive to each other.
2. The couple's marriage or relationship is more apt to be reinforced by being with another couple (as opposed to being with a single friend).
3. Each partner interacts with the opposite sex friend, which can lead to greater understanding of his or her own partner and men and women in general.

In addition, and related to marital happiness, couple friendships can strengthen individual friendships that the couple has with one or both members of the other couple. Many of the couples interviewed for this book described friendships that began on a one-to-one basis; the men knew each other from college or the women met at work and then introduced their spouses to each other. The opportunity to still go out alone with the close friend as well as with the other partners of the friends reinforces the earlier friendship.

What Affects Friendships?

Despite some of the obvious advantages to great couple friendships, making friends with another couple is not always easy. To understand why it is difficult, we first need to break the friendship-making process down to the individual level. This is where many friendships begin.

Research (ours and others') confirms that men's and women's friendships are constructed differently and, because of this, working together to make friends as a couple can be daunting. For example, women's friendships have been portrayed as based on face-to-face interactions as opposed to men's on shoulder-to-shoulder activities. Women will get together for coffee, sit across from each other, and talk. Men will watch a game (sitting shoulder-to-shoulder on the couch while they do so) or compete in a sport. Men are activity driven, perhaps because our cavemen relatives hunted side-by-side while our cavewomen relatives conversed and cared for the children in the village (or the cave). Women's friendships are more verbal, physically expressive, and self-revelatory than men's. In addition, and not insignificantly, women need more frequent contact with their friends to maintain their friendships than do men.[10] Men do not need as much conversation and, instead, are in greater need of sharing an activity.[11]

Differences Between Women and Men

Other differences exist between how men and women manage their friendships with their same-sex friends. From research specifically comparing men and women, men are more likely to engage in sports with their men friends than women are with their women friends. Women are more likely to shop with their friends than are men. Men are more apt to help their friends by giving advice while women help their friends by being verbally and emotionally supportive. Finally, women are less likely to express concerns about appearing homosexual when with their same-sex friends than are men. This concern prevents some men from being as expressive with their male friends as they wish to be.[12] This affects what they do with guys and to what extent they pursue friendships with other men. This is why, in part, sports play such an important role in their friendship activities—it is a socially acceptable way for men to spend time together.

These differences, which are just a few of the ones we could have cited, affect what couples want from their couple friendships, what they do when with other couples, and how often they need to see other couples to maintain the friendship. For example, based on these findings, conversations between couples may be more satisfying for men if concrete advice is given about how to solve a work-related problem. Women tend to process the problem more, be supportive and less direct with suggestions. Women may feel they need more contact with the other couple to maintain the friendship than do men. When socializing with the other couple, women may feel more comfortable being emotionally expressive. In numerous interviews for the book, men described feeling as if a boundary had been crossed when their partners began discussing issues they thought were just between them. Women, in turn, sometimes felt the focus was too much on politics or sports and not enough on emotional sharing.

In one situation we know, the wife is concerned the husband is not talking about his feelings enough with others. At some point in the evening, and acting out of loving concern for him, she may engineer a discussion of a topic so that he will have an opportunity to hear how others feel.

Age as a Factor in Friendships

It is not just that women's and men's friendship styles are different. Other considerations are also at play when we think about couples' friendships. Take age, for example. Remember the intensity of friendships in the teen years? Forget homework, housework, or studying for the SATs. Being with friends took precedence. Knowing that Sally told Jerry about what Susie and Billy did behind the backs of Johnny and Monique at Michelle and Henry's party after the prom surpassed in all importance what happened in Sarajevo that sparked World War I. Friendships do not remain at that level of intensity throughout adulthood for many of us. With age, they tend to reduce in intensity when we marry (or partner), get to the world of work, and have children. We have less time to extend ourselves outside of the home. We are trying to earn a living, attending parent-teacher conferences, and grabbing a few minutes of alone time with our partners. Friends often become temporarily less vital to our well-being if our lives are filled with other obligations. But friends return in importance later in life. When the children are grown, jobs are stable, and retirement looms, we become interested in friends again, as we have more free time.[13]

With age, we also become more relaxed about friendships. Age brings greater acceptance of others. According to research, both men and women are more tolerant of friends (we are less judgmental) and make greater attempts to resolve differences with age.[14]

Gender and age can intersect. Though we are less likely to show the gender-specific behavior we displayed when younger,[15] differences based on gender do remain. Older women continue to have larger, more emotionally close, friendship networks than men.[16] Older men, like younger men, are more apt to try and "go it alone." For example, if they are taking care of an ill spouse, they are less likely to reach out to others for help than are women. This could result in greater social isolation for a man.[17]

Sometimes men end up relying on their wives for help. We found that men are more likely to credit their partners as the social secretaries than the reverse. One woman, responding to one of our blog postings about friendships recently wrote:

> My husband doesn't have any real friends in our city because he says he already had a group of good friends back home (it's across the country and they barely see each other) and doesn't think he'll ever find anyone like that. Thus, he doesn't really try. It has been this way for years here. As a result, 99% of his social life is with me and what my friends include us in. He doesn't insist in joining me for everything I do, but he looks to me to be his activity partner for everything. What do you make of his reason for not having friends here—that he isn't trying because he doesn't think he would find anyone? He's not hugely outgoing, but not shy either.

For this couple, couple friends may be the only way to persuade the husband to socialize.

Race as a Factor in Friendships

Race is also related to the maintenance of friendships, according to some research. African American men and women are believed to disclose more interpersonal information to their friends than do whites.[18] Why is this? It could be that blacks have a greater sense of collectivism than whites, who tend to be more individualistic.[19] In other words, blacks feel a greater connection to the community and to their families.[20] Minority groups frequently have banded together while majority groups have not needed the support of the community to the same extent. It could be anticipated that, with this greater level of disclosure, African Americans would also place a greater emphasis on friendships with others than would whites. But one team of researchers[21] who looked at white and black women has called this into question—they found that black women had fewer friends and similar levels of support as white women. As the United States becomes increasingly diverse in the 21st century, how race moderates friendships is yet to be seen. Interracial couples add even greater complexity to the intersection of race and friendship.

Socioeconomic Class in Friendships

Gender, age, and race matter in how individual friendships are carried out. So does money. The research on class and friendships tends to show that working-class men are more apt than upper-class men to develop friendships at work[22] and to place a higher value on those friendships.[23] Working-class women's friendships are likely to remain centered on the context in which the women meet (e.g., work, a shared activity, or membership in a group) while middle-class women extend their friendships beyond their immediate context by reaching out more.[24] In addition, working-class women tend to rely on family and relatives for ongoing support while middle-class women, who generally have greater geographical mobility, rely more on friends.[25] In essence, with higher income comes more opportunities for meeting people in a greater variety of contexts.

Are there other variables that affect making friends? Sure. Common sense tells us that living in a big city versus a small town affects one's ability to meet new people. More options exist in the city, but proximity as well as more frequent random contact would occur in a small town. As Jerry tells us (see Chapter 8), a small town allows him to run into his friends more often. They are more apt to eat at the same restaurants and drink beer at the same party because there are fewer other dining spots and socializing opportunities.

Larger changes in society also make a difference. For example, many years ago, marriage was seen as a sign of commitment. Couples who were partnered and not married were seen as being unwilling or uncertain if they were ready for marriage. Cohabitation without marriage is becoming increasingly common and often a precursor to marriage, as the median age of first marriage has crept up. The latest data from the U.S. Census Bureau indicate that couples are waiting to marry until they have completed their education and feel financially secure, leading to a decrease in the divorce rate.[26] The presence of children who need tending could also affect a couple's ability to engage with friends. Couples with older children out of the home and those who have not given birth would likely have more time to be with friends than couples who are actively engaged in child rearing.

The work environment would play a role, too. Imagine serving in the armed forces versus working alone from home. Relying on others for survival will build strong connections with others that writing the great American novel in a garret will not. Common sense would say that moving around a lot when young could affect how well someone enters new situations and makes friends. We could add to this environmental stew of location, employment, and mobility, the nature of the individuals involved. Within families, personality variations between siblings often exist. One sibling is outgoing and at ease in most situations, while the other is shy and prefers her or his own company. One excels at sports or math and is a friend magnet, while the other is neither particularly introverted nor extroverted. One takes after an outgoing mother while the other takes after the quiet father. All of these variables (gender, age, race, class, the environmental stew, and personality makeup) can affect how individuals make friends.

What happens then when a couple, with their own disparate friend-making abilities, tries to make friends with another couple? How might these variables come into play?

MARRIAGE/PARTNERSHIP (COUPLEDOM)

To understand how friendships with other couples are built, we must next consider what happens during the early stages of coupledom to the two partners. Initially, people are often attracted to each other for their similarities. The attraction has a sociological basis. Marriages between people with similar religious approaches[27] and races,[28] tend to be more stable than those between people of highly dissimilar backgrounds. People feel most comfortable spending time with people like themselves, though this is changing as we become a more diverse society. The increased rates in interracial and interreligious marriage attest to this.

Similarities in personality and interest may connect people. A book lover wants to be with a book lover, a triathlete with a Division I tennis player, a satiric wit with another satiric wit, and a Republican with a Republican. Of course, opposites attract, too. Many people look past race, religion, and politics when they fall in love. Personality traits loom large. The quiet guy may be attracted to the boisterous gal because she has qualities he longs for. The conformist gal is drawn to the rebel because he can free her from an upbringing she found restrictive.

Building an Identity as a Couple

As the couple forms, partners begin to share experiences with each other which builds their identity as a unit.[29] The more they interact as a couple (both when alone and with others), the more the partners solidify their identity as a couple. How they tease each other in front of friends will become part of the way they are known as a couple. Their level of affection with each other will become charming as will the way they surprise each other with well-thought-out gifts. When they complete a bicycle ride for charity together, it helps their friends seem them as a duo. Friends begin to "see them together."

One outcome is that, as they form an identity as a couple, they may start to seek out friends who are also coupled. One engaged 28-year-old we interviewed told us that for her wedding, almost all of her invited peers were partners in a couple. These are the people with whom she and her fiancé are more apt to spend time. Couples want to be with others who remind them of themselves and reinforce their being a couple. This expands their circle of friends. But, consciously or unconsciously, as with this 28-year-old, they may also shut out individual friends who are not partners in couples.

Take the case of two women friends and what happens when one becomes a newlywed. If the three of them go out together, it may not be much fun for the husband as the women recount their pasts together and talk about people the husband does not know. The woman wants to keep her friendship but also wants to spend weekend evenings with her husband. Everyone has a story about being dumped by a close friend when he or she starts to date (or marries) someone and has less time available for the friendship. In this case, the couple's friendship circle may shrink[30] as they drop individual friends in favor of couples.

The friendship circle especially may shrink if they cannot find couples with whom they enjoy spending time. To make forming couples' friendships more difficult, some couples may be shunned because of their choice of partner (e.g., if they are dating someone of a different race or where a large age disparity exists).[31] This process of "relationship marginalization" (when partners perceive their romantic relationship as a subject of disapproval) was looked at by psychologists Justin Lehmiller and Christopher Agnew[32] who found that couples who were viewed with disapproval by their social network were less apt to survive. This makes sense as they find themselves with fewer people with whom to spend time. Another study led by Agnew reinforces this finding. In this study, he and two colleagues explored how well friends of the couple were able to predict the success of that couple's relationship.[33] Not surprisingly, the more the couple did together, the more likely the success of the couple.[34]

We found support for this in our research even among those whose marriage ended. As one divorced 61-year-old man who was married for 25 years told us, "It is important for couples to value one another's friends and to integrate these friends into the relationship. It is helpful when the couple shares common interests. That creates an opportunity to have fun when getting together with 'his' friends and 'her' friends."

Ultimately, couples' interactions help to solidify their togetherness in their own eyes and in the eyes of others who, in turn, reinforce that togetherness.

Even with the support of the community, happy marriages may be hard to sustain. Not only does a significant minority (close to 40%) of couples end up in divorce,[35] but of those couples that are married there is a range of happiness. Happy marriages are characterized by shared checking accounts,[36] communication,[37] and spending time together.[38] These couples enjoy each other and can talk through issues as they arise and are egalitarian in nature.[39] These same couples are more apt to have friends in common, which would increase their opportunities to spend time together. Good marriages will breed more couple friendships than bad marriages. No one wants to hang out with an unhappy couple who fight all the time. A number of couples we interviewed who were in happy marriages specifically said they cannot stand being around couples that bicker. Unhappy couples often understand this. One divorced man who was interviewed told us that he and his former wife lost friends because they fought in front of their friends.

According to John Gottman, who was cited earlier and who has spent years in his laboratory videotaping and studying how couples get along, people can improve their marriages by communicating in a nondefensive manner, by validating their partners, and by staying calm during a disagreement.[40] To Gottman, staying calm includes not hitting below the belt by making a nasty remark that crosses the line of acceptable arguing.

Once You Find Friends, How Do You Fit Them In?

Finding couple friends who are highly compatible and can fit into a couple's life may be easier said than done given the different paths partners take to and with their individual friendships, with their own relationship, and with their couple friendships. Plus we have not even discussed a person's need for time alone. In the simplest scenario, how does a newly married man in his 20s balance time with friends from college AND his old friends from high school AND his new wife AND his family of origin AND friends he and his wife have made AND his wife's friends and family? If he weighs these competing allegiances and spends less time with his wife (without her explicit permission), it may mean their identity as a couple is slower to develop, and this can spell trouble for their future.[41]

Suppose we add to this common scenario what actually happens when this young couple finds another couple with whom to spend time. They make plans and choose a restaurant. Maybe there is a level of nervous excitement like on a first date. Then, half way through the dinner, they both experience the "Love her, find him overbearing (or boring) syndrome." Or they experience one of its variations—the "Hate her, love him syndrome," the "Like him but don't talk about politics syndrome," or the "Don't get her started on her work syndrome." Whatever the vagaries of this budding (now doomed) relationship, a couple may steer away from too much contact with another couple because they cannot tolerate long periods of time with one of the partners. The couple may even end up fighting about whether to use their little available time socializing with a couple when they really only like one of the partners, yet feel loyalty through a lifelong friendship with one of the partners. This is particularly vexing when the person they like in the couple is a lifelong friend whose partner they both intensely dislike. This situation is not uncommon.

When things work well, partners learn to accommodate to each other so they can spend time with both their spouse and their good friends, though the tenor of the interactions may not be wholly open and free floating. Let us offer another scenario that illustrates how many couples successfully reconcile competing demands for socialization and their time. This one is from a midlife marriage.

Sue and Mary, both in their 50s, are lifelong friends. They share a great deal about their marriages, including the ups and downs inherent in most relationships. These ups and downs include infrequent innocent flirtations with other men, occasional unhappiness with their partner as a lover or father, or disappointment with his career progression. They also talk about their disappointments about their own careers, doubts about their competence as mothers, and sticky problems with their siblings and aging parents. These are issues they do not usually talk about with the husbands when the two couples go out together. As a result, these couples' friendship, built on the strength of the relationship between Sue and Mary, is not a friendship where all topics can be discussed between both couples. Some topics are taboo. Yet these couples still consider each other friends as a couple. The joy in getting together for these women is in spending time with a friend with whom there is a strong affinity as well as with her own partner. It is a couple friendship where not everything is discussed among the four of them. It also is a relationship where the women spend additional time together because their husbands are compatible with each other.

Before we delve deeper into our thinking about the purpose of this book and how we came to study couples and their friendships, another variable needs to be considered—the family's impact on the couple.

Family and Couple Friendships

When a couple starts to build a relationship, they often initiate a healthy and natural separation from their families of origin. The amount of separation varies widely from one couple to the next: Some stay closely involved and include family members in many social activities, whereas others reduce their time with their parents or siblings. When they have children, as in Tracy and John's case, the couple may want to be with other couples with young children because of shared life situations while still retaining their parents' involvement for child care and possibly even financial assistance.

One couple we know spends every Sunday dinner at her parents' house. Other siblings and grandchildren come for dinner, too, if they are available. There is no extraordinary pressure for this couple, now in their 50s, to go for dinner, but such obligations, especially when they are seen as pressure, could prevent a couple from making friends, as it would tie up one night a week. On the positive side, such visits provide emotional support and build family cohesion, both of which can bode well for the healthy development of family members.

Whereas some couples seek being with family, others avoid it. Another couple we know in their 30s and with two young children want nothing to do with his parents. He is still smarting from perceived injustices from years past and sees those injustices being potentially visited on his own children as they grow up. He is trying to separate from his parents and has the support of his wife in these actions.

In trying to understand how couples structure their time with family, friends, and each other, psychologist Catherine Stein and her colleagues, working in Ohio, interviewed 49 middle- and working-class couples between the ages of 20 and 49 and married for at least 5 years. The couples named an average of 7.7 shared family members and 1.5 shared friends. Wives were apt to have more separate friends than husbands. Couples with a large shared family network (as compared with couples with few shared family members or couples with separate friend networks for both spouses) were the most common. This configuration considered family as central in their everyday lives. Those couples characterized as having separate friend networks reported the highest levels of marital satisfaction, a point requiring additional consideration.[42]

In our research we asked couples whether they spend a lot of time with their extended family and whether time with their family interferes with their developing friendships with other couples. We were interested in how couples balance what could be seen as competing demands on their time together as well as their time with friends. From the interviews we learn that extended families can impede friendships with other couples, though this is not a common occurrence. We also learned that some couples we interviewed viewed their parents as good role models for couple friendships, whereas others used their parents as examples of what they are trying to avoid. When thinking about forming friendships, the present and the historic push and pull of family connections must be considered.

In addition to looking at the interpersonal characteristics that can affect couple friendships, as well as such immutable factors as race, age, and sex, we need to look also at the broader social environment in which couples have been raised and in which men and women live. Popular culture is one portion of the broader social environment.

WHAT HAVE WE LEARNED ABOUT COUPLES OVER
THE YEARS FROM TV, MOVIES, AND BOOKS?

By looking at popular culture we can gauge what may have influenced some couples and what may have changed over time about how couple friendships are portrayed. TV is both a leader and a follower of current trends. Couples are not the same as they were 50, 30, or even 20 years ago. A brief look at television sitcoms offers some reflection on how couples during those years were portrayed in relation to other couples. The portrayals of characters on popular television shows have enormous social impact. TV shows were discussed the next day in school and the workplace. White couples may have wanted to be the Cleavers on *Leave it to Beaver* or the Nelsons on *Ozzie and Harriet* in the 1950s and black couples may have wanted to be the Huxtables on *The Cosby Show* in the 1980s.

In the early years of television, we saw the role that women played in the family. They were stay-at-home mothers whose husbands worked outside of the home. The couple in the sitcom was likely to have a close friendship with another couple. The men or the women in those couples got into "trouble" with each other, setting the comedic stage. By the 1970s, when women began to be portrayed as working outside of the home, a shift occurred where the couple's own relationship gained ascendancy, often over the friendships between the women or the men.

In the 1950s, families sat around their television and got their first sustained look at how couples interacted with other couples—what might be shared with them, how men and women bantered with their friends around other couples, and where a couple might draw a boundary around their own relationship. As Jackie Gleason and Audrey Meadows portrayed Ralph and Alice Kramden on *The Honeymooners,* they were offering a glimpse of a working-class couple: a bus driver and an occasional secretary. The Kramdens closest couple friends, Ed and Trixie Norton, were played by Art Carney and Joyce Randolph. Here it is Ralph and Ed who often plot behind their wives' backs and are ultimately brought into line. In contradistinction, and also in the 1950s, Lucille Ball and Desi Arnaz were starring in *I Love Lucy.* Vivian Vance and William Frawley portrayed Ethel and Fred Mertz, their landlords and closest couple friends. Here it is the women who are usually involved in some escapade, plotting and hiding behind the men's backs. On those shows and in those days, men worked and women stayed home. If the woman worked, it was often at a job that paid well below the man's wage. The takeaway message from the 1950s is that couples' friends are vital to happiness both because of their individual friendships as well as their couple friendships. This was the last decade where this message came across so clearly.

The Dick Van Dyke Show, which ran from 1961 and 1966, starred Dick Van Dyke as Rob Petrie, a television writer. Laura Petrie, played by Mary Tyler Moore, does not work outside of the home. Their best couple friends are their neighbors, the Helpers, Jerry and Millie. The four occasionally socialize together. Both members of the couple join with their same-sex friend from time to time, forming a bond that signals the importance of friendships with individuals in couples. Here the couple's own relationship, including some of the first television scenes of a couple's bedroom, is portrayed as having closed boundaries, much more so than what was portrayed on *The Honeymooners* and *I Love Lucy*. By boundaries we mean that the Petries are a unit, pull together, and are not split apart by friendships with other people.

In the 1970s, *All in the Family,* starring Carroll O'Connor and Jean Stapleton as Archie and Edith Bunker, exploded on the social scene. Archie, presented as acerbic, racist, and beyond politically incorrect, is kept in check by Edith (whose dottiness is used to soften the underlying compassion of her message). In this series, significant women characters, such as Irene Lorenzo, a neighbor of the Bunkers, works outside of the home with Archie. Interestingly, her husband is portrayed as a househusband—a major role shift. Both the Lorenzos and the Jeffersons (an African American couple who later spun off into their own eponymous TV show) are neighbors who are "couple" friends—if Archie is capable of having friends. What is learned about couples' friends here? Unlike the previous examples, the Bunkers are not as much on the same page when it comes to the importance of friends; that is, Edith values them much more than Archie.

Family Ties, the Michael J. Fox vehicle, ran for almost the whole decade of the 1980s (and was supposedly Ronald Reagan's favorite TV show). Both of the Keatons work outside of the home and in comparable jobs, she as an architect and he as a TV station CEO. No couple friends appear as recurring or central characters. This could be a reflection of a story line more focused on the cultural divide between Michael J. Fox's Republican character and his parents' Democratic characters; it could be that such a story line would have diverted attention from Fox; or it could be that, as a working mother, Elyse Keaton (portrayed by Meredith Baxter-Birney) did not have time for couple friends. As we found from our research, when couples are raising children who are past the toddler stage, they have less time for couple friends—there is too much going on.

The Cosby Show, which ran for 8 years until 1992, featured two parents, a doctor and a lawyer, who were successfully raising their children. Child rearing issues, not relationships with other couple friends, were the show's focus.

In the 1990s we have the dueling top sitcoms of *Seinfeld* and *Friends. Seinfeld* did not have couples as central characters. *Friends* had Courtney Cox and Matthew Perry as a married couple a few years into the show, but the other cast members are not consistently coupled during most of the show's run. Not much to look at there in terms of couple friendships with other couples. That leaves us with *The Simpsons* or *Home Improvement.* While we do not deny the cultural importance of *The Simpsons, Home Improvement* provides a more realistic portrayal of everyday life, though the Simpson family captures many of its features.

In *Home Improvement,* a vehicle for comedian Tim Allen, no couple friends are portrayed as significant characters; the emphasis is again on the children and Allen's individual relationships.

Will and Grace was popular in the first decade of the 21st century but not for portraying a couple who are partnered. Here we consider *Everybody Loves Raymond.* (*That 70s Show,* also popular, is retro and deals with the wrong decade.) Ray Romano plays Raymond Barone, a sportswriter who is married with three children. In this sitcom, it is relationships with his parents and brother that cause the comedic tension. Again, no couple friends outside of the family are given ascendancy, but we are shown how family affects a couple's ability to hang out with friends.

A couple looking for themselves in relation to other couples would have few role models for how to carry out their friendships from the recent decades. Outside of TV, where else do we learn about couple friendships? Movies? Older couples who we interviewed mentioned the 1969 movie *Bob and Ted and Carol and Alice,* the story of two couples at the cusp of the sexual revolution who push the envelope on their friendship. But surprisingly few movies, as reflected in Best Picture Oscar nominees, deal with friendships with other couples. Friendships are often depicted, but they are male-to-male friendships (e.g., *Butch Cassidy and the Sundance Kid,* starring Paul Newman and Robert Redford) and female-to-female friendships (e.g., *Thelma and Louise,* starring Susan Sarandon and Geena Davis).

What about politics, popular culture, and literature? The Obamas hang out with friends from Chicago, but it is hard to know if those are individual friends they have maintained rather than couple friends. George and Laura Bush were not often seen with couple friends. Adam and Eve, Anthony (or Julius Caesar) and Cleopatra, Lancelot and Guinevere, Douglas Fairbanks and Mary Pickford, Liz Taylor and Richard Burton, John Lennon and Yoko Ono,[43] Will Smith and Jada Pinkett Smith, Brad and Angelina—the list of famous couples goes on. But when we think about them, they are a unit without a significant other couple that immediately comes to mind as their close couple friends. (John Lennon and Paul McCartney were best buds but not after Yoko and Linda got into the mix.) These couples may have close couple friends, but they do not loom large in our consideration of their relationship or teach us what to do with our own couple friends.

We also learned about ourselves and others from literature. Many sources offer lists of the greatest books of all time but none of these (think *Madame Bovary, War and Peace, Lolita,* and *The Adventures of Huckleberry Finn*) offers insight on couple friendships.[44] Short of what we learned from television in its earliest decades, movies, literature, and political and popular couples do not offer a template for how such relationships operate.

Women and Work—The Shifting Forces

Having offered this cultural digression, we can return now to the more serious topic of the impact of societal changes in relation to work on women's and men's relationships with other couples. The culture since the 1950s has dramatically shifted. Segregation of the sexes at the workplace was once common, regardless of the level of employment. If women were employed in an office, the boss was usually a man. Factory work was often segregated. If women were employed as saleswomen, the executives were often men. When Ralph and Alice and Lucy and Desi were America's couples, women were less than 10% of the medical profession.[45] By 2006 they comprised 28%[46] of doctors, and half the medical students. In 1930, 2% of lawyers and judges were women.[47] Twenty years ago, 43% of the first-year law students were women;[48] now close to 50% of law students are women. Medicine and law, like engineering and business, were once considered male professions in the United States. Women and men were not equal in the workforce and in generating income for the home until recently. (Even with these changes, women often earn less money for the same work, including in medicine, law, and business.)[49]

Until recently, men and women did not have a chance to socialize at work on equal footing. They tended to not interact at home on equal footing either. With more women in the workforce and greater equality, though not complete equality, has come the rise of the companionate marriage, or the marriage of equals. Partners in a companionate marriage believe roles are interchangeable and share similar views on child rearing and work. They value each other's friendship, too. Partners are more likely to view each other as close friends than their predecessors, in part because the workplace treats men and women more equally.

What this means in terms of couple friendships is the following:

1. Women have less time to socialize with their women friends.
2. Spouses/partners are more apt to view each other as best or very close friends.
3. Socializing as a couple takes on greater importance because less time is available for the couple to be alone with each other (as two work schedules need to be juggled) and to socialize with other couples.

As a result, when the couple goes out, a friendship with another couple has gained increased importance. With this greater friendship and equality comes a new challenge of how to be friends with other couples. When couples socialize, they want to maximize time with their spouse as well as with others. Couples' relationships may be even more important than in the past as the friendship between the partners of the couple is being balanced at the same time that the relationship with another couple is being navigated.

What has also changed over time is that, according to recent research, the number of friends individuals have is on the decline. Americans today are estimated to have 2.08 confidants as compared with 2.94 20 years ago.[50] Even if we were looking at just men's and women's friendships, this fact alone would point out a significant difference in the way people live today.

Thus, when people (a man and a woman) with fundamentally different ways of interacting and little time on their hands (and fewer friends than the previous generation) try to form a friendship with two others who also have fundamentally different ways of interacting, negotiation is needed from all four members to make the friendship(s) work.

Healthy couples are good at accommodating each other, but the individuals in the couple still may not want to spend what little free time they have to socialize, trying to accommodate. Do women want to get together on a Saturday night and watch the baseball game? Do men want to go out for an intimate dinner with another couple and listen to their wives revealing more than they think they should about their children, their health, and their sex lives?

We asked couples about these friendships, and many can identify at least one, if not a number of, couple friends they have. They go to dinner, travel, watch their kids' sporting events, and hang out with them. But question the couples more closely, and the friendship may not always be highly satisfying for both members of the couple. If free time is short, figuring out how to parcel out time with those friends as well as individual friends, children, extended family, work contacts, and time alone for just the couple may be difficult and stress-producing. Finally, if the individuals in the couple have different personality styles, how they engage with other couples and what they do when all four are together may be a source of disagreement.

TWO WAYS OF THINKING ABOUT COUPLE FRIENDSHIPS: STYLE AND INTERACTION

Style: *Seekers*, *Keepers*, and *Nesters*

From our research with close to 400 members of couples, both married and partnered, we have come to understand that couple friendships mean different things to different couples, and we have categorized them into three distinct groups. We discuss these in greater depth in the next chapter and wish to offer a thumbnail sketch here. The most outgoing couples we call Seekers. These couples seek other couples for social, intellectual, and emotional stimulation. Both partners enjoy the company of others. A second, and the largest group of couples, are ones we call Keepers. They tend to see couple friends as an important but not vital part of their lives. They have a significant number of friends, are close with those friends, and are not too interested in making new couple friends. A third group of couples that we see from our research are those that are not particularly interested in couple friendships. Either or both partners do not place a high value on them, and they are content to just spend time with the other partner, with their individual friends, or with one or two close couples. They are not oriented by personality style to a great deal of socializing with other couples. We call them *Nesters* because, without putting any value on their behavior, they are content to be in their nest with just each other or with a small group of friends. Some *Nesters* found each other late in life or in a second marriage and are fiercely protective of the time they have.

As we offer these categories, we are aware that couples are comprised of individuals who bring their own style of interacting into the couple relationship as well as into their own individual friendships. Introverts may tend to be *Nesters* while extroverts may tend to be *Seekers*. Temporal or developmental shifts can cause an individual, for example, to change from being a *Seeker* to a *Keeper* or a *Nester* as work piles up, children are born, or a relationship deteriorates and socializing with another couple is no longer fun. The context may also shift. A person who grows up in a small town where she was well known and an extrovert may become more withdrawn or shy moving to a new metropolis with a new husband where people are familiar with him and not with her.

Interaction: Emotion Sharing and Fun Sharing

The other way of thinking about couple friendships, which we also explain in greater depth in the next chapter, is to look at what they do with each other when they get together, how they interact. We believe that couples tend to be on a continuum from emotion sharing at one end to fun sharing on the other end. When we asked couples how they defined couple friendships, many said they were friendships where they could spend time with another couple and have fun. The emphasis was on "doing something" with the other couple. A smaller number of couples we interviewed defined couple friendships as being relationships where they had close, sharing relationships and where there was a mutuality of friendship among all four partners. We consider the first group to be closer to the fun sharing end of the continuum and the second group to be closer to the emotion sharing end of the continuum.

We recognize here, as psychologists Jean-Philippe Laurenceau, Lisa Barrett, and Paula Pietromonaco point out, that considerable variation exists in how people develop and sustain intimacy and even in their need for warmth and validation from others.[51] In studies conducted by these researchers, self-disclosure and partner's self-disclosure were related to greater feelings of intimacy between the partners. Some couples were better at, and more interested in, self-disclosure than others. Emotion sharing couples may also be fun sharing. What we wish to illustrate here is what couples do when they are together with their couple friends.

THE TOPIC

To recap, why are couples' friendships important? Friendships are important to the individual's well-being, and couples' friendships, by extension, are important to the individual's, the couple's, and the family's well-being. The marriage may be the greatest beneficiary of a couple's friendship. According to one group of family therapists, "Friends can potentially be a great hindrance or help to a couple's marital adjustment ... friends can prevent escalation of conflict, can help reduce enmeshment, and may be used as a therapy resource."[52] Couples' support systems will help them to weather crises.[53] Socializing with other couples is a key part of the development of the couple as a unit and is different from socializing with individuals. Just as a friend can provide a mirror on the self, another couple can provide a reflecting team that supports or impedes couple growth. As each couple interacts with another couple, their own relationship is reconsidered. This topic gets to a core component of the marriage. Couples engage in "relationship presentation" either consciously or unconsciously. According to Agnew and colleagues, couples put on a public face "to maintain a sense of intimacy and exclusiveness regarding their relationship or to conceal aspects of their relationship."[54] Unhappy couples tend to be more isolated from friends and coworkers.[55] On the flip side, we know from the study of 49 couples by Stein and colleagues that couples with individual networks of friends experience a high degree of marital content. Couples do not operate in social vacuums; they are subunits of families and often have children, relatives, and their own friendships. Happy couples will maintain more functional families and, by extension, healthier children.

Couples' friendships allow the couple to go to dinner, see a movie, bowl, golf, and travel while also enjoying the company of two others who, when all goes well, enhance the experience. Is it fun shooting a hole in one when a spouse is the only witness? Certainly, but it is even better when it is a shared experience. Ditto to seeing a great movie and having a lively discussion afterward, sharing impressions of the new first-grade teacher, commiserating about the minister who is about to retire, laughing at the soprano who missed the high note, and bemoaning the batter who struck out.

Spending time with another couple provides benefits beyond greater enjoyment of shared events and activities. It provides a cross-check on one's own marriage by offering a lens on the inner workings of another intimate relationship. Do they treat each other well? Are they affectionate with each other? Do they compete with each other, interrupt, and deprecate each other? Or do they encourage, take pride in, and compliment each other? Are any of this couple's relationship patterns worth emulating? Or avoiding? Couple friendships, by giving us a unique perspective into another couple's operational definitions of closeness, allow us to understand our own relationship better and offer a different model of how couples can relate.

From our interviews, we will show how *Seekers, Keepers,* and *Nesters* live out their friendships and how a couple's interaction style affects what couples do when they get together. Such an understanding will help to connect couples more meaningfully with friends, short-circuit potential problems within the couple as to how to incorporate couple friendships into the couple's life, and help couples build new friendships if that is their desire. While we believe friends can enrich one's life, we also understand that some people and couples are comfortable with a small circle of friends or just with each other. From conducting the interviews, we know that many couples have never considered how they balance conflicting pulls on their time in relation to family, friends, and each other. We hope that reading about other couples will help all couples understand what their style is and how to work as a team to maximize their own potential as friends and as a couple.

ABOUT THE BOOK

This book is the first of its kind to explore the meaning of couples' friendships with other couples. Every couple is involved in some form of couple friendship. Yet virtually no research is available on this important relationship. What little is known is drawn from anecdotal comments in books on marital therapy and couples counseling, friendship blogs, and the occasional reporter-written article for a magazine like *Ladies' Home Journal.* When we started to learn about couples' friendships, we realized very quickly that we had little to guide us. We started by building on the first author's research on men's and women's individual friendships and talking to couples ourselves. Between 2008 and 2010, we directed, trained, and supervised graduate students as they sought out and interviewed current members of couples or people who were once in a couple and are now divorced. We continued to interview couples ourselves. In addition to our interviews, the graduate students interviewed nearly 400 members of couples.

One important decision we had to make was whether to focus on heterosexual couples only or to include both heterosexual and same-sex couples. We consulted with gay and lesbian friends, who mentioned some important differences between couples' friendships in that community due to dense friendship networks. We consulted previous research and found so little information about couples' friendships that exploring both opposite and same-sex couples in one book seemed like a daunting task. This led to our decision to focus this book on heterosexual couples with the hope that our work will stimulate further exploration of couples' friendships, including those of same-sex couples.

CHAPTER GUIDE

The next chapter offers the theory we used to help us understand the couple's relationship, the categories for couple friendships that we have developed, and a way of looking at how couple friendships operate. Some key findings are also presented. Additional information about the research methodology appears in Appendix A.

Chapter 3 focuses on the young couple. Our interviews are used in this and the next two chapters to highlight the categories and the complexities of couple friendship formation and maintenance. In this chapter, examples will be provided that illustrate the *Seekers, Keepers,* and *Nesters.* This chapter will be particularly important reading for the newly formed couple who is struggling with understanding how to balance their commitments to others as they forge a commitment to each other.

Couples who are 35 to 60 years old, typically those in the middle years of marriage, will be the focus of Chapter 4. Examples will be provided that illustrate the *Seeker* Couple, the *Keeper* Couple, and the *Nester* Couple. Many couples at the younger end of this age group have established routines that are focused on child rearing and career development. Older couples in this age group may find themselves with more time on their hands as their children become independent and their careers become more solidified (though an uncertain economy can affect this). Their need for friendships is growing. Their identity as a couple has been well formed.

Chapter 5 describes older couples, those 61 years and older. These couples are struggling to find couples friends, as very often, especially in the later years, one of the partners in a couple has died. One couple who is highlighted has been married 65 years and is in their 80s. The oldest couples push the limits of our categories as, in some cases, deaths have forced a couple (in the *Seeker* Category) to only socialize and befriend widows.

The next two chapters of the book explore some of the struggles that couples and individuals have with their couple friendships. Chapter 6 centers on what happens when a couple friendship ends. Many couples have either dropped a couple who were friends or been dropped by them. Why don't they return our calls? Is it us or is it them? And, more commonly, what do couples do when they like one member of the couple but not the other? These are difficult moments for couples. Chapter 7 is based on interviews with people who have divorced and are often coping with the loss of couple friends.

We then offer two chapters focusing on specific couple interactions. Chapter 8 is an in-depth interview with two couples who have been friends for nearly 40 years. As they describe how their friendship works, how it has changed with time, and the nourishment it provides, we get a great picture of how these friendships work when they are at their best. Chapter 9 provides a look at couples who meet regularly as a group. We looked at the dynamics of seven couples and what they gain from a formalized group setting.

We conclude the book with suggestions for making and keeping couple friends. How can couples build better friendships with other couples? How can they understand each other's styles when it comes to establishing couple friends? How should couples balance when one wants to be a *Keeper* and the other a *Nester*? We include in Appendix B questions that marriage enrichment groups can review as they help each other understand the balancing act between individual friends, couple friends, family, and alone time. Appendix C is a quiz that couples can take together to help them discuss their relationship and how they integrate couple friends into their lives.

We offer our conclusions modestly. We have come to refine our understanding of couple friendships over the years. We have worked closely together, bringing two sets of eyes and ears to the subject matter, as well as the eyes and ears of more than 50 other interviewers who assisted with the research. When we present our results, sometimes they are drawn from specific questionnaire responses, for example, "How important are couple friendships?" and sometimes they are drawn from interview questions, for example, "What do couple friendships mean to you?" What we have is our best take on what this mix of methodologies means.[56] Couples are complex and dynamic. What we heard from one couple may have changed for them by the next week if some aspect of their relationship or friendships with others has changed. We are humbly aware that other researchers and clinicians looking at the same topic may have asked different questions and may have derived different impressions from the responses we have received.

We hope that the answers to these questions will improve friendships between couples and individuals. We also hope the answers will improve marriages and relationships as well.

2

How We Conducted the Study and What We Discovered

We began our research on couple-to-couple friendships with some questions. This chapter explains how we tried to answer those questions by interviewing many couples who generously shared their experiences with us. As qualitative researchers, after our initial findings about how and why couples form friendships with other couples, we checked the accuracy of our answers in additional interviews, refined our questions, and continued to build our ideas about what couple friendships mean and how they begin and develop. In this chapter we describe that process, explain some of the major themes we found during our study, and consider how our findings fit with previous theory and research on friendships and marriage.

QUESTIONS

We began our study in 2008 with several broad questions.

1. What do couples actually mean when they say they are friends with another couple?
2. How do couples begin friendships with other couples, and how do they keep them going?
3. In what ways do their friendships with other couples affect a couple's own marriage or partnership?
4. How do couples balance the demands on their time—time spent together, with children, family members, work, individual friends, and couple friends?
5. What happens when couple friendships are not working out satisfactorily for all concerned?

We began by having the first author train graduate students to conduct in-depth qualitative interviews. In 2008, these 17 students talked at length with 76 heterosexual couples. Each couple (21 years old or older and living together for at least 1 year) was interviewed together and asked to respond to 15 open-ended questions about their friendships with other couples. As part of our data collection, each member of the couple was also asked to separately complete a 31-item paper-and-pencil questionnaire. (See Appendix A for a more detailed account of how we conducted our study.)

Based on this first group of interviews, we began to see a way to differentiate among groups of couples and tentatively began to classify couples based on how actively they sought out new couples for friends. In later interviews, we tested this hypothesis. We also became concerned that partners interviewed together may have felt inhibited in answering questions because of a partner's presence. In 2009, a second group of graduate students was trained and interviewed one member of a couple. Twenty-one students conducted 122 interviews of such individuals. To understand more about the relationship between marriage partners when they interacted with their couple friends, we asked interviewees additional questions about how they perceived their partners when they socialized with another couple.

As we examined this second round of interviews, we found a gap in our knowledge about what happens to couple friendships when a couple divorces. Some couples in our study reported being in a second or third marriage, and we were beginning to see that divorce often led to the end of a friendship with another couple. To understand these effects more fully, we designed a third wave of interviews in 2010 in which another group of 19 graduate students interviewed 58 persons who had gone through a divorce. We also wanted to test the validity of our early hypotheses, which categorized couples based on how actively they sought other couples for friendships. So students also interviewed 47 couples together and specifically asked them if they saw themselves as fitting within one of our three hypothesized categories.

In addition to the previously mentioned interviews conducted by our graduate students, we (Geoff and Kathy) conducted extensive interviews with numerous couples, as well as interviews with two couples who are close friends, and an interview with a couples group. Most of the couples described in depth in the book are from interviews conducted by the authors, either jointly or separately.

WHAT WE LEARNED FROM PREVIOUS RESEARCH

As we gathered information from our interviews, we looked to theories and earlier research to provide a context, paying particular attention to several areas. To what extent might the differences between men's and women's friendships apply to friendships between heterosexual couples? Are these friendships more likely to resemble the intimacy of women's friendships, the shared activities of men's friendships, or some unique hybrid? What is a useful framework for understanding how a couple keeps a healthy balance in their marriage among competing time demands? What is the effect of outside friendships on a couple's marriage? We found little research on couple-to-couple friendships themselves. But we did find theories and earlier research on the effects of outside friendships on marriage, the role of shared friends in a marriage, and why spending time with joint friends may enhance a couple's own relationship.

KEEPING A HEALTHY BALANCE: FOUR TYPES
OF HIGH-QUALITY MARRIAGE

One way to understand the role of friendships in a couple's marriage or partnership is through the lens of University of Maine Sociology Professor Stephen Marks's "three-corners" framework of marriage,[1] which considers how couples relate both to each other and to people outside their marriage or partnership. Marks describes each person as having a "three-cornered self," a triangle composed of a person's inner self, his or her self in relation to the spouse or partner, and a third corner, which is any focus beyond the individual and the partnership. At any given time, this third corner could consist of children, friends, relatives, jobs recreation, religion, and so on. The third corner could be jointly shared by both partners (e.g., children or couple friends) or pursued independently (e.g., a job, hobbies, or individual friends). This third corner offers opportunities for spouses or partners to at times be connected to each other through a friendship, activity, or interest they share and at other times to explore interests or friendships on their own. Marks defines quality marriages as those in which each partner is able to maintain a balance among a focus on his or her self, a partner, and people or activities outside the marriage. Couples are able to strike this tricky balance with varying degrees of success. Marks, in looking at relationships where a workable balance is struck, describes four types of high-quality marriages. In his first example, a couple with a *balanced connection* evenly distributes their energies among all three of their corners. The good feelings from their interior selves and their shared interests from their third corners flow into their partner relationship and enrich it. Marks believes that such balanced connections are unusual, as most couples tend to prioritize their commitments and may focus more on their own needs or their outside interests.

The second type of high-quality marriage is a *couple-centered connection*. Here both spouses concentrate on their partnership by putting most of their energy into their marriage and maximizing time with each other. This type of marriage is considered "high quality" because the couple do not isolate themselves from others but remain involved with their other two corners (individual self and outside interests). The third type, a *family-centered connection*, describes a couple whose major focus is around a shared third corner, usually their children. When partners are raising young children, they may tend toward this type of connection as they dedicate themselves to child rearing. A _loose connection_ characterizes the fourth type. This is a marriage in which both partners have as their primary focus a separate third corner. This type of marriage is seen as healthy when the couple is still connected to one another "principally through conversation in which they fill each other in on their daily third-corner adventures … and feel much involved in each other's outside lives."[2]

Marks's ideas are consistent with what we discovered in our research. Couples we interviewed strove to balance the often competing demands of their lives, particularly when their responsibilities involved the care of children or elderly parents. Some couples told us that at certain times in their lives they had little time to develop or maintain couples friendships and let such friendships go. Others gave a high priority to friendships with other couples and considered them integral to family life. A small minority fit Marks's definition of a couple-centered connection in that their main link was with each other and couple friends were relatively unimportant.

EFFECTS OF OUTSIDE FRIENDSHIPS ON MARRIAGE

As mentioned in Chapter 1, couple-to-couple friendships have rarely been a focus of research. Instead researchers have primarily studied the effects of individual friends or friends held jointly (who may or may not be another couple) on a couple's marriage. Marks[3] states that activity in one of a person's corners affects the other two corners in a dynamic continual process. Therefore, a spouse's involvement in his or her third corner (outside interests or friendships) will affect the second corner (the marital relationship) and vice versa. For example, a wife may have individual friends separate from her husband and couple friends that she and her husband share. Both friendships would be considered third-corner interests, but each might affect the wife and her relationship with her husband in different ways. The wife's individual friends could be a source of potential interest, energy, and resources for her while joint friends, such as another couple, could offer a shared experience with her husband, which can enhance time spent together. When a couple spends time with friends they share in common, their identity as a couple is strengthened and supported.[4] Friends held in common are more likely to be viewed as allies rather than competitors for their partner's time or interest.[5] On the other hand, when one member of the couple spends time with individual friends, that member gets support for herself or himself as an individual, which can strengthen the person's separate identity.[6] As we discuss further below, in the best case scenarios, individual friends may provide additional emotional support separate from the support a person receives from her or his partner. A partner's individual friendships, however, can affect a couple's marriage either positively or negatively.[8]

In reviewing the research on how friendships outside a marriage affect a couple's relationship and vice versa, we found that researchers asked some important questions. Does the interest and support partners receive from each other (or fail to receive) affect the ways they relate to their friends? Are individual friendships outside the marriage likely to relieve or intensify tension between partners? For example, when a spouse vents about problems in his or her marriage, under what circumstances do friends support a couple's marriage versus interfere with the marital bond? Friends, as we see later in the chapter on divorce and couples friendships, do encourage friends to leave spouses who they believe are wrong for them.

Gender seems to be an important factor in answering these questions. Women and men tend to get different things from their friends. Women find their relationships with other women to be more rewarding and supportive than men describe in their friendships with men as well as with women.[9] Women, more so than men, are socialized to be empathic, nurturing, and supportive of others.[10] Therefore, it is not surprising that married men tend to rely on their wives for emotional support while married women also turn to their female friends.[11]

Stacey Oliker, a professor of sociology at University of Wisconsin–Milwaukee coined the term *marriage work* to describe "reflection or action to achieve or sustain the stability of a marriage and the sense of its adequacy."[12] A couple can engage in marriage work together, or one partner could use friends for this purpose. Women talk about their marriages with friends more often than men do. Oliker learned that women used their female friends to explore issues around autonomy and identity while they avoided such discussions with their husbands. In a later study, Christine M. Proulx, a professor at the University of Missouri Department of Human Development and Family Studies, and her colleagues found that wives were equally as likely to discuss "marital communication, spouses' childrearing philosophies, family decision making, social life and leisure, support for wives' work roles, support for wives' parenting, division of household chores and division of child care" with their husbands as with their close friends.[13] The exceptions found were that wives were more likely to discuss family finances with their husbands and relationships with their in-laws with their close friends.

Early studies found that rather than harming their marriages, women's engagement in marriage work with friends improved marriages by providing wives with additional needed support.[14] Later studies have found important distinctions in the effects of spouses' marriage work on their marriages.[15] For example, in a study of married couples by Helms and her colleagues,[16] wives who engaged in marriage work with their friends, while also discussing the same marital concerns with their husbands, reported no negative effects. However, wives who discussed their marital concerns with their female friends, but infrequently discussed these concerns with their husbands, either failed to feel better about their marriages or reported conflicts with their spouses. Husbands engaged in marriage work with male friends to a lesser extent than did wives. Husbands differed from their wives in that their discussions did not affect husbands' feelings about their marriages. In a study by psychologist Danielle Julien and colleagues,[17] 88 wives and husbands engaged in conversations about a problem in their marriage with a best friend. Spouses satisfied with their marriages were successful in getting reinforcement for their marriage even when they revealed marital conflict, while dissatisfied spouses were less effective in getting such support from their friends. Husbands and wives who were satisfied with their marriages felt closer to their spouses following these conversations compared to dissatisfied husbands and wives.

Taken together, results from research on the effects of individual friends on a couple's marriage support Marks's[18] ideas about the dynamic relationship between friendships outside the marriage and the marital relationship. Although we found no research specifically addressing the effects of couple friendships on a couple's marriage, Marks's model suggests that the marriages of both couples would be affected by their friendship with another couple. What might be unique is that within this shared friendship a couple's marriage could be affected directly (e.g., one couple is influenced by how the other couple support or fight with each other), or one member of the couple could be affected, with implications for the marital relationship (e.g., a wife understands her husband better by hearing the perspective of the male member of the other couple). Our study of couple friendships is an initial attempt to understand the extent to which couples see their couple friendships as affecting their marriages, either positively or negatively.

Another important question is whether having shared friends contributes to a couple feeling more satisfied with their marriage.[19] In general, the answer is yes. Couples who have friends in common tend to be more satisfied with their marriages. Some specific studies were mentioned in the previous chapter and will be discussed in later chapters. However, these studies do not indicate which came first—shared friends or marital satisfaction—so that cause and effect are not clear.[20] Interestingly one study found that couples in which both husbands and wives had primarily separate friends were also highly satisfied with their marriages; however, the men in these marriages had a high level of depression, while the women did not.[21] These findings suggest that the gender differences in friendships noted earlier may play a role—women seek and get more emotional support from their friends than do men.

EFFECTS OF COUPLE FRIENDSHIPS ON MARRIAGE

We looked at previous research for answers on how spending time with another couple might enhance a couple's own relationship. One answer is that spending time with others as a couple helps solidify a couple's sense of themselves as a couple. Research supports the fact that couples with a greater proportion of shared friends are happier in their marriages.[22] We found the same connection in our research: Couples who reported a higher number of couple friends also rated themselves as more happily married.[23]

Another possible answer to this question, however, has to do with the idea that sharing novel experiences with someone makes them more attractive.[24] Consider partners' relationships with one another. One reason partners are attractive to each other is that they bring interesting people, activities, and interests with them and thus help stimulate the partnership.[25] This attraction may start at the initial stages of a relationship. For example, a guy from a small family may be first attracted to his future wife because she comes from a large family, something he always longed for. Such an attraction may grow through the course of a marriage.

Taking this idea a step further, Arthur Aron, a psychologist at Stony Brook University, and his colleagues[26] developed a "self expansion" model, which states that as relationships between romantic partners develop, each partner expands her or his sense of self to include aspects of his or her partner. In other words, each begins to identify aspects of his or her partner with himself or herself. To illustrate, Rhonda loves to dance and encourages Robert to take salsa lessons with her. Robert agrees and, through this new shared experience with Rhonda, their relationship not only deepens, but Robert now begins to see himself as "graceful and sexy," qualities he previously attributed to Rhonda. The novelty and enjoyment they experience in learning to dance together makes them more attractive to each other. Several studies have confirmed that a couple's relationship is enhanced when they share experiences that are novel and challenging.[27] This, again, is consistent with Marks's three-corner theory.

What happens then if Rhonda and Robert as a couple share a new and interesting activity with another couple, such as hiking the Grand Canyon or talking about an interesting movie? Richard Slatcher,[28] a psychologist who runs a relationship laboratory at Wayne State University, designed an experiment to see what happened when a dating couple shared a novel experience with another couple. Would they experience strong positive feelings toward their own partner and the other couple, since all four were sharing the experience? Using a sample of college students, Slatcher randomly assigned one couple to talk with another couple they had not met previously. One group of couples was given questions to discuss that asked them to disclose personal information, such as "How close and warm is your family?" A second group of couples was given questions to discuss that required only small talk, such as "When was the last time you walked for more than an hour?" Compared to the couples who engaged in small talk, the couples who disclosed personal, emotional information about themselves reported feeling closer to the other couple and to their own partner as well. One month later these results still held, although the feelings of closeness to their own partner had lessened. An important factor in creating feelings of closeness was that their conversations increased the participants' positive feelings, for example, excitement or enthusiasm, which then became associated with their partner and the other couple. Slatcher's research was conducted on unmarried couples who did not know each other prior to the study; additional research is needed to determine if the results would be similar for couples who were already friends.

A variation of the idea that couples enjoy each other more when engaged with others in fun activities or conversation was captured by researchers Larson, Mannell, and Zuzanek,[29] who asked married couples to separately record their moods in a diary. In discussing this study, Milardo and Helms-Erikson clearly describe what these diaries revealed: "Spouses report the highest positive feelings toward their partners when in the company of mutual friends. These friends had the effect of transforming the attention of spouses from the mundane, constant, and ordinary business of family life to the more playful, unpredictable, and unique qualities of the partners."[30] Taken together, the research suggests that when a couple spend time with another couple and engage in interesting activities or conversations that are outside their routine, they are likely to experience their spouse with fresh eyes and feel positively about them.

SUMMARY OF TRENDS WE FOUND IN OUR STUDY

In this section, we summarize the most important trends we found in studying couple friendships. These trends are based on interviews with 123 couples interviewed together, 122 individuals who were interviewed without their partner, and 58 divorced individuals. Of the people we interviewed, almost three quarters were Caucasian, one-sixth were African American, and one-tenth were Asian, Hispanic, or self-identified as another race or ethnicity. Approximately 12% were in interracial marriages. The ages of persons interviewed for the study ranged from 21 to 95 years old, with two-thirds of the sample being 50 or younger. About half considered themselves middle class, one-third upper class, and one-sixth lower class.

We mentioned earlier in this chapter that after we began analyzing data from our first group of interviews, we hypothesized that couples fall into one of three categories based on the degree to which they actively seek out other couples as friends. As the study progressed, we tested this hypothesis and found that our categories resonated with the experiences of many couples. We call these three categories of couples *Seekers, Keepers,* and *Nesters.*

Seekers, Keepers, and Nesters

From our research with close to 400 members of couples, both married and partnered, we have distinguished differences between what couple friendships mean to couples; based on these differences, we have categorized couples into three distinct groups. The most outgoing couples we call *Seekers*. These couples seek other couples for social, intellectual, and emotional stimulation. Both partners enjoy the company of others. They are generally comfortable in their marriage and with each other but like the stimulation that another couple provides and are often open to and actively seek out new couple friends. They may easily start a conversation with a couple at another table at a restaurant and end up exchanging numbers. They may follow up with new couples they meet on vacation. They believe that their friends (both their individual friends and couple friends) are important to their well-being and look for ways to include them in many facets of their lives.

A second, and the largest group of couples, are ones we call *Keepers*. They tend to see couple friends as an important but not vital part of their life. They have a significant number of friends, are close to those friends, and are not overly interested in making new couple friends. Maybe they are caring for aging parents or raising difficult children and feel their plate is full enough in the friend category. Maybe the add-ons of soccer practice and late work hours or a troubled economy are wearing them down. Making new friends can be time consuming and, while it can also be fulfilling, they feel satisfied with their social life. They have old friends with whom they spend time and, while open to making new friends, will not go out of their way to do so. They are content with their relationships and want to "keep" what they have. For some couples a *Keeper* is not a permanent orientation to friendship but depends on current life circumstances, especially the demands of young children or the responsibilities of work or extended family. Jenny and Ike, in Chapter 3, are a *Keeper* couple.

A third group of couples that we see from our research are those that are not particularly interested in couple friendships. Either or both partners do not place a high value on them, and they are content to just spend time with the other partner, with their individual friends, or with one or two close couples. They are not oriented by personality style to a great deal of socializing with other couples. We call them *Nesters* because, without putting a value on their behavior, they are happy to be in their nest with just each other or with a small group of friends. Some *Nesters* found each other late in life or are in a second marriage and are fiercely protective of the time they have.

Seekers, we found, are the most likely of the three categories to rate couple friends as very important; *Nesters* are the least likely to rate them as very important.[31] At the same time, we found a trend suggesting that *Seekers* were the least likely to say they believed their spouse was very happy in the marriage while *Nesters* were the most likely to see their spouse as very happy in the marriage. *Keepers* are the most likely to have their marriage reaffirmed by being with other couples and *Nesters* are least likely to give this response.

As we offer these categories, we are aware that couples are comprised of individuals who bring their own style of interacting into the couple relationship as well as into their own individual friendships. Introverts may tend to be *Nesters* while extroverts may tend to be *Seekers*. Temporal or developmental shifts can cause an individual, for example, to change from being a *Seeker* to a *Keeper* as work piles up, children are born, or a relationship deteriorates and socializing with another couple is no longer fun. The context may also shift. A woman who grows up in a small town where she was well known and an extrovert may become more withdrawn or shy after moving to a new metropolis with a new husband where people are familiar with him and not with her.

These shifts can occur on both the individual level and the couple level. One partner in the couple affects the other. If two *Seekers* marry each other, they are likely to be a *Seeker* couple just as if two *Nesters* or *Keepers* marry someone similar to themselves in this manner, they are likely to stay in those categories. Quite common though are couples where partners in different categories marry. Perhaps an introvert was attracted to the extrovert because of her outgoing qualities. The couple then has to negotiate how to implement their different styles of friendship making. They have to negotiate how to balance their social life with their life as a couple and with their lives as individuals. The couple can also shift from one category to the next as they pull together to take on the caretaking of older parents or child rearing responsibilities.

These categories do not, of course, describe all couples. They provide a broad template for understanding the dynamic situations of couples' interactions with others. Couples are often driven to spend time with couples for reasons other than their style. These reasons might include escaping an unhappy marriage where seeking a stimulating conversation serves as a respite from one's spouse or partner. On the other hand, that same couple may start to withdraw from others as their marriage deteriorates, and because of their unwillingness to show their unhappiness to others, they become *Nesters*. Couples thus may shift from one category to the next based on what is happening in their lives.

Sometimes both members of the couple are active *Seekers,* for example, Will and Zoe in Chapter 4 and Michael and Nadine in Chapter 5. Other times the partner who is a *Seeker* will take the lead and bring her or his partner along. You can read how a newly married couple, Charlie and Diane, are working out their *Seeker-Nester* differences in Chapter 3 and how Sonia (primarily a *Seeker*) and Raymond (primarily a *Nester*) in Chapter 4 have learned to negotiate their different orientations during their years together. You can read about Adam and Betty, an example of one type of *Nester*, in Chapter 3.

We would like to illustrate these categories by quoting a few of the couples we interviewed who were asked specifically about which category they felt was the best fit for them. We will start with *Seekers*.

Cindy, married to Dan for 30 years and in her early 50s, told us, "I think at this exact moment in time, we resemble the first group where we are actively seeking new couples friends because we haven't made any couple friends here yet." Dan clarifies. "It's not like we are cold calling people on the phone and running out in the yard and tackling people saying, 'Please be our friend!' but, yes, I would agree."

Carolyn and Paul, married for 2 years and in their 20s, have to negotiate different personal styles of interaction. They identify themselves as *Seekers*. Carolyn reported, "I get my energy from being around people and Paul is more of an introvert so when we go to parties I'll want to stay longer. But I think we try to compromise. I'm more sensitive to when he is getting tired and he tries to put in an extra effort to stay longer because he knows I want to. It probably makes us a better couple because we are really happy with our friends in the community." Paul chimes in, "I agree, having the big circle of friends. When I see everything I love about Carolyn it puts it all in perspective for me."

Sarah and Ben, married for 3 years and in their early 30s, are an example of *Keepers*. "We like other couples," Sarah said. "We have friends and if we make new friends that's great but we don't go seeking them out." Ben replies. "I have to say the same thing. I enjoy hanging out but do not seek new friends."

This next couple, newly married and in their early 20s, are *Keepers* but are less sure if that is the best way for them to be. In describing themselves as *Keepers*, Davey told us, "We should probably lean more toward making new friends because we just moved and don't have any friends where we live but I am just not that kind of person. I don't instigate hanging out with a person. If they want to hang out, that's fine. Also I am not one of those needy people that needs you to text me all the time so, if you need that, then we are not going to be friends." When asked how the move has affected their couple friends, Astrid replied, "We are still very close with everyone so far. It has only been a few months. Some people have come to visit us already and we have plans for the holidays to see other friends so I have not noticed any change so far except that we don't have couples to go out to dinner with or see a movie, or things we used to do."

In essence, and as the 24-year-old husband in one other couple told us, couples in this category are not closed to making new friends, but they are content with their current situation. "It is not that we don't want to make new friends, but we are not in a rush to do so because we are more than satisfied with the friendships that we have."

The *Nesters* sometimes mention family as a reason for not being a *Keeper* or a *Seeker*, as do Neil and Sayra, married for 30 years and in their 50s. Couples also realize that they may change from one category to the next. Sayra described their situation, "I would say I used to be a *Keeper* and am now a *Nester*. I don't think either of us is really looking to make new couple friends. We feel right now we are happy with each other and if we go out as a couple every once in a while, that's fine. And we have family."

Jack and Kathleen are in their mid-20s and have been married for 1 year. "We prefer spending time with each other," he told us. "We are not especially interested in making new couple friends." "Yeah, definitely," Kathleen added. "We don't go hunt for couple friends. They aren't a necessity." As Jack sums up his feelings, "I'd rather just spend time with Kathleen."

Mixed Responses

Couples, of course, don't always agree. The introvert in the couple may staunchly defend his position that the couple are *Nesters* or *Keepers* while the extrovert will argue that she is a *Seeker*. Quotes from three couples illustrate that these categories may exist on a continuum and that not only might couples disagree, they also change with time as we heard above from Sayra.

Denny, 30 years old, and Marie, 24, hold different views and express varying social needs—he's a *Keeper* and she is a *Seeker*. Denny explains, "I think we have enough couple friends. I feel set. I don't think we need to make any more." Marie's perspective is different. "I thought you might say that, ha ha. We live in an area with many of Denny's friends so obviously he would feel set with our friends but most of my close friends live farther away so I would like to make new friends."

Suzanne and Randall, both in their 50s and married 26 years, describe how making new friends takes time and energy, which he may have but she does not. Randall speaks first. "I'm interested in associating with other couples and making new friends where she may not be." Suzanne responds thoughtfully,

> And I'm trying to think of how I would phrase that because I would say that we like spending time together and we have a small group of friends and I would like to make some more friends. It's just not that easy for me to make friends. I like people, but making real friends takes time and really getting people to a deeper level and especially in this (geographic) area, I have found it is hard to find that much time to build friendships unless you cut out a whole lot of other things in your life.

When questioned further, Suzanne says she may be a little bit of each category. "I would like to have some new friends, maybe a couple of couples, and although I am not running out every day trying to beat the bushes for them, I would like to—so I am not saying we have enough friends, but we are content. But I like the *Nester* notion because we like to spend a whole lot of time together alone."

INTERACTION: FUN SHARING AND EMOTION SHARING

Another way of thinking about couple friendships is to look at what two couples do when they get together, how they interact, and what they discuss. Based on what we learned from our early interviews, we hypothesized that couples tend to be on a continuum from emotion sharing at one end to fun sharing on the other end. When we tested this idea in later interviews, we asked couples directly if they saw their couple friendships as being more fun sharing or emotion sharing and gave them descriptions of each. More than two-thirds opted for the fun sharing definition as the primary one. When they were asked how they defined couple friendships, the couples who self-identified as fun sharing were also the couples who tended to describe couple friends as people with whom they could hang out with and have fun. The emphasis was on "doing something" with the other couple. Some couples in this group made a distinction between the nature of their individual friendships compared to the nature of their friendships with other couples.

Thomas and Anne, a couple in their early 30s who married 2 years ago, are typical of this group. Thomas explains, "I would say [we enjoy couple friendships] to have fun. Maybe her personal girlfriends are there for emotional reasons, but as a couple, I think they are mainly to do activities with and hang out and have a good time." Anne adds, "I would agree—primarily to have fun, I think. My individual friends are the ones I talk and gossip with."

Claudia and John, a couple in their mid-20s, have a similar view. Claudia begins, "If I want to be emotionally close to somebody, I'll seek it out, but that's not the purpose of going out with another couple. I don't need them to validate our relationship." John agrees. "If I want to be close to somebody and have a close personal conversation with someone, it would be one-on-one, not couple-on-couple. I guess there's a certain closeness there being with couples, but I still feel it's not too close. But yeah, I'm out there to have fun."

From other couples we frequently heard descriptions of couple friendships that included "couple friends are people with whom we share things," "where we care about each other," "where we have things in common" (interests, family values), and "where we all four people are equal." Couples who invoked definitions like those just given, which imply a different quality to a friendship than only having a good time, tend to be closer to the emotion sharing end of the continuum. We believe that most emotion sharing relationships also involve a good deal of fun sharing (which would enhance the emotion sharing), and many couples who identified as emotion sharing confirmed this.

Bill, a physician in his early 50s and his wife Barbara, who have been married for 25 years, are a good example. Bill responded first to our question about whether he and Barbara were more fun sharing or emotion sharing in their couple friendships. "I think the two are not mutually exclusive, meaning that we look for both at the same time." Barbara added, "I think that feeling emotionally close with someone allows you to feel safe and therefore have fun, so I agree that they aren't mutually exclusive."

Moira, a woman in her mid-20s who has been married to Laurence for 1 year, takes a similar perspective.

I think that having fun comes from having an emotional closeness with people. I mean there are definitely some couples that we just do things with that we have fun doing, like bowling or going to concerts. But I feel that the friends that we have an emotional closeness with we also have fun with and I would consider the friends where we have both to be better or closer friends than those where we are just friends because they are fun to party with.

We do not think the opposite is necessarily true; fun sharing couples are often not interested in feeling emotionally close to another couple. Some fun sharing couples just want to have a good time with friends. They may have very busy and emotionally fulfilled lives and want to be with other couples only for the fun that is involved. We found that fun sharing couples were more likely to have children 18 and under living in the home than were emotion sharing couples. Such family obligations could easily consume their time and emotional energy and cause them to seek out couples to have a good time as a respite from raising children. As we mentioned earlier, some couples we interviewed told us that they prefer to discuss personal issues and share feelings about what's happening in their lives with their individual friends. Other couples may prefer to confide primarily in their partner and not with others outside of the relationship, or they may have a partner who is uncomfortable sharing emotions.

Research on gender preferences in friendships suggests that fun sharing couples are closer to the male model of friendship, which focuses on engaging in joint activities, whereas emotion sharing couples are similar to women's friendships with their focus on intimacy. However, interviewing couples together, as we did in our study, makes it difficult to determine the impact of gender-based friendship styles on couples' preferences for emotion sharing versus fun sharing with their couple friends. We did discover characteristics of emotion sharing couples, however, that distinguish them from fun sharing couples. Emotion sharing couples tend to identify couple friendships as more important to them than do fun sharing couples. They tend to describe a strong emotional investment in the couple friendships that they have. Further, they tend to be more affected by the breakup or divorce of their couple friends than are fun sharing couples. They have invested more in their couple friends and thus lose more when the friendships dissolve. Emotion sharing couples frequently mentioned how important couple friendships were to their lives, at times referring to another couple as "like family." Their description of the closeness they felt, often over many years of friendship, is consistent with Slatcher's[32] research that sharing emotional information helps people feel closer.

We became interested in what these couples could teach us about how to establish close, caring, often long-lasting friendships with other couples. What could we learn about whether these friendships enhanced their own relationship as a couple and, if so, how? There are many examples of emotion sharing couples in the book. See Chapter 8 for an example of a very close 38-year relationship between two couples who were interviewed together. Read about Paula and Oscar in Chapter 5 and Sonia and Raymond in Chapter 4.

OTHER FINDINGS ABOUT COUPLES

Age and Child Rearing

The importance of couple friendships changes with both age and child rearing responsibilities. The older the couple is, the more important couple friendships are. Couples with children age 18 and younger are most likely to feel they do not have enough time for couple friends and less likely than couples without children in the home to say couple friendships are important. People without children in the home (those who never had children and those with children older than 18) are more likely to say that couple friendships increased in importance over time. We believe these findings are a reflection of differences in life stages. Couples with child rearing responsibilities are the group most likely to be busy caring for children and do not have as much time for socializing with other couples.

Partnered Versus Married

Partnered couples comprise 22% of the sample and tend to be younger than the married couples. Partnered couples are less likely than married couples to say couple friends are important. Partnered people are more likely to have opposite sex friends and are more interested in socializing with other couples than married people. They are less likely to share friends in common. We believe these differences reflect greater independence on the part of partnered people and less interdependence in relation to their significant other.

Married or Partnered for the First Time

Those married or partnered for the first time (compared with those married or partnered more than once) comprise 76% of the sample. They are more likely to say couple friendships are very important. Those married or partnered for the first time are less likely to admit to competing with each other when socializing with other couples. We found a trend showing that those married or partnered for the first time are more likely to say their relationship was reaffirmed when they were with another couple. We believe that people who have had more than one marriage or partnership have most likely experienced the loss of couple friendships. As a result, they may value them less and not be as influenced by spending time with another couple.

What About Men and Women?

We inquired about gender differences with a number of different items on the questionnaire. Men and women agree that women do most of the friendship maintenance and socially women are more likely to "call the shots." Although not statistically significant as a difference, there were clear trends with men and women agreeing women are better at making friends than men and that the couple's socializing revolves more around women than men. In many aspects of these relationships then, things are left in the hands of women.

We also asked about individual friendships. Women are more likely than men to say their partners do not have enough friends. And, as an interesting commentary on relationships, women were more reluctant to introduce their partners to friends than were men. This may be because, according to one of the trends we found, men are less picky about friends than are women. Two final differences that are perhaps no surprise: Women are more comfortable than men are with sharing self-doubts with friends, and men feel more competitive with their friends than do women.

As discussed in the first chapter, these friendship-making trends would be expected given past research on gender roles. Women tend to take the social lead in relationship maintenance; may care more about what their friends think about them, as they are more relationship oriented; and feel more comfortable being with their feelings.

In addition, we found gender differences in the divorced sample. Women who divorced viewed couple friendships as less important than divorced men did. We're unsure why this is so. It may be because, if women lost couple friends because of the divorce, they were more likely to protect themselves from valuing them in the future. Divorced women are more likely than divorced men to say that their spouses flirted during the marriage and that alcohol interfered with socializing. Divorced women were also more likely to say that the couple had no couple friends during the marriage. This last difference between men and women may be due to women, who, sensing trouble in the relationship before the men (and, as we just saw, are more involved in maintaining couple friendships), pulled away and separated themselves from other couples.

Does Money Matter?

People grouped themselves by their socioeconomic class (lower, lower-middle, middle, upper-middle, or upper). We collapsed these into three categories of lower, middle, and upper. Class is a difficult variable to understand because people may have lived the majority of their life in one economic situation and then recently moved up a class (depending on education or a new job) or down a class (depending on the impact of the recession or retirement). Also, a couple may be comprised of two people raised in different classes. We did not find many relationships between the key variables explored in this book and social class. We did find that couple friendships are least important to people in the lower socioeconomic group and are most important to middle-income people. Middle-income people would be the least content not socializing with others. People in the highest economic group are more likely to seek out couple friends and to say that they wanted to be closer with their friends. These findings may reflect that money buys time to socialize with others outside of family and work.

Potential Trouble in Marriages

There are correlations between happiness in marriage and beliefs about friendships. We do not know if one causes the other. Most people (58%) said they thought their spouse or partner was "very happy" in the marriage or relationship. Most notably, and a finding that has a significant application to the couples reading this book, those who thought their partner or spouse was less than "very happy" were also those who rarely agreed about how to spend time together. We asked, "Do you and your spouse/partner agree about the amount of time you should spend with other couples versus spending time alone with each other?" Those who did not agree frequently were likely to be the same couples who rated their spouse less happy in the marriage.

Those who were less than very happy were also more likely to say their couple friends were based on either their or their partner's friends rather than shared couple friends. They also believe they do not have enough friends as a couple and that their spouse or partner wants more friends. Put another way, if people in our study said their partner or spouse is very happy in the marriage, they were more likely to agree about how to spend time together, more likely to have couple friendships that were formed jointly, and more likely to believe that they have enough couple friends and their partner or spouse has enough individual friends.

A few couples who were interviewed told of sexual tension and even sexual infidelity between couples. In Chapter 3, Charlie describes tension between him and the female in another couple. Ken and Leah in Chapter 5 describe an affair involving two couples who were part of their social network, and Gloria in Chapter 7 admits to an affair with her best friend's husband. Flirting occurred in couples who divorced as well as couples who stayed together, with men described by their partners as being more likely to flirt than women.

FINAL THOUGHTS

To add to the complexities of trying to understand human relationships, we found considerable overlap between couple friends and individual friends among the couples in our study. Couples we interviewed described fluidity in how they socialized with their couple friends. Sometimes two couples got together. Other times, the two women or men from these couples socialized together without their partners.[33] This is not surprising, as the majority of couples in our study first met through one member of the couple. For example, two women who met at college or at work would bring their husbands or partners into the joint friendship. Marking exactly where an individual friendship ends and a couple friendship begins is often impossible. But couples did share examples of drawing boundaries, both around what they share in their individual friendship and what they shared with another couple. At times, the couples we interviewed made a joint decision as a couple not to discuss a sensitive topic when out with another couple. As individuals, they sometimes decided to hold in confidence something one member of the other couple had shared with them.

We asked, through a series of open-ended questions, how individual and couple friendships differ. Many reported the context affects their conversations and their activities: One-third feel that when they are out with couple friends, their friendship with one member of the couple is constrained, that the individual friendship is reined in. Half said they talk about different topics with individual friends than couple friends, and half said they engage in less gender-specific activities when with couple friends. One-quarter offered that one of the differences is they converse on more emotional topics with their individual friends. With individual friends, for example, they may talk more about their partners. When couples are together, they may be more interested in talking about topics relevant to the four of them. Some partners will use the couple friendship to seek another perspective from a friend of the opposite sex about a couple issue. They may not get such a perspective from a same-sex friend, especially if that friend is not in a relationship. A few couples said there was no difference between what they said and did with their individual versus their couple friends.

Little information in prior research relates to couple friendships with other couples, that is, two couples relating together as couples. Our study sought to understand the nature of friendships in which each participant is linked in an intimate committed relationship (partnership or marriage) to her or his partner and also connected through friendship to both members of another committed couple. Such friendships combine the dynamics of the marital relationship with the gender expectations both men and women bring to ideas about friendship. How these dynamics played out for the couples we interviewed was one of the most interesting parts of our study.

3

Starting Out
Couples in the First Years of Marriage/Partnership

A newly married couple in their 20s lived in three cities in 3 years while she finished her education. He is a school teacher and easily found work as they moved. In their newest location, they had single friends and wanted couple friends so they could go out with people they both enjoyed and with whom they could converse on a variety of topics. One of them would meet someone through work who was married or had a partner, and suggest that the four of them go out, hoping to begin a couple friendship. "I would get nervous before we went out. It was like it used to be before a first date. Here we were on a first date with another couple," the woman said. "Only it is tougher because my husband and I each need to like both of them for us to get to the second date."

In this first of three chapters discussing the life stages of couples, we focus on the early years of the marriage and partnership. We include the initial years of living together before marriage, the first years of marriage (or committed partnership; we will use the terms interchangeably but are referring to both partnerships and marriages), and the raising of young children.

Who are these young couples? One-half of our sample is between 21 and 35 years old, and about two-thirds in this age group are between 21 and 29. The Pew Research Center in a 2010 publication[1] refers to 18- to 29-year-olds as "millennials." We excluded people under 21 from our sample and have added the mid-30s to include couples who are more likely to be starting families. In our study, half are partnered and half are married in the 21- to 29-year-olds, and about two-thirds of the 30- to 35-year-olds are married. About one-sixth of the couples between 21 and 35 have children, and all of those have at least one preteen child in the house. Most have been married or committed for 5 years or less, and two-fifths have been committed 2 years or less.[2]

To older readers, these young couples may seem younger than their chrono-logical age. They may live at home longer, stay wired in to their parents more through e-mail and cell phone, and rely on parents for guidance to a greater degree than did previous generations. According to the U.S. Census Department, people are forestalling marriage longer, as the age of first marriage has crept up during the last 10 years. This age group may have extended their childhoods so that 25-year-olds seem younger and more dependent than ever before. This may not be a bad thing. The Pew Report states that this generation feels emotionally closer to their parents than previous generations felt to theirs.

COUPLES JUST STARTING OUT

Many of these new couples consist of individuals finding their own way in life as they find their way together as a couple. Pressures are varied. As they transition from being single to being a member of a couple, they are starting careers and securing first jobs with companies that might not exist in 6 months due to a reces-sionary economy and a rapidly changing marketplace. For example, at the end of the first decade of the 21st century, school boards are cutting teachers' positions to balance budgets. Cities are reducing services. Law firms are forestalling hiring new associates for 6 months to a year. Construction on new homes has slowed, leaving skilled workers on the sideline, and the unemployment rate remains stub-bornly higher than it has been in decades. Once-secure jobs or professions are no longer certain. As partners attempt to find their way for the first time in this job market, they may also be "coupling" with a partner for the first time.

Many pressures affect how newly forming couples deal with each other while they try to establish friendships with other couples. These include economic and work pressures, pressures to communicate electronically, and entanglements with former sexual partners. In addition, family history and societal shifts affect how couples manage these friendships.

Economics and Employment Affect Couples and Their Couple Friends

Some members in these couples were interviewed in 2008 and 2009 when the economy was at its weakest; others were interviewed in late 2010 when the econ-omy was slowly improving. A few had decided to return to college or enter grad-uate school to enhance their job prospects. Some were "in between positions." Others were treading water until the economy turned around, holding on to jobs where they were unhappy but had health benefits. A few stayed in their relation-ships longer so they could share living expenses. The Pew Report describes mil-lennials as experiencing a higher rate of unemployment, 37% for those 18 to 29, than any generation in the past 30 years.

As these economic conditions potentially affect a couple's relationship, they affect couple friendships, as we will show in this chapter. Couples seek other couples who travel in their same financial strata. For a couple where both members are working (if they are both lucky enough to find jobs), there are limits to their free time and discretionary income. How they spend time and money is significant for their identity as a couple.

Choosing the right restaurant in the right price range can be vexing if one couple is comprised of two foodies and the other is not. What if one couple drinks and the other does not? How is the bill split, and will the anticipated costs of drinking affect where and how they decide to socialize? What if time off from work to vacation together is more a problem for one couple than the other?

Other changes intrude on a friendship for young couples starting out. If one couple is skipping up socioeconomic classes as a result of success at work and wants to try new places while old friends prefer their favorite haunts, a schism as well as jealousy can put the friendship in the deep freeze. These issues are not unique to newly forming young couples, but this stage of economic and social separation could be the first time the couple must figure out together how to negotiate their couple relationships. How these potential rifts are handled speaks to the couple's identity and relationship as a couple.

Electronic Communication Affects Couples and Their Couple Friends

The Pew Report notes that this generation is more "connected" than previous generations. Specifically, they are more apt to sleep with their cell phone near them and to have a social network profile. Social pressures from these electronic ties arise. New couples communicate with their friends more often than previous generations did. Facebook, Myspace, Linkedin, high school and college reunion Web sites, Google, WhitePages.com, e-mail, text messaging, and cell phones affect the speed of responding to requests from friends.

The partner in Couple A asks about Couple B's plans for the weekend. The spouse in Couple B tries to reach her spouse to see if he is interested. (Many couples negotiate about their social calendar between themselves before making a decision about with whom to socialize. The exception may be when a request comes in from old friends and a spouse has carte blanche to accept.) What is the time lag before Couple A feels insulted by not getting a response? What if Couple A wants to approach another couple for the weekend and time is running out? In the "old days," voice mails would be left at home and calls returned after work when partners were home. In the "real old days," pre–voice mail, someone had to be home to answer the phone. Today, the waiting period before a couple appears rude by not responding has been shortened, which gives the couple less time to negotiate between each other.

As a result of increased connectivity, separation from friends is harder to forge. If a couple wants privacy or boundaries between themselves and their friends, they must actively unplug. There are few excuses for not communicating. And, not communicating is communicating, according to psychologist and philosopher Paul Watzlawick, who wrote, "You cannot not communicate." He meant that everything we do, how we dress, act, and, by extension, what car we drive and house we live in, is a form of communication about ourselves.

Today there are so many active ways to communicate that it is hard to imagine Watzlawick making that same statement. The pressure to communicate is so great and the ability to communicate is so varied. Attempts to not communicate with friends may subtly take the form of not returning a text, an e-mail, or a phone call within a matter of minutes; those attempts send a clear message: I am not as interested in you as you are in me. They even take the form of being jilted in relationships. Drew Barrymore's character, Mary, in the 2009 comedy, *He's Just Not That Into You*, laments that she now has to check text messages, e-mail, and voice mail before she is convinced a guy she has just met is not trying to reach her; she gets rejected in three mediums.

Sexual Relations Affect Couples and Their Couple Friends

Not only are economic matters and communication modalities adding pressure to young couples and their couple friendships, so, too, are sexual matters. This generation's social scene includes dating in groups in high school and college, rather than pairing up; hooking up for one-night stands; and maintaining "friends with benefits" (a reference to having sex with someone with no explicit emotional commitment). When couples form, there has often been a sexual history to contend with that may include current or past friends. Incorporating these friends into couple friendships may be tricky. If platonic friends had sex without an expectation that a love relationship would form, does that friend get invited to the first-one-to-marry's wedding? An explicit ex-boyfriend or ex-girlfriend might be kept off a guest list, but what about an ex–friend with benefits?

Family History Affects Couples and Their Couple Friends

Family history can also play a part in the formation of the couple and their friendships. Although the divorce rate, now close to 40%, has dropped slightly from its high a generation ago, many of those now in their 20s and early 30s were part of the divorce generation where, according to the Pew Report, just 4 in 10 children were raised with both parents in the home. Although divorce no longer carries a stigma, a newly formed couple may have expectations about the permanency of marriage or relationships derived from their family history.[3] Numerous studies show that children of divorce are more apt to consider divorce than those raised in two-parent families. Opting out of a relationship becomes a viable choice and may account for the rising age of first marriage in the United States (because adult children with divorced parents are more reluctant to commit). A family history of divorce may also help explain the high percentage of couples in our sample (not a random one) who are partnered and not married. In fact, we found specific characteristics related to couple friendships that do distinguish married from partnered couples in our sample. (See Chapter 2 for this information.) And what do couples learn from their parents about friendships? Although our findings do not show a clear relationship in the friendships between couples whose parents had a lot of friends and those who did not, interesting stories emerge about these influences from the couples we interviewed.

Social Changes Affect Couples and Their Couple Friends

In addition, there are social changes as couples sort out single friends from couple friends. Who is kept and who is dropped in the transition to partnering and marriage will affect the individual partners' identities and their well-being. Stories are legion of single friends being dumped as their former best friend finds a partner who replaces them with a love interest. The time available to the friend vanishes, especially if that friend poses a threat to the new relationship.

Behaviors change, too, as people reach their late 20s and marry. Partying is less likely to involve heavy drinking and staying up late, as numerous people in the study told us. Weekends with the "boys" or the "girls" often come under scrutiny as they are perceived as a potential sexual threat to the relationship (though, as we will hear from Jenny later in this chapter, by the time children arrive and the marriage is stable, getting together with "the girls" becomes okay again). Single friends, while still important to the identity of the individual, get crowded out.

Friends of the opposite sex? Newly marrieds, and members of younger couples in general,[4] are more apt to have friends of the opposite sex than people married longer. This makes sense. Such opposite-sex friends have been an important part of most young adults' social lives. They are around prenuptially, so it is natural that some of these friends remain initially with marriage. Dropping friends after establishing a love relationship with someone else might demonstrate disloyalty to those old friends. But over time, these friendships may fade anyway.

What Others Have Learned

The research on couple relationships is instructive here. According to Robert Milardo, a professor of family relations at the University of Maine, the more interaction a new couple has with each other and with others outside the couple, the more their identity as a unit will be solidified. One way of thinking about how couples balance their needs to be with single friends versus couple friends is the "competition hypothesis." Essentially, couples have to choose between competing demands on their time. As newly formed couples spend more time with each other, their network of friends shrinks, according to previous research.[5] More recent research has challenged this, indicating that the number of friends increases.[6] In a study of young dating couples, researchers Agnew, Loving, and Drigotas found that couples with a higher proportion of joint versus individual friends were more committed to and satisfied with their relationships, suggesting the potential influence of shared friendships in stabilizing a relationship.[7] It may be that when couples share interactions with other couples and receive support for their relationship from their social network, their relationships are validated. That validation solidifies it for them and, as a result, further solidifies the couple in the eyes of others who then reinforce that togetherness. A feedback loop is established.

Figuring out how to balance time for both individual and couples' friends is key to a new couple's development. Couples tend to form these overlapping "friendship networks" (friends in common) before and during their first year of marriage, after which the interdependence of husbands' and wives' networks remains fairly stable.[8] The phenomenon of couples sharing overlapping social networks is complex, however. On the one hand, whereas sharing of friends is good for marital satisfaction, too much intensity of interactions can be a problem. If the networks are too small and the interactions too enmeshed, the couple may experience marital dissatisfaction.[9] On the other hand, having shared lifestyles with friends in common can keep couples together because the emotional cost of breaking up is greater.[10] Jenny's example later in this chapter speaks to these issues as she drops one of her friends who wanted to spend all her time with her.

The success in developing friendships with other couples has also been linked to the degree of communication members of a couple have with each other. Couples who talk about their problems are more stable than those who do not.[11] Research has also explored how couples spend time together and apart. As might be expected, those who spend more time together are happier (and probably those who are happier spend more time together).[12] These couples are likely to have more friends in common, which would increase their ability to spend time together. This assumes that the choice of a partner is supported by the "friendship group." This does not always happen. Some couples are marginalized by their choice of partner (as historically occurred for interracial couples where each racial group may have rejected the other partner's choice.)[13] This "relationship marginalization" (when partners perceive their new romantic relationship to be a subject of disapproval by friends and others) has been linked to couples being less apt to stay together.[14]

It also may be that partnered couples, as compared with married couples, have slightly different views on friendships. Cohabitating (partnered) couples in the Netherlands who are not yet married were found to spend less time together than married couples, because, it is believed, of the uncertainty of the future of their relationship.[15] In essence, when compared with married couples, partnered couples make less of a commitment and may be more likely to want to keep their options open for a separate life by retaining outside friends. Once these couples are married, the friendship process can change. Sociologist Sarah Matthews, writing about friendships across the life span,[16] describes what newlyweds go through. She writes that before the wedding, the partners are concerned with whether they will be accepted by their partner's friends. After the wedding, and with the commitment formalized, they look more critically at how much they like their partner's friends. They begin to consider who will stay friends with one of them and who will become friends with both. In addition, the partner's partner also will be considered for his or her merit as a friend. Who is kept and who is dropped is a natural stage in friendship making that evolves in the early stage of marriage.

When a couple spends time with one friend, it is different from being with another couple. When two friends are alone together, they often provide a mirror on the self, something an individual friend cannot provide the couple as a unit. Another couple is needed to provide a reflecting team that can support or impede a new couple's development. As each couple interacts with another couple, their own relationship is reconsidered.

ARRIVAL OF CHILDREN

Once children arrive, the playing field shifts. Just as single friends may be dropped when someone becomes part of a couple, friends without children may be dropped in favor of those with children, especially if they are close in age. Friendships are forged around newborns and children who enter day care or school. Activities change. With newborns, going out to dinner and traveling with another couple are off the list unless children are included. And, when out with another couple, the conversation centers on children, which, to a childless couple, can be a conversation killer. One couple we interviewed, who is introduced in the next chapter, has been trying for years to have children. They recently and understandably made friends with another childless couple, whom they met in a dog park. Had they had a child, they would possibly have met a different couple in a child-oriented park.

In a study of 137 couples, those who described greater network support prior to the birth of their first child were more apt to report having larger and more supportive networks 2 years after the birth.[17] One interesting note was the finding that contact with family, and by extension the social network, increased when a couple had emotional difficulties relating to the birth of a child. While this research speaks to the importance of establishing friendships early in the marriage, it cautions against drawing conclusions about the amount of contact with family and friends being related to adjustment of the couple to their relationship. A couple may feel they have a large and loving network yet not see the people in the network frequently.

Children are an important part of life for this generation. According to the Pew researchers, being a good parent was a higher priority for those under 30 than for those over 30. The under 30s also rated being a good parent a higher priority than having a successful marriage. In our research, the couples that remained childless were most likely to believe that couple friendships increased in importance with age. Without children, they most likely have more time for these friendships.

We now hear from three pairs in various stages of forming as a couple. The first, Charlie and Diane, are expecting their first child. The second, Adam and Betty, are struggling with their relationship, and we see tensions that can develop around friendships if the couple is not on the same page. The third, Jenny and Ike, have young children and are trying to figure out how to find time to be with their children and with friends who have been important to them.

THE COUPLES

Charlie and Diane

Charlie and Diane, both white, in their early 30s, and living together, were engaged the first time we interviewed him. Interviewing one member of a couple offers a different perspective than having both in the room. Charlie was remarkably open about his relationship with Diane. We interviewed them together 9 months later and much had changed. They were married and expecting a child in 6 weeks. Charlie is one of three children and Diane the middle child of nine. Both were raised by both parents—his were a teacher and a nurse, hers a postal worker and a military employee. Family life was stable for both of them and neither moved around when young. Charlie and Diane have college degrees and work as teachers.

Both interviews took place in a noisy pizza parlor in downtown Baltimore on warm afternoons in September and June. Charlie had volunteered for an interview after hearing the first author give a lecture on male friendships and noting our request for couples to interview for this book. He was initially more interested in being interviewed than was Diane and arrived without her.

As all our interviews begin, we asked Charlie how he defined couple friendships. He used the word *equality*, which is consistent with our findings about emotion sharing couples. Emotion sharing couples look for a deeper level of disclosure between couples than do fun sharing couples. Equality among members can facilitate openness. His answer about equality is an exemplar of how couple friendships can be constructed when relationships are evenly balanced.

> Our couples' friendships consist of people who are friends to both of us; there is a feeling of equality. It is like a friendship that we can enjoy when we are together. It makes Saturday night really fun or anything that is supposed to be good and relaxing. A couple friendship makes time enjoyable for couples and is defined by those with whom we feel that way. Diane and I have a number of friendships (he later names three couples). It is a huge privilege, we are all around the same age, and have similar interests and can be found in similar places.

Have Friends Broken Up?

We asked Charlie if they had ever known a couple with whom they were close who broke up and, if so, what the impact was on his relationship with Diane. Just as they derive great pleasure from friendships with couples, when their friends broke up, it shook their foundation. We believe that when a couple breaks up, even their friends in healthy relationships should consider its meaning. In our study, over one-third of those who said they knew a couple who had broken up were affected in some way.

> The impact on us was kind of shaky. We weren't clear what happened but then we learned that they had broken up and we know that it was internal. There was no one else involved, just them. It affected us in that it was a concern without there necessarily being an assumption of a problem, or it being a superstitious or worrisome thing. It had importance because there but for the grace of God-go us. The people were important to us. We were not going to say to them, "You are such a great couple, don't break up." We just know that it is hard in a relationship when someone is confused. So we felt empathy.

We asked Charlie what he meant by his statement, "There but for the grace of God, go us."

"That problems in relationships are inevitable, they can be too much, they are a natural part of relationships; the good relationship that we can call 'real love' is in great danger. It can be humbling."

We tried to clarify further what Charlie meant and asked if he was saying that relationships between two people are in danger because of what is happening in society.

His answer implies that relationships are fragile and that what happens outside of the couple can affect what happens inside the couple and that when couple friends break up, there can be reverberation. Part of Charlie and Diane's response was to take the breakup as a cautionary tale. In our research, younger couples are more affected by couple friends breaking up than are couples who have been together longer. These newer relationships are more fragile and have weathered fewer ups and downs.

> I may be a little flamboyant with that but the stakes are high because it seems like the whole world is to be gained or lost at any moment whether or not we have the same fears. My fears are not going to be shared by everyone in a relationship but they can be universal. And so, the impact of our friends' turmoil on our relationship with them made it harder for us to be as close to them so we tend to err on the side of caution and tend to be a little more reserved with friends and a little less spontaneous. When it is unclear what is going on with them, we pull back. Their turmoil was disruptive and made us rethink and be more aware of our own relationship.

How Open Are They With Friends?

Another standard question is designed to learn how the couple negotiates their openness with other couples. We asked Charlie if they decide what to share or not to share with another couple before going out with the couple. Newly minted couples have a harder time negotiating this than do well-established couples. Well-established couples usually understand better what their partners feel willing to discuss.

"There are times when I will mention something and maybe Diane will be uncomfortable that I mentioned it. I tend to talk more than she so I am likely to be the one to share too much (when out with another couple). Diane will then wait and make it clear to me what she wishes I had not done and why."

So Charlie is the more open one. But will they decide in advance what to talk about? His answer was forward looking and a sign of a well-functioning couple trying to figure out how to make things work better.

> In a moment like that, things will be decided for the future. We are not harping on each other; we are trying to be constructive. She will say, "Please don't say that in the future." She will not tell me to scold me but just so we can better understand each other in the future. Let's get to the root of the problem and let's find something to agree on.
> That's happened, but it is not par for the course. Maybe it has bordered on a quarrel or we have just had an intense discussion about something emotional, which may have been triggered by the social pressures of going out with someone—then she'll say, "You won't say anything about what we were just doing." That's happened a couple of times.

Opposite-Sex Friends and Individual Versus Couple Friends

Another standard question is whether the couple has opposite-sex friends. We found younger couples are more apt to have them than older couples because these friendships often were started before they became a couple. As Charlie relates, old friends are accepted, but new friends would raise concerns.

"I do have friends who are women. The ones that go back from before Diane and I were together are more accepted by her (laughs) but I don't think there are any new ones. I just don't see how I could make friends now, unless it was someone at work. And this would be an object of scrutiny."

Charlie gave one of his more interesting responses to our question about old friends and whether they were part of the package when they first established their relationship. His answer shows again how forward thinking Charlie and Diane are.

> We specifically dismantle our thoughts that would be expressed in that sort of language—is that part of the package deal. We purposefully dismantle it. The term

deal is the language of business brought together in matters of the heart and it seeks to communicate emotions in terms of currency, contract, obligation, is litigious, and we totally reject that. What is understood is that I can say that for all of the turmoil there may have been with a friend of mine, that it has never been questioned as to whether I should have those friendships. And yet, we have never discussed this but I just know that the only new individual female friendship that will come up would be destined to come about. Because I am not looking for it and because I act different because I am not going to be available in the first place for the kind of sparking connections that make those friendships.

The last comment is a cogent insight into how one makes friends or chooses to not make friends. Charlie will rein in his behavior around women to clearly communicate that he is not available. He is also commenting about how he could act around women in couples he and Diane would like to befriend, in relationships where there is no flirting.

In building our case for the importance of couple friendships, we are not suggesting they replace individual friendships; some people will always rely on individual friendships more. We believe couple friendships can be an important adjunct to those friendships. To tease out the differences between individual friendships and couple friendships, we ask what distinguishes one from the other. Charlie, like many in our research, answers that he interacts differently with individual friends. He adds that he is highly aware of Diane when he is out with her and their friends. This awareness is a distraction because he is trying to balance her needs, too.

Mainly, when I am with one person I am going to talk about my spouse. I am going to be more spontaneous with the one friend because it doesn't take much room to be sensitive to my own emotions but when I am out with Diane and another couple, it's much more mind power devoted to what she is doing.
What I say about our relationship when I'm with the couple, what I select, is quite different from what I say to an individual who is going to hold it in confidence. The fact is, I will be more spontaneous with individuals than with her and another couple.

We ask if being with another couple makes Charlie inhibited. When Diane is there, he constantly monitors what she may be feeling.

If nothing else, the main thing is that she's different from everyone else and she's on my mind. It's a fact that she matters more to how my actions might affect her. I don't have to think about how her actions are affecting me, it is right there and I can deal with it, but how my actions are affecting her requires a little more forethought and energy because when she is there I am being more careful, more sensitive. There are many actions that might affect her more than anyone else.

Charlie continues about the advantages of being with couples rather than individuals. "We have more in common; there is a parity with the couples. We have things in common, economically. The table stays level with more legs. The individuals? Who knows? One who is a friend is dealing with a heroin problem. So we have less in common. Individuals might be doing anything, they might be in the army or rich. I have nothing in common with them."

To us, it sounds like a couple friendship is a regression to a mean, whereas individual friendships can follow more extremes.

> It is the only place where the four of us are going to find each other, where all four of us would have found each other in the beginning. We have to coincide at least in the beginning. And only in such a place are four people going to find each other. It is like, if one person in the couple does not like each other, they won't find the other couple worth hanging out with. But if we all like each other, we say, "Weren't they great?" And then the other couple becomes something that we share as a couple, it makes us happy by ourselves and we are going to like hanging out with each other more.

We needed to clarify this key point and learned from Charlie that, in essence, being with another couple helps him enjoy his own partner more.

"Yes," he responded. "The power of groups."

Sex Roles

Charlie seems like a pretty progressive guy when it comes to men's and women's roles in couple friendships. That being said, he comes down squarely on the side of science when it comes to how our sex roles are played out in friendships. He also believes that sexual tension is often lurking in the background.

> I never forget what someone said about women having a bigger brain and a bigger limbic system and forming attachments. Then I heard from a friend who went through a sex change operation, female to male. He got testosterone and said that before [when he was a woman] he used to look at women on a train and say, I think she is pretty, I wonder what she is reading. Now he has his mind assaulted with pornographic images. Makes perfect sense to me. It is concrete chemistry that I can understand, and evidence of the psychic nature of women and men being different. A man will approach couple friendships differently because there is the female element to the other couple. Does he think she's attractive? Does he think that she thinks that he's attractive? Does he perceive sexual tension? Does he enjoy that? Does he prefer that there is none?
> I guess when it comes to the bottom line men will [make the phone calls for couple dates] less frequently because they don't want to get into trouble. What if the man calls and gets the woman? Will that look like he and she are making plans? He is vulnerable to being accused or misinterpreted or he's vulnerable to crossing the line or being flirtatious. Whereas if the woman makes the call to the other woman, they will be the bosses together, which is stereotypical but that's how it is.

Charles has felt sexual tension with another couple. As part of the interview, we ask couples to think of a particular couple and answer questions about them. When asked if there has been sexual tension with that couple, couples rarely state there has been. (Perhaps a couple would not choose to talk about a couple where it existed.) Charlie has experienced it.

"At one point Diane thought the woman was flirting with me but that was in the past. We talked that through and she is okay with it now."

Their friendship with this other couple improves their own relationship. "Being with them makes us stronger because it is another couple doing what we are doing. They are faithful to one another and authentic, sincere, and genuine human beings and the fact that we can see their relationship as good makes us more confident in our relationship. They have integrity. It is harder to hide when you have integrity. We know that they endure the difficulties as well; we know that the difficulties happen."

For Charlie, his couple friendships have improved with time and age. They have reached a greater level of emotional maturity. As he tells it, "They have deepened and opened. We have real good friends and enjoy friendships that aren't plagued by boredom and gossip and envy. We don't seem to be up for that sort of thing."

Nine Months Later

We interviewed them together 9 months later, at which point they had been married for 7 months and Diane was pregnant. Diane is the quieter of the two and describes herself in *Nester* terms while Charlie is a self-described *Seeker*.

Charlie gladly yielded during the couple interview to let Diane express herself and seemed to revel in her comments. Whereas couple friendships are very important to Charlie, they do not hold as much salience for Diane. She needs space from other people from time to time and does not like to do many things with groups—she wants the freedom to go off on her own.

> When I have free time, I don't think, "Who can I hang out with?" I think, "I can do the things I want to do." I don't think to call up people even if I care about them. When Charlie gets a free moment, he thinks about whom he can call. I will usually call someone when I am bored. When I am alone, I can be very happy. Maybe it's because I was raised in a large family and shared a room with three others. Charlie is the more social of the two of us. But now that I am pregnant I want to be with Charlie. I don't want to be alone. I think I am more of an introvert in general. Some people get their energy from others. Not me.

Diane can be quite self-contained. But since her pregnancy, her desire to be with Charlie has shifted. Shifts in sociability are not uncommon. We see a shift in the interview with Jenny and Ike, where they are becoming less social with other couples as they focus more on their young children.

While Diane wants to be with Charlie more often, she also is more willing to be with others, too, if the environment is contained. "Society is not set up for pregnant people. It is difficult to be in crowds and do things when you are pregnant," she told us. As a result, she increasingly prefers to be home. This natural tendency is heightened because of the fatigue she is feeling. She is happy entertaining others there because she can decide whom to invite and when the entertaining will end. They are as likely to have couple friends, she believes, as individual friends. What they do with their friends has changed as they age into the 30s; they tend to party less when they go out.

We wondered if they sought couple friends.

"I am the more social one and I do not look for friends. We do not make an effort to make friends. It just has to happen," Charlie told us. "You cannot expedite or accelerate it. We recently saw a couple we liked at a few different events and began hanging out with them more because of that. Circumstances got us closer. We value individual friends as much as couple friends and will be inclusive when we can be. I am thrilled when Diane reaches out to friends or calls them. I'm usually the one who does it."

When an outgoing person is married to an introvert, how do they balance the competing interest in socializing?

"We have to negotiate it," Diane replied directly. "We talk about it."

When we asked them about our *Seeker, Keeper,* and *Nester* categories, Diane offered insight into what external factors may affect the couple's category. She told us that her parents were *Nesters.* With nine children, they did not have time to do anything other than stay home and try to manage the family. She added that the house where she grew up was always a mess, with 11 people running around. She sees herself as someone who is comfortable with people as long as they are in the house she shares with Charlie. By hosting people, it allows her the freedom to begin and end the entertaining and control how she spends her time. This is a slight refinement then of the *Nester* category. She does not naturally seek out people to spend time with, but if she is with people, she wants it to be on her terms. Like Charlie during his interview, Diane added that individual friendships are a lot more "free flowing" for her. "I think that I am really a *Nester* and don't want to bring people in that much. I don't like to travel or get into social situations where I can't leave. I know that about myself and it frees me up to do whatever I want."

Charlie added, "I am more willing to go with the group than is Diane. I might be hoping to find a group and join it. The prospect of having more friends, I like that." Diane was shaking her head, disagreeing with this. "I don't want to give over control to the group. A leader will emerge. I don't want to be led and I don't want to be that leader."

We again asked, as we had asked Charlie earlier, if they discuss in advance what will and will not be shared with another couple when they go out with them. Their answers also reflect the nature of fun sharing and emotion sharing in couples. While both like to keep conversations light, Diane would go to her siblings for assistance with a serious issue. They also believe that emotionally laden topics can be worked through between the two of them.

"If we get into a fight, we might agree to not talk about it. Diane will say to me, 'You are not going to want to bring this up, are you?' She knows she does not need to say it but it is more like one of us is asking for assurance."

"Charlie really likes to have a good time when he is with people so I think there are things he wouldn't want to bring up, difficult things."

"Right. I don't want to sit there and complain about my problems unless the example serves the conversation," Charlie agrees.

"My siblings are where I would bring up something that was bothering me," Diane adds. "I would not sit with a man and a woman in a restaurant and talk about emotional issues that I have, our relationships, or child rearing."

According to Charlie,

There is a lot of stuff that goes on between us that we don't need to discuss with other couples. Your question, do we plan in advance what to talk about? We don't need to and even if we are susceptible to something we don't need to work that out in advance. Neither of us feels that we cannot work this out if it happens. We work well together and so a lot of this does not need to be negotiated. There is no danger of us going to sleep without processing something. We are not trying to mess with each other, so we can work it out.

As the interview winds through other questions, Diane's impressions about their relationships with other couples and each other closely reflect what we heard previously from Charlie. But as we turn to the upcoming birth, Charlie adds a comment that places this couple on the cusp of making new relationships. "I look forward to our couple friendships turning into family friendships. What breaks my heart is that family has to edge out friends." Diane adds, "I agree. I will like our friends interacting with our child. It does my heart well to know that this can happen." And Charlie continues, "I like the notion of our kids growing up knowing our friends' kids. This is so important that I don't want to push it because I think it has to happen naturally. You can't push friendships, they have to happen. But if they become friends, that will make my life. That will make my life!"

Charlie and Diane are a new couple, partnered for 4 years, engaged, and now married and expecting their first child. They reflect the life cycle of young couples as they begin a family. They have their typical struggles, but they seem to have worked them through with a realistic view of what couples endure as normal growing pains—working out differences and trying to communicate with each other while accommodating to each other's needs. If we were to think of them in our categories, they would sit between *Seeker* and *Nester* status as individuals and as a couple.

Contrast Charlie and Diane with what we hear from the next couple, Adam and Betty, who are younger and struggling in their relationship; friends are one of their flashpoints.

Adam and Betty

This young white couple is negotiating different styles of friendship making. She is highly interested in meeting couples and he is not; they are a *Seeker* and a *Nester* who are partners. In a healthy relationship made up of partners with varying styles (and we have many such couples in our sample), the couple talk through their expectations about time with friends, time with each other, and time alone. As will be seen, Adam and Betty's relationship is problematic. The number of couple friends they have? One.

Adam, 23 years old and with a high school degree, has been living with Betty, 22 years old and a store manager, for 3 years. Both have lived in their home-town in New Jersey their entire lives. They consider themselves middle-income. Adam's parents divorced and remarried when he was growing up. Betty's parents were in a stable marriage. His parents had a handful of couple friends after they each remarried; Betty's parents were involved with many other couples, giving her a perspective of a large social network. Their early years may have affected how they view couple friends now. Betty values couple friendships and Adam does not. In our study, couple friends tend to be valued more by those married for the first time than those partnered or married more than once.

Adam reports he has no female friends and two male friends. He feels that two friends are enough, that he is comfortable with this level of closeness, and that he could call one of his buddies any time if he needed help. Betty counts three female friends and one male friend, and, while comfortable with her level of closeness with them, wishes she had more friends. Both Betty and Adam have siblings but do not feel close to them.

Making Friends

Their differences about the importance of couple friends emerge early in the interview.

"I think that couples friendships are those that couples have as a unit. They spend time doing activities and enjoy each other's company. I feel it is positive and to me they mean a lot. It would be nice if they meant more to Adam."

"I just don't care so much about that," Adam replied. "I like doing things with just us or my friends alone. Those friendships with other couples don't mean much to me."

These different views from a *Seeker* (Betty) and a *Nester* (Adam) affect how they approach these couple friendships. "She tries to start them (couple friend-ships) by introducing me to a couple. She'll meet new women and try to get us all to go out as a couple. She's the one who tries to begin them," Adam explains.

"I agree. I usually try relentlessly to get a couple as friends through either work or other friends. I want to go out with other young people our age, but it is so difficult to get him to want to go. I just don't understand his aversion to it." Betty goes on to indicate that they continue to pursue individual friendships, which are not always as satisfying to her. "I'd say that we all four go out together and then Adam and his friend go out together as a pair."

"I'd say we usually go out more separately, not together, but we do go out sometimes together," Adam added.

From these answers, as contrasted with other couples, Adam and Betty sound like they are struggling to get along regarding their individual and their couple friendships. Other questions confirmed this, and when asked on their questionnaires about their partner's happiness with their relationship, both indicated they thought their partner was not very happy.

Looking at this couple through the lens of Marks's "three-corners" framework of marriage[18] (discussed in Chapter 2), Adam and Betty are having difficulty navigating both their second corner (their relationship with each other) and third corner (their connections with people and activities outside their relationship). They differ in how they want to use their individual third corners. Betty would like to socialize as a couple with another couple—a way to strengthen her relationship to Adam. Adam prefers to spend time away from Betty with his individual friends—a way to establish his separate identity. This tension affects their satisfaction with their own relationship.

How Open Are They With Other Couples?

We asked them if they determine in advance whether certain topics will be shared with a couple they are going out with. About 4 out of 10 of the couples in our study talk in advance about what they feel comfortable sharing with their couple friends when they go out. This question revealed further tension in Adam and Betty's relationship.

> Usually we don't do this ahead of time. Sex is considered taboo when all four of us are together, but I assume he talks about that with his friend. When we are out, Adam may get upset if I say too much or complain about something he did. It's pretty annoying when we're in a conversation and I feel like I'll get yelled at later for something I said that he thinks I shouldn't have.

Adam tries to clarify his reaction. "It is not that I'm mad; I just assume she won't say certain things and she does. She should know better. But I agree with everything else—we don't discuss sex and we don't set limits in advance."

Women tend to be more open when couples go out. But that can cause problems when the openness runs counter to privacy needs of the male partner. We asked them how often it has happened that one partner was interested in being friends with just one member of the couple and the other is not interested. As expected, Betty comes across as more invested in friendships. "I'm usually the one interested so I'd say Adam is the one that is quite often reluctant." Adam defends himself by saying, "I just don't think that having a lot of couples friends is important so I don't really see the need. I just wouldn't be friends with the person I didn't like. Life's too short."

"So I would end up just going out with the friend I liked," Betty said as a way of explaining how they deal with this.

Before we leave Adam and Betty, three more answers are worth noting regarding the balance between individual and couple friends, the couple's view of themselves as a couple, and their view of another couple they identify as friends. First we asked if they have opposite-sex friends, which are more common for younger than for older couples.

"He doesn't want me to have guy friends. Not even his best friend. He gets anxious if I talk to him on text messages!"

"I just don't like her talking to other men," Adam rejoins. "It is just not right. I don't have girlfriends so I don't expect her to have guy friends."

When we asked whether they think their couple friends are a reflection of them, Betty jumped in with, "I think I am a lot like Adam's best friend and his girlfriend is a lot like Adam. So perhaps they are a good reflection."

This pushed Adam's buttons. "Why do you think I am like her? She's annoying."

"Sometimes you are, too," Betty replied. "I just think she's a little insecure about him leaving her or something silly and you're a lot like that, too."

Rather than escalate this, Adam backed out by saying, "I don't agree but whatever."

When talking about their relationship with a specific couple with whom they are friends, they were asked if being with that couple reaffirmed their own relationship. About two-thirds of couples say being with another couple whom they identified as close friends strengthens their own relationship. This is one benefit of such relationships, a reaffirmation of the couple's own relationship. Betty's answer seems born out of jealousy and indicates another area in which the couple may need help.

"Usually being with them makes me mad because the guy is so good to her and treats her really well and sometimes I don't feel that Adam does that."

The blame cycle continues with Adam's response. "I feel like I treat Betty well but she doesn't appreciate what I do or the way I treat her well."

Despite their friendship with the other couple, they are not optimistic about that couple having a successful relationship. Adam doesn't think the other couple should marry, and Betty thinks the relationship is unhealthy, that she's too immature and untrustworthy to get married. We wonder if some of the comments made about the couple were a mirror on their own relationship.

Betty and Adam seem to be moving in opposite directions. Disagreeing to this extent in front of an interviewer is rare. Usually there is a level of relationship presentation that allows for a united front. Here, the gloves were off. They do not agree about the time to be spent with other couples, they believe the other partner is fairly unhappy in the relationship, and they actively snipe at each other at most turns of the conversation.

Six months later, they broke up. Two years later, she has moved out of her hometown and he has enlisted in the military.

Jenny and Ike: A Couple With Young Children

We met Jenny on a flight to Atlanta where we were going to interview another couple. We were talking about the research for this book and she hopped into the conversation, fascinated by the topic. (This is not an unusual situation for us; while waiting for planes we have met a number of people who have spontaneously offered us insight into their lives.)[19] We were intrigued by her descriptions of her own relationships and asked if we could follow up with a telephone interview.

Jenny, a white woman, in her mid-30s, was born and raised in New York. She is the second of three children. When she was 11 years old, and painfully aware of the difficult marriage her parents were having, she came across indisputable evidence that her mother was having an affair. She demanded her mother move out, which she did, leaving Jenny's father to raise her, her older sister, and younger brother. Despite what could have been Act II in a Greek tragedy, the family got itself on an even keel and the rest of her childhood was normal. Even though she had taken charge at a critical time by insisting her mother leave, Jenny subsequently never felt burdened to take care of her father. Described as lower-middle class, the family struggled but remained in their ranch-style house; Jenny went to a local college and married her high school sweetheart, Ike.

"I met him in high school at a leadership retreat and we became best friends, adored one another. We each had a bunch of girlfriends and boyfriends in between, but I came back to him because he was a perfect guy. He went to the University of Georgia and when I read that Atlanta was a great place to live, he was happy to stay in the South."

Ike was an only child of parents who are still married. He is the shyer of the two, by Jenny's description, and loved being pulled into her group of boisterous high school and college friends. As an only child, the instant "family" of so many friends was highly appealing.

Jenny and Ike now are raising two children, a 3- and a 6-year-old. They have figured out how to maintain separate relationships with their own friends. Once or twice a year, they tag team and one of them goes away on weekends to the beach with just "the boys" or "the girls" while the other parent stays at home with the children. They also travel with friends and their children. Their new home is large enough to accommodate family and the friends from New York. Ike is a business man earning a good income, and Jenny, once also in business, is now, by her description, a "domestic goddess aka housewife." She is thankful every day that, although she came from modest means, she and Ike can afford a more comfortable lifestyle. As a child, she had wanted a large and open house. As we will hear, acquiring a nice home can affect friendships.

Defining Friendships

Jenny adds,

> Relationships in general are such that we can learn and grow from each other and I think that applies to our couple relationships as a means to grow ourselves intellectually and emotionally in a group format. I like to surround myself with good energy and I like to have good times. I think it is so important for the soul to have fun and that's what friends do for me. I laugh a lot and have fun and that's what life is all about for me it is everything. I have my family and I have my base but without other people life would be lonely.

In Jenny's description of her and her husband's couple friendships, we see many benefits. She is an extrovert who wants to create as much togetherness as possible. Her network is quite large (20 couple friends) compared to most people we interviewed (less than one-quarter of the couples in our sample said they have 10 or more couple friends). As she counts her friends aloud to us, she makes a telling commentary about this stage of life and her ability to still seek friends.

> We are close with our neighbors and get together with them, seven couples, whom we see weekly, biweekly. And we have our high school group, and I have mommy friends, and college friends. So it is a lot of couple friends—the mommy friends are not that close—actually, I don't want any more friends, I can't maintain them. I can't open myself up to them; my son just started kindergarten and I am meeting all these moms who want to be friends and I have to say no to them because I can't maintain it with them. I wouldn't be able to give them what I think a friend deserves. I want to be able to maintain a quality relationship. It is an interesting time to have to say no. It is hard for me because I love everybody. Twenty couples.

Recently, Jenny has gone from being the epitome of a *Seeker,* always wanting to enlarge her circle of friends, to being a quintessential *Keeper.* She says she has enough friends and cannot add any more. She also echoes what Aristotle says about not being able to give close friends what they deserve if someone is spread too thin. This is similar to other couples, including Charlie and Diane, whose categories shift based on each circumstance.

"Despite this number, we have not found this one right couple in Georgia like close couple friends we had who we lost. We thought we had them but they beat us up over the beach house—we found out how jealous they were and we were really devastated. We have all these friends around us but none that we feel we are bonded to like our friends in New York."

Here Jenny has introduced another relevant issue for people wanting close couple friends: She and Ike miss having one close friend. It is more painful for her because they had such a relationship once with a couple and broke up with them over envy about a second house Jenny and Ike bought. She returns to this later in the interview.

Unlike what we heard from Charlie, although they have had couple friends who split up, it has not affected their relationship. Their strong, established partnership can withstand this turmoil. "We have an amazing marriage," she told us.

Dumping Friends and Being Dumped

As befits the space they have in their life for new friends now, they are selective about new couples with whom they spend time. She recounts the end of two relationships with couples, one because she did not like the husband and the other because the relationship between the women was too intense. She also describes how she was attracted to "mommy friends" who filled her needs once, but she has grown away from them since.

> When I don't like the spouse, because I am usually the one who makes the friends, I know we will not pursue the friendship. I had a couple of mommy friends and did not like their husbands, so I would only do things when dads were at work. I would make excuses. I made it clear that our weekends were family time and for friends from out of town. Two of my mommy friends did not like that. One broke up with me because I would not have her over on the weekend because I didn't like her husband and that was bull. The other girl, I broke up with her because she was so attached to me. My second child had colic and it was very difficult as I could not make him comfortable. I was attracted to these two moms who were not happy because I was not happy. I was in a very low place. They weren't the happiest of people. When my son got better, I felt free again. I broke it off with one of them and one broke it off with me. I needed space. I was working on the house and I couldn't get together with her three times a week and she got upset and freaked out and couldn't survive without me and I thought this was unhealthy. We had only known each other for 8 months and this is not good. And her husband is someone I don't want to be around, it was not good. Her lifestyle is really not what I was into and I dropped her.

So in one relationship she was dumped and in the other she did the dumping. Jenny then recounted a more recent upsetting experience of being dropped by a couple. Here is the pain and problems that can develop with close couple friends when envy intrudes.

> We just got dumped a bit ago. It took me a while to get over that. It sounds ridiculous—we loved this couple, we were friends for 11 years, she honored me with the title of the sister she never had. We loved the husband, their child was baptized here, and when we moved into this house, it all changed. She said to me, "You have

the life I always wanted. All I ever wanted to do is stay home and raise a family and you are doing that." And when we went to look at the pool, she cried. She sat in my backyard and cried. And I thought, is she crying because she is happy for me? What was this? And so they ended up not really showing up as friends. We would invite them over and they would come late and so I considered they dumped us. I was devastated. We were like family to each other. I felt like she dumped us so they weren't invited to our annual Christmas party and she started calling me to find out what was up with me. But I was done. I was not going to be treated like that.

The issues around jealousy between couples came up again later in the conversation when we were discussing other couple issues. As couples are consolidating their identity as a couple and building careers, they often change socioeconomic class. They may be cheered on by their old friends, but they also may be resented, which puts a strain on the friendship. Not only did this happen to Jenny, it happened to one of her friends.

A friend invited her three oldest couple friends to come over and christen her new house and only one showed. She said how devastated she was and didn't know how to handle it. What do I do? Do I call and ask them what happened or wait for them to call me. If I don't call, is the friendship over? She doesn't know why they didn't come over, other than that they have jealousy issues. It was all good and fine when she was in a normal house, but then they inherited some money and got a dream house with a large deck and pool, and she wanted a fun, party house and she got it. It was embarrassing for her when her friends didn't come—even her daughter asked, "What happened to the party, Mom?" "I got stood up," she said and she's such a quality person.

And here I was in the same position 5 months ago when our friends were blowing us off. What do I do? Do I call her? Do I deck her? One of my friends said, "When a door closes, another one opens." I think that door has shut.

We asked if the door could open again.

Sure. I love them. My children love them, but I was so devastated by their behavior when we put in a pool. And then she was calling me—why wasn't I invited to your Christmas party or the Easter egg hunt? She knows we had these parties—but she only shows up when it was convenient for her. That is not a friend. My only regret is I never had the courage to tell her how I felt. She was calling and I called her back and we talked about general stuff; the next time she called I waited a few days to call her back. I just wasn't rushing to call her.

While Jenny has many female friends, she admires the way that men act with their friends.

When women first meet, they are judgmental and standoffish and don't open up and that is annoying. Men are more conversational. It is like, "What's up?" and they go from there. Women check you out, study you. Eventually they come around and become your friend. And there are differences. Girls talk about husbands. The husbands say, "You guys tell everything about us to our friends. I know all the intimate details about our friends' lives." That is what women do and we have been doing this since we were kids—who else would you share those intimate details with?

Although they have many close friendships, Jenny wants to have one close couple in Atlanta to befriend.

We find it exciting to meet new people. We are more picky after being dumped and are not interested in jealous people. Now that the close couple is gone, we have room. We have such wonderful friends but they are not here. We adore our neighbors, and they are like family, but for those real comfortable evenings sitting around the table drinking wine, we miss it. I want to jet off to New York for the weekend. My husband said, when I asked him about moving back to New York a few years ago, that he would do anything for me but please do not ask to move back there. It is the only time he has said no to me. We have a wonderful life here and I knew that if we stayed here we would never go back. I can't complain but here we are. And, I do not know anyone else who has been able to maintain a group of such quality friends and no one has as much fun as us.

Jenny looks forward to growing old with her friends.

The people you surround yourself with are a direct reflection of you. As we get older we are all growing at the same rate. Those who have not grown have fallen off, like the high school and college buddies who did not keep up, because there was something missing. You kind of know where the connection is with the same morals and core values. Birds of a feather. We went through everything together; we found our careers, lovers, husbands, and children together. We lose our parents together and go through all the stages together. It makes sense that the jealous people are falling off the grid but it is heartbreaking.

Friends are extremely important to this emotion sharing couple. Once *Seekers* of couples (she is a *Seeker* by nature and Ike more a *Keeper,* but as a couple they are *Seekers* by dint of her outgoing nature), they are now, at this stage in life, *Keepers.* They are, however, looking for one close couple to replace the one they lost. At this stage, with young children and making new friends through their children, they are trying to set priorities on their time.

CONCLUSION

Young couples just starting out are forming their identity as a unit as they get to understand themselves as adults. They are figuring out how to balance time with each other and still remain loyal to their individual friends and family commitments. They value couple friendships, though not as much as older couples do. If they remain childless, the importance of couple friends grows stronger than it does for couples with children. Stephen Marks defines quality marriages as those in which each partner is able to maintain a balance among a focus on his or her self, a partner, and people or activities outside the marriage. For newly forming couples, this can be a particular challenge.

As we look at couples in the middle years, we will see how demands increase, especially for those couples with children. When children are young, parents can dictate what their children do. Once the children develop independent interests, new couple friends may emerge in relation to those interests, which might mean dropping old friends who have been acquired through the children. The stronger the couple relationship is and the ability to talk through changes in friendships, the easier it will be to accommodate to these changes.

4

The Middle Years
Couples Raising Families and Balancing Friendships

While the previous chapter focused on the early years of a couple's marriage or partnership, this chapter explores couples who are in their middle years. Great variability exists for couples in these middle years of marriage. Some are in a first marriage or partnership, whereas others have remarried. (We address divorced couples in a later chapter.) Couples today, especially those who complete college or graduate school, tend to delay having children while completing their education. They may become parents for the first time in their 30s or even 40s. Such couples may have married later or established themselves as a couple years before having a child. Other couples in this stage of marriage may not have children, due to choice or medical difficulties, and find their relationships between themselves and their friends who do have children have changed. Those with children may start to seek out couples with children just as those without children may prefer the company of those who have not traveled down the child path. Older couples with children at the end of this middle stage often see their children becoming more independent in their teen years and then leaving home, potentially freeing up more time for their adult friendships.

Who are these middle couples? About 4 out of 10 of the people we interviewed together are between the ages of 35 and 60. About one-quarter of this group is between 35 and 40, almost one-third is between 41 and 50, and almost one-half is between 51 and 60. The youngest group has been committed to each other on average 7 years, and the oldest together an average of 30 years. By this age, 9 out of 10 are married, with the rest partnered, and 9 out of 10 have children in their family, though not necessarily living in the home anymore.

A major societal change that affects couples at this stage is the increase in women who work outside the home. According to the U.S. Bureau of Labor Statistics, in 2009 almost 60% of women were in the labor force.[1] In 2006 both husbands and wives were employed in 57.4% of marriages, up from 43.6% in 1967. In 1975, 39% of women with children under the age of 6 were employed; in 2007 that percentage increased to 63.5%.[2] Not only are more women working outside the home, but they are contributing an increasing amount to household income, due partly to the fact that Americans between the ages of 30 and 44 are the first age group in which more women than men are graduating from college.[3] By 2007 22% of working wives earned more income than their husbands, leading to an increase in women's decision-making power in and out of the home.[4]

MAKING TIME FOR COUPLE FRIENDSHIPS: IS IT WORTH IT?

As described in detail in Chapter 2, all couples need to find ways to balance time and energy for themselves as individuals, their marriage, work, friendships, family, and outside interests. During the middle years these competing interests may be at their peak, as the demands of child rearing, advancing in a career, being active in the community, and possibly caring for aging parents increase. With many responsibilities competing for time, the importance of how middle-stage couples decide to spend their "free" time also increases. Will they socialize with extended family or friends as a family unit and include their children? Enjoy time with a close friend or several friends and have a "girls" or "guys" night out? Share dinner or go bowling with another couple whose company they enjoy, so they can combine time spent together and time with friends? Attend a cook-out or party with a large group of couple friends? When both partners work outside the home, especially if they have children living at home, who manages their increasingly complex schedules? With less time available, working wives may have less inclination or energy to maintain the couple's social relationships, which has traditionally been women's role.

Some research has found that adults in middle age tend to spend less time with friends than do younger adults.[5] In our interviews with couples, the oldest couples[6] were most likely to have 10 or more couple friends, the youngest couples were next most likely to count that many couples as friends, and the middle age group were least likely to count 10 or more couples as friends. As mentioned previously, the importance of couple friendships increases with age, although it is lowest for couples in our study who had children under age 18. It is also lowest for couples who have been partnered or married for between 3 and 10 years (some of these are later adult relationships). This could suggest that age alone is not the only determinant of how couples view the importance of friendships; where they are in the stage of the relationship could also have an influence with couple friends becoming less important as the couple forms an initial identity as a unit. Balancing the demands of family and friends may be particularly demanding for couples with children living in the home, which is why they value couple friends the least.

Given competing demands and the limited amount of time available for friendships for many middle-stage couples, are there any benefits to a marriage when a couple spends time with another couple? The previous chapter mentioned that when new couples are supported in their relationship as a couple, that relationship is strengthened. A study of couples married an average of 20 years found similar results: Couples whose friends supported their marriage felt more satisfied with and committed to each other.[7] So support from friends for a couple's marriage seems to benefit the marriage relationship even when couples have been together for years. Our study found an additional benefit for couple-to-couple friendships. Almost two-thirds of the couples we interviewed agreed that time spent with a couple who are good friends reaffirms their marriage and makes it stronger.

In preparing this book, we found no research that specifically explored couple-to-couple friendships. It is a very new area of study. What we did find were studies that determined that couples who socialize together with mutual friends (which could include other couples) are more satisfied with their marriages. In one study of couples with children who were married an average of 9 years (similar to our couples in this chapter), both husbands and wives reported greater satisfaction with their marriage when their friendship networks included other couples with whom they were both friends.[8] In other words, sharing mutual friends is linked to a happier marriage. In addition, having closer ties to family and friends is also linked to a happier marriage. Couples with children in the home who had good relations with significant support systems were happier in their marriages than those couples with children who felt less close to family and friends.[9] It may be that family members play an important role in providing emotional and instrumental support to couples, separate from friendship.

There may even be a link between having fewer friends in common and going to marriage counseling. Psychologist Finy Josephine Hansen and her colleagues compared couples in marital therapy with couples who were not in therapy and found that the more mutual friends a couple had, the less likely they were to be in therapy and the more satisfied they were with their marriage.[10] These authors suggest that couples who are experiencing marital distress may not choose to spend time with mutual friends. Consistent with this research, the respondents in our study who believed their partner was not happy with their marriage tended to report fewer couple friends than those who believed their partner was happy in the relationship. Findings that couples who share friends in common feel more satisfied with their marriages may be a cyclical process. Couples in happy marriages get support and approval for their marriage from their mutual friends, and that support helps them feel more satisfied with their partner.

We asked Charlotte Spiegelman, a Los Angeles couple and family therapist, if couples ever mention their friendships with other couples during therapy. Charlotte said that in her experience the topic of couple friendships comes up in only one context: One person will unfavorably compare her or his partner to one of their friends, as in, "Why can't you compliment me the way Jeff notices nice things about Jane?" This observation resonates with comments made by

Betty and Adam, the couple in the previous chapter who broke up. Betty said that being with another couple makes her angry because she feels that the guy in the other couple treats his partner better than Adam treats her. Charlotte added that a couple experiencing marital distress may compare themselves to their couple friends and find it painful to socialize with couples who are comfortable with and enjoying each other. Likewise, couples who enjoy a positive relationship with each other may drop a couple who are obviously unhappy or, even worse, are openly hostile to each other. Numerous couples we interviewed, including Bianca and Mick in Chapter 8, discuss not wanting to be around couples that fight.

When the "Nest" Empties

Couples at the end of this middle stage of marriage may find themselves with an "empty nest" after their children leave home. An increasing number of couples will be entering this phase of marriage as the Baby Boomer generation ages. Although studies on the effects of children leaving home on marital satisfaction show mixed results,[11] recent research suggests that an "empty nest" leads to couples experiencing greater satisfaction in their marriage. Psychologist Sara M. Gorchoff and her colleagues studied middle-aged women over the course of 18 years and found the women reported greater marital satisfaction as they transitioned to an "empty nest."[12] Interestingly, it was not having more time with their partners that made their marriages more satisfying but rather the quality of the time they shared after the children left home.

Having more time and money available may allow "empty nesters" to enjoy dinner or plan a vacation by themselves or with another couple. With fewer worries about overseeing children's activities or worrying about teenagers' whereabouts, couples can get together with friends more spontaneously. Other changes also contribute to parents' positive feelings after their children leave home. Contemporary couples in their 50s are likely to still be working, often have more disposable income, and enjoy good health. With cell phones, Skype, and Facebook, parents and young adult children can keep in touch much more easily than was possible in earlier generations.

We interviewed many interesting middle-stage couples for this book and you'll meet four of them in this chapter. All four couples have been together at least 16 years. Compared to the young couples in the previous chapter, these couples have developed more consistent patterns in the way they relate to each other and their friends. They have met many life challenges together and value the role their friendships played in helping them along the way. Some of the couples have experienced friendships with other couples that became richer over many years. One finds balancing couple friendships with the demands of work and raising children very difficult. Another couple has trouble finding couples with whom they feel compatible while one couple describes learning to negotiate with their partner to accommodate their different personality styles. As Will, whom we present first, puts it, middle-stage couples are able to take the long view of the "arc of their lives."

COUPLES IN THE MIDDLE YEARS

Will and Zoe

Zoe and Will are a white couple in their early 40s, married for 16 years, and parents of two elementary school-age children. They live in a small town near the Shenandoah mountains. Both are educators. They agreed to be interviewed in their home, which was clearly designed for the needs of their children and their desire to offer a warm and inviting place for people to gather. From the beginning of the interview, both emphasized the importance of friends in their lives. Like many of the couples we interviewed, their experiences of the role friendships played in their parents' lives have affected the kind of relationships they want for themselves. Will, who grew up in a small town, doesn't remember his parents having any couples friends. Zoe remembers her parents socializing with friends from the neighborhood but recalls that they hosted few parties or dinners and that these social events were not "very relaxed." She does remember one of her grandmothers, whom she has tried to emulate. At this grandmother's house, there were "couples all over the place and my grandmother would have a party like that and so that's how we developed things here."

When asked what couple friendships mean to them, Zoe reflected on how central these relationships are in their lives.

> They are extraordinarily important to me, and to Will. We've lived here a long time, we're teachers here, and we live in a small community. We've chosen that. It's something I didn't have as a kid and I want to make sure my children have that. And for me, I don't have family in the area, so it was really important that we have friends that we can count on like family. So I guess they're extremely important. They're like family to me. Like I can count on them as support like I would if I had close family. … [They] add enrichment to the life we have here and it makes our home, our community, just a little closer.

A high number of couples in our study (about three-quarters) primarily met other couple friends through one partner. Will and Zoe are different in that they formed their friendships with other couples together. Will identified three distinct sets of couple friends they have in their lives and how each began.

> We have a cohort of friends that we got to know as teachers, as colleagues, before we had kids. A lot of those teacher friends are a little bit older than us, had young kids at the time that we became friends with them and their families. So we might go to the beach every summer with them and do traditional things. And now, interestingly, their kids are in high school or out of high school and our kids are

young. So it was almost a kind of apprenticeship in a weird way. We saw them as a collection of friends. Then having our own kids introduced a whole new entry point to a different set, and now we've just actually got a handful of friends who are just having their first children even though they're closer to our age. ... Our friendships are equally strong, although different, throughout those three threads.

Zoe added the importance that this first group of older couples had for them in the 7-year period before they had their own children. "I like them for that reason because ... I saw them as sort of a model—this is how families can work. I didn't have that growing up. This is how happy families are organized, how they work, how their friendships work. I was very observant of that and wanted to surround ourselves with that."

When asked if their relationships with their couples friends have changed over time, Zoe explained that some of their friendships "drifted a little bit—not intentionally" when they began to have children and another couple did not, because much of their social life revolves around their children. Will added that they try to maintain friendships with each of the three groups of friends he described earlier. They may not see couples in their older group of friends as often, because they're in different places in their lives, but both Will and Zoe agreed that they will always consider these couples to be close friends. As Will explains, "I don't think it affects the emotional connection. I think it affects the interaction."

Will makes an interesting observation that how often a couple sees their friends is not identical to how close they feel to them. The bonds that Will and Zoe forged with the older couples who modeled family life and close friendships for them formed an emotional closeness that still remains.

They are aware that in small towns friendships can tend to be exclusive, and they try to counteract that. Zoe describes how they reach out to newcomers.

> If there's someone new coming into the area, we try to have them come over and introduce them to everybody else. We've done that for quite a few couples. Because I know what it feels like to be new in a situation—we moved a lot as a kid—and not knowing people and having to bridge into that group. You see somebody that's having a picnic in the backyard and you'd like to come over. So I always make sure if there's somebody new that we invite them.

Zoe and Will talked about how varied their social activities are, sometimes getting together with just one couple, several couples, or a large group, with or without their children. They seemed to be in the middle of all this activity, so we asked them if they often organize the cook-outs, concerts, parties, and dinners they enjoy with their circle of friends. Will agreed that he often takes the lead. He gave an example, "If I find out that a music festival we go to every summer, the tickets go on sale on Thursday, I let everybody know. So I guess that's organizing it." Zoe added that he's very good at this but that his taking the lead is different than most of their couple friends, where it's the women who "pull it all together." In our study we also found that women typically organized social events, so we were curious how this arrangement developed for Will and Zoe. As Will sees it,

People know if they want to do something, call me. I've got the calendar. I also have a schedule that requires a lot more attention because I travel a fair amount and my days are very unpredictable. But the other factor here is that until last year probably most of Zoe's closest girlfriends were stay-at-home Moms. So they had time during the day to coordinate and think about that. Now almost all of them have gone back to work and that's really shifted the frequency that we do things and the way that we do things. Zoe has always worked, so she was always a little bit different than her other friends who did not work outside the home.

Will added two other factors to explain his taking the lead in maintaining friendships; his outgoing personality and the egalitarian nature of their friendships with other couples. He recognizes the stereotyped differences between how men and women act in their friendships but doesn't see them as applying to Zoe and him or their friends.

For the most part, when we get together in medium, small, or large groups, we don't have the men go down and watch sports and the women stay in the kitchen thing. Usually it's very integrated in terms of gender. And I would say in general all of our friends, male and female, are activity oriented and certainly enjoy doing things. When you first asked that question [Do you think men and women approach these friendships differently in terms of starting and maintaining them?], I thought the traditional male role is to do things to be friends and women's role is traditionally to talk to be friends. But actually, we blur that pretty well with all these folks.

Contrast Will's response with Charlie's in the previous chapter when he expressed concern about talking to another woman to make plans for his fiancée and him to get together with another couple. He feared being seen as "crossing the line or getting flirtatious" and thought it was safer if the women did the planning. Both these couples stress the egalitarian nature of their friendships with other couples. However, over 16 years Will and Zoe have developed a level of comfort with each other and their couple friends that allows for greater trust and flexibility.

The Vault

With so much time shared with friends, we asked Will and Zoe, as we did all couples in the study, whether they decide ahead of time what they'll share or not share with other couples. They talked about how their conversations with friends are generally very open but that some information is confidential and isn't shared. Will explained, "We have what we call 'the vault' and if there are things we're not sharing, it's in 'the vault.' And that vault has layers, too, so there are vaults that might include certain people and not others." Zoe added, "There are times when things have been shared with Will by another friend 'in the vault,' which he can't share with me and he doesn't." As another example of not sharing certain information with friends, Will mentioned that sometimes they decide ahead of time not to discuss a certain topic because, "my sense is not that we don't want them to know, but rather it's we don't want the night to be impacted by a heavy thing, whatever it is. Let's not get to the heavy thing tonight. Let's just go out and have fun, rather than not wanting them to know."

In our understanding of couples who are essentially fun sharing versus emotion sharing, emotion sharing couples often want to go out with couples and have fun but also are interested in emotion sharing. While Zoe and Will, with their comment about not wanting to affect the evening and just have fun, might appear to be closer to a fun sharing couple, we see them as in the middle of this continuum because they are also comfortable with sharing "heavy things" about their situation with friends but purposely decide if and when such sharing will occur.

Another Couple's Breakup

We asked all couples in the study whether the breakup of another couple affected them. Zoe and Will reported that a couple with whom they had a long relationship separated. After the couple broke up, Zoe described how couples in the community tended to take sides, and this affected many friendships at that time. However, she and Will "were able to stay close to both members of that couple and now they're back together and it's something from the past and it's probably strengthened our friendship as couples."

Based on our study, we found that this is not typical; in most instances a couple stays friends with only one partner. Charlie and Diane, an engaged couple from the previous chapter, reacted to the breakup of a couple with whom they were friends by feeling somewhat shaken; they saw their friends' breakup as a "cautionary tale." Both Charlie and Diane and Will and Zoe empathized with what their respective couple friends were going through. But Will and Zoe's long-term investment in their friendship with both partners, coupled with their own experience that marriage has its ups and downs, gave them a long-range perspective. Zoe explained how and why they worked to stay connected with both partners.

"I think we had empathy as a couple. We were married for 7 years. We went through our own troubles. When they were going through their difficulty, you have empathy for both sides. I mean, there weren't any good guys or bad guys. We just want you both to be happy. We're going to make everything as equally good as possible. I mean not to badmouth one partner or the other partner. Try to be supportive without …"

"You never know how it's going to come out." Will inserted. "We've been there and had support from friends, and so I think we're able to give it to them."

Will and Zoe are a middle-stage couple who work hard at balancing the demands of marriage, children, jobs, and friends. Although their family is their top priority, they also recognize how friendships enrich their lives, bringing fun and emotional closeness. They purposely set out to create a rich network of friends in common, even though neither of them grew up in families where that was the norm. Will also mentioned another way their marriage benefits from their friendships.

"Both of us, regardless of how happy and committed we are in our own relationship, we're all complicated, layered people. It's nice to have other people provide different aspects of your own fulfillment and needs. Having people in your life like that allows us to give each other a break, too."

Will and Zoe recognize their needs as individuals, as a couple, as parents, and as friends. They are both *Seekers*—open to others and actively looking for and cultivating friendships. The next couple also has worked steadily to build a community of friends but have had to find ways to accommodate their different styles and preferences in doing so.

Sonia and Raymond

Although only in their late 30s, Sonia and Raymond have been together as partners for 19 years and married 10 years ago. Both are African American. Raymond is a physician and Sonia a graduate student. Sonia is a warm, extroverted woman whom the second author met on an airplane. She showed great interest in the topic of couple friendships and agreed to be interviewed with her husband. Several months later, the interview took place in their home in a large southern city. This couple was clearly at ease with one another, sometimes finishing each other's sentences and other times comfortably and playfully disagreeing. Sonia described herself as "90% *Seeker* and 10% *Keeper*" and rated couple friendships as extremely important to her. Raymond saw himself as about equally *Nester* and *Keeper* and rated couple friendships as important, but not as important as Sonia rated them.

They have a large network of couple friends, and their home tends to serve as a gathering place. In contrast to Will and Zoe, many of this couple's friendships began through Sonia's friendships with single women. Over the years, as these women became partnered or married, these friendships expanded to become couple-based friendships.

Similar to Will and Zoe, Raymond and Sonia used their parents' relationships with friends as models (both positive and negative) in developing their own couple friendships. Sonia and Raymond identified ways they observed their parents interacting with friends that they strive to emulate and some problems or limitations that made them determined to do things differently. Raymond's parents and both sets of grandparents had long marriages. He talked about the importance of creating the sense of welcome he witnessed in his grandparents' house.

One of the things I remember about my Mom's parents was the amount of people they had over at the house, the children and the jovialness of everybody around; whether it's tension or not tension and always trying to create that sense of family and community throughout our household. So a weekend doesn't go by where we don't have folks just coming in and out, kind of stopping in and saying "Hey."

Sonia, whose mother is white and father is African American, described her parents as extremely social, working class southerners who relocated to the North. In their interracial household, they created a community of predominantly African American friends where open communication was encouraged.

One of the things they worked really hard to do was to minimize the tension around race in our household, but to have really honest authentic discussions about it. So that looked like seeing people get into heated discussions around race and the influence of politics and classism, which a lot of families I've heard don't have that level of discussion or that level of turmoil about. But it felt like that was just a basic thing in our household and I feel that I'm stronger because of that.

Differences in Friend Making and Personality Styles

Although both Sonia and Raymond value the importance of friendships, they discussed some tension between them based on personality styles and differences in the degree of openness in their families of origin. Sonia is an extrovert raised in a family that valued open communication about any subject. Raymond is a self-described introvert, whose family highly valued a sense of community but rarely communicated about feelings or day-to-day responsibilities or activities. In their couple friendships, one way this gets played out is by Sonia initiating and maintaining their couple friendships and Raymond tending to hold back initially and proceed slowly when anything is "outside my comfort zone." Sonia has learned to accommodate their differences in personality style and levels of comfort with open discussion by recognizing the importance of "allowing him to develop relationships more slowly." But they are clear that this is a work-in-progress, and some tension remains.

Both Sonia and Raymond discussed what they gain from their couple friendships. When we asked them why these friendships were important, Sonia described how maintaining friendships with other couples helps their marriage. "If there is discussion about how folks or how the couples deal with different issues that we may have already encountered before, it helps with our relationship, saying we've kind of done that, maybe looked at it in a different way, or maybe their way was better."

We asked whether the breakup of couples they knew affected their relationship. Raymond described how this happens. "It has caused us to reevaluate our relationship, to reaffirm things, to try to figure out things that are not settled in our own relationship—to see if those things can be managed or thought of differently."

Unique to the couples we interviewed is that this couple also discusses what they would do if their own relationship ended. These conversations include the perspectives of Black feminist thought and the role of male privilege that are consistent with Sonia's upbringing in a family where issues such as racism and classism were openly discussed. Sonia reported how she and Raymond talk about "financial solvency and what that means for me to be financially secure and what expectations we have to set me up so that I am in a position of …"—at her hesitation, Raymond added, "stability." Sonia said that she's reassured by Raymond's ability to criticize the patriarchal attitude displayed by some of their male friends who are going through a breakup when it comes to "finances or everyday interactions. In that sense it is affirming to me because then I have the ability to see the man that I'm partnered with, and think 'thank goodness our relationship won't be that way.'"

Mentoring Couples

An important aspect of their couple friendships for Raymond and Sonia lies in the intergenerational giving and receiving of care and support, a sense of couples learning from other couples. Although they see themselves as informal mentors to younger couples, Sonia also describes the help she receives from older friends.

> There will be strengths that elders will have and they will just kind of talk like, "Sometimes, Sonia, there are times when you just don't have to speak; just let the man do what the man is going to do and he's going to make his own decisions." I take some of that in. I tend to be a little hard-headed. But then the gift that I receive from them is that they have also shared things like, "You and your friends and colleagues speak with a level of independence that people in our peer group have not always had."
>
> I think we have been really lucky in the black community to have a lot of really great examples of intact marriages, and so part of what we do is we have just made a commitment to being authentic in sharing our partnership with our friends. So if we're arguing, we're arguing in front of our friends. If we're laughing, that sense of humor doesn't stop just because friends come into the room. So I tend to think of our partnership as being community based—that we are members of community and everything that happens within our household folks in the community are privy to. And what that means is that we're also able to speak to and have involvement in their lives as well.

Sonia describes looking for couple friends "who want to be partnered and people who are interested in being their best selves and helping their partners be their best selves." Through hosting potluck dinners, Raymond's teaching their male friends how to cook, going to amusement parks or baseball games, they describe building these friendships through combining activities with open discussions.

They described further evidence of their sense of being part of a community when, due to improved financial circumstances, they moved to a larger house. Sonia initially felt guilty at having so much space, which seemed "too big … too much … and a bit ostentatious" and brought this up with her female friends.

"We had conversations about what a home means and the agreement was that they were proud of us and they wanted us to do better and they saw this as a stepping stone and that the home belonged to the community. So the agreement was that our home would be a community home. When we had gatherings, everyone knew that it could be used as a communal gathering space."

Their experience stands in contrast to Jenny's experience, recounted in the previous chapter, when a friend's envy of her new home was a factor in ending a long friendship she and her husband had had with another couple. It's possible that Sonia's willingness to openly discuss her improved financial situation with her friends, including her worries, played a role in keeping her friendships strong.

Dealing With Infertility and Its Impact on Friendships

A recent problem has affected the nature and intensity of Sonia and Raymond's friendships. They have been dealing with issues of infertility at a time when many of their couple friends are having children. In talking about the pain of this situation, Sonia relates, "I haven't seen a lot of models of black folk talking about infertility. It's been something that we've been reticent to talk about with our friends." They pulled back from their friends during the worst of this time, because it was painful for them to talk about, but are slowly starting to reengage.

Even when they found it difficult to talk, their friends have been supportive. As Sonia says, "It helps that they check in and that they force us to talk at times when …" Raymond finishes, "we don't want to be bothered." They identified a particularly helpful couple who have a child but have been sensitive to what they're going through. Raymond identifies how they've helped. "They've been so amazing with the whole process, protecting our space and boundaries and being more of a listening ear, which was very helpful."

Sonia showed particular appreciation for what the man in this couple was able to offer Raymond when other male friends backed away.

> That was when I sifted through our male friends and our female friends and was able to take a clear sense of who I could trust with Raymond's heart. [She turned to Raymond.] Because you're right. You did try to talk about the challenges we were having with three men and one of them kind of freaked out and said I don't really want to talk about this. Another just kind of left you there, literally with the sound of crickets. And it's hard for me to forgive that. So the men that have

stepped up and have pushed Raymond—who would prefer not to say anything to anyone, particularly with our challenges around fertility—have been the ones that I've thought, "I don't ever want to let go of them because they really take care of him in ways that he needs and that I can't."

Sonia's observations illustrate both the helpfulness of couple friends during a time of crisis and the recognition that a friend outside the marriage can offer a perspective and support that a spouse, who is also in pain, may be unable to provide. Her experience echoes that of Will's, described earlier, when he mentioned that friends can speak to different parts of himself, which complements the relationship he enjoys with his wife.

As Sonia and Raymond discussed their couple friendships, we noticed that they were describing times when they socialize with a couple together and times when only one of them will get together with a member of the other couple. Although we found this pairing off common in many of the couples in our study, such friendships were more frequently same-sex pairings. Sonia and Raymond mentioned that their socializing with one member of another couple might be with either a person of the same or the opposite sex. Sonia explained that how they managed this depended on the race of the other couple.

Because [in] our white couple friendships, the male feels more comfortable having a separate relationship with me. Whereas in black couples, you're very mindful of the way that you communicate with the black female's partner. … So there's a lot of awareness about when you come by the house, if she's not there; whether he comes by my house, if Raymond is not there or she's not with him. If I initiate conversation with him, I typically CC her in an e-mail; call to make sure she's aware. So there is always this kind of checking in. One of my girlfriends was going to have lunch with Raymond. She didn't necessarily tell me but Raymond told me, so then I had a conversation with her where she said, "Raymond and I were hanging out" at her and her partner's date restaurant, is what she called it. But it is very interesting that with black women and black couples we're a little more mindful of the boundaries. Now our white friends, the guys are coming over, they're calling all the time, they're having separate relationships. They're like, "Hey, let's just hang out." [I'm thinking] "Really, without your partner? OK. Gotta talk to my partner about it."

When we asked Sonia how she understood this racial difference, she recalled what other black women have told her.

It's something about wanting to be very sure that people are not trying to invade your relationship and somehow take your man. And I know that because the black women's wisdom that's come from elders and you hear amongst girlfriends is you don't ever let another man that's not your husband live in your house with another woman. You don't ever take another woman into your house in a coupleship. And so those are the messages I've been taught amongst black folk. But I think we've challenged that in a lot of ways, but we've had to really talk about it. Had to talk those stereotypes and those fears through.

Sonia and Raymond describe a partnership that began in college and has matured over time. In dealing with the crisis of infertility, they've sharpened their sense of which friends can help in such a crisis and which are likely to avoid such a sensitive and personal issue. Both Zoe and Will and Sonia and Raymond offer examples of couples who have purposely set out to develop a community of couple friends who are an integral part of their lives. Will and Zoe are both *Seekers,* and their approach to developing these friendships is very similar. Sonia and Raymond have different personalities and have learned how to manage the tension around accommodating each other's style. The following couple is less active in seeking couple friendships while they work hard to keep up with the demands of raising children and managing several jobs.

Hank and Phyllis

Hank age 53, and Phyllis, 48, have been married 20 years and have three children ages 17, 13, and 10. They are an interracial couple (Hank is white; Phyllis is African American) who live in a racially integrated community. They describe lives that focus primarily on their jobs and children. Hank is a musician with a full-time teaching job, which he combines with teaching private students and performing as a musician. Phyllis works in sales, a job that entails working every weekend. Their social activities tend to revolve around their children; in fact, they've met most of the families with whom they socialize through their children. They count four couples as friends, not all of whom live in the area. Although on the written questionnaire they checked that couple friendships are only slightly important to them, they noted that they would like to have more. Consistent with those responses, they described themselves as somewhere between *Keepers* and *Nesters.* As Hank put it, "We aren't seeking friends; we are seeking other things and finding friends along the way."

Hank elaborates on how he and Phyllis desire more contact with other couples but find it extremely difficult to fit anything else into their busy schedules.

"We have been talking in the last couple of years of doing more and going back and inviting people over and we have had a few nice parties, like my 50th birthday party, which was great having a lot of people. But we end up spending so much time on paid employment and kids' stuff it is hard to make time for anything. We need to make a deliberate effort. To some extent, part of it is the struggle to survive. Currently, I'm working three jobs. Phyllis is working one full-time job and I am working one full-time and two part-times and they require your physical presence, so that just takes up so much of our time."

Consistent with their busy schedules, Phyllis describes how their couple friendships typically begin by meeting another couple in the course of their activities. "Most of the people I met are typically other parents at school activities. If we happen to hit it off, we might—because the kids are playing to together—we might end up at a birthday party together or something like that." Hank adds, "We don't seem to have any way of deliberately going after people … it's how things arise in the course of events."

Because most of their friendships revolve around their children's friends, the friendships seem more vulnerable to drifting away as their children get older. Phyllis discusses how this happens.

"Older friendships we could have done better at keeping up with—they just know we are there. A lot of the friendships I have made have been kid driven. As the kids become more independent—like friends we made when my daughter was younger—we will still see them and chitchat and say hi, but we aren't coming over for dinner or anything like that because the kids have grown."

Because Hank and Phyllis are an interracial couple, we asked them about the racial makeup of their couple friends. Not surprisingly, their friends reflect the racial mix found in their integrated community. However, when asked if they thought the country was changing in terms of its acceptance of interracial marriages, Phyllis pointed out, "I think if you drive across America, you will hit pockets where things have changed and pockets where, 'oh my' it really hasn't changed a bit." Perhaps because of their choice to live in an integrated community, Hank and Phyllis did not report experiencing the negative reactions and weak support for their marriage that interracial couples have been found to experience.[13] Their long marriage is consistent with the research of Sociologist Jenifer L. Brattner and Health Scientist Rosalind B. King which found that couples composed of a white husband and a black wife were 44% less likely to divorce than couples where both partners were white.[14]

Navigating Differences in a Close Friendship

When we asked Hank and Phyllis to choose a particular couple with whom they are close and reflect on their relationship with them, they described a friendship with Janice and Robert that began before their marriage. Similar to most of the couples we interviewed, this friendship began as an individual friendship: Hank and Robert were childhood friends. As both men found partners, the couples became friends. Although this couple now live several states away, Hank and Phyllis described many enjoyable times spent with them over the years—hiking, going to amusement parks, vacationing together, and visiting each other's homes. They view both Janice and Robert as equally likable, one of the characteristics we found in couple friendships that go beyond fun sharing.

Despite the closeness of this friendship, there is one topic that the couples tread carefully around, and that is politics. As Hank describes the situation, "It can go to a certain point, but then we get to land mines and it's all over." He describes Robert as "pretty much on the opposite end of the political spectrum from us. So, you can talk to him in person but you can't e-mail him about it … that's what I've found." Given that political divisions have become intense and often acrimonious in this country, we were curious how Hank managed to navigate these waters.

"Well, I guess it is the stock phrase, 'agreeing to disagree,' and so if those kinds of things come up, we don't go in depth enough to get to the point where the conflict is. It's being a good listener. You can listen. There are people in this world, when you listen to them respectfully, they don't automatically interpret that as agreement."

Hank and Phyllis are a self-described "low key and laid back" couple trying to balance the multiple demands of making a living and raising children. They offer a contrast to the next couple, who have time and energy to devote to making couple friends but find such friendships hard to develop.

Victor and Yvonne

Victor and Yvonne are a couple in their mid-50s, married for 31 years, with three young adult children. Yvonne is an educator and Victor works as a manager. Both are African American. They were interviewed in their home in a large city in the mid-Atlantic region. They identify five couples with whom they have satisfying friendships. Neither believes they have enough couple friends, but they only occasionally seek out such friendships. As with many couples in our study, Yvonne believes that couple friendships become more important as one gets older. Consistent with much of what's written about "empty nesters," they have more time to socialize with couple friends now that their children are grown and they no longer have financial worries. Yvonne recalls the shifts from when they had young children to the time when she was the caregiver for her parents to now when their children are grown.

> When you are busy changing diapers and doing carpool, and that is either your children's or your parents' diapers, you are in that sandwich and don't have that much time for couples friendships. You cannot get your head above water or are trying to get the oil bill paid. Once the kids grow up, you look around and wonder who is left and who you can create a friendship with. You go through a sort and see who is left.

When they talk about what they value in couple friends, both stress compatibility and equality. Yvonne starts,

"I think in terms of two couples who are friends and where the husbands like each other and both wives like each other and everyone has a compatible relationship. The four of them have a compatible relationship."

Victor adds, "The cross-gender piece is important and, in the relationships that we have with friends, one of those relationships started at some point and then the cross-gender relationship grew. So it helps when the friendship works for the other person in the couple. It also helps when the couple is friends with each other."

Their definition of friendship is akin to one that gives a high value to equality between all members of the couples. This is one of the characteristics of emotion sharing couples. While they are looking for fun in couples, they also want a couple with whom they can have a more meaningful relationship.

Yvonne and Victor have individual friends, but they laughingly describe themselves as "snobs" and "elitists" when it comes to forming new couple friendships. At different points in the interview, Victor described their preference for "people who think outside the box" and his fondness for Yvonne's family because "they are very sharp and we can discuss politics and not get bent out of shape about something." Victor describes what he calls their "prescreening" process for finding new couples friends.

"If Yvonne doesn't like them, that is pretty much it. It is not worth it to go through whatever we have to go through to become friends because I have come to learn that her intuition is just so much better than mine. If she says there is something wrong with the picture, then there is. It may come out later."

They provided an example about a beginning friendship with a new couple that they both believe is unlikely to work out. Victor's take is that this couple is one step behind Yvonne and him.

"The couples that we hang out with really have to keep up with us on some level because it is just no fun otherwise. We had a couple here for dinner and I don't think they are going to make it into the final couples group because they don't operate at the same rpm. They are nice enough, but they are doing 33⅓ and we are already at Blu-ray."

Yvonne added more information about their interaction with this couple.

> I have a medical condition that sometimes makes me seem socially awkward. We invited this couple for dinner and they turned us down twice and then called us back and asked if they could come over. So I prepared this lavish table for them and they came late and never apologized. I was furious and I told her that. That is just how I am and people can take it or leave it. But that inhibits Victor socially.

Victor, however, supported Yvonne's approach. He responded, "I don't see that as a drawback because the other part of this is couples that don't have the maturity to deal with prickliness are not going to be fun for us to hang out with."

When asked whether their parents had couples friends, Victor and Yvonne, like the other couples in this chapter, made a connection between their parents' attitudes and interactions with friends and their own behavior. Although this has been hard to validate in our study of the more than 250 couples who have been interviewed, many couples do say that there is a connection. Some want to be like their parents, and others want to forge their own style. Yvonne described both of her parents as extremely shy. Her father played cards nightly, and her mother worked evenings. Her parents had no couple friends. Victor's father was a minister who spent a lot of time with his brothers. He described his mother as being picky about whom she would become friends with, just like he and Yvonne are.

> Out of the couples that my father would associate with, my mother would hand-pick a few couples that she would associate with. My mother used to consider my father's minister friends as pompous, and I would agree, and she did not want to associate with them. I think what I drew from this was that I really wanted to be with couples that were meaningful to us [a sign of their emotion sharing style]. The second thing I learned from that was that I had no idea how to do it.

Many of the couples they knew from the church where they first got married are now divorced. When asked about the effect of friends' breakups on their relationship, Yvonne described how news would make her angry at Victor and worried about her own marriage.

> It [the breakup] is usually through the man, who is the dog in the story and doing something on the side. From my point of view, I would realize whenever there was a breakup or a husband who misbehaved, Victor would get a spanking, even though he wasn't into that at all. I would get angry at him and he would get a whole lot of drama that he does not deserve, but it is because I am hurting for my friend and I am feeling a little insecure. Every time I hear about a breakup and he is Mr. Wonderful, I get insecure—because it's like, well wait a minute, her husband was a good guy, he had my seal of approval. How did that happen?

"In many cases, it is the guy who does not step up with the right stuff," Victor agreed. "So in that way, I get disgusted because these guys are messing it up for the rest of us guys. … Yvonne may be hurting, but I am borderline angry about it."

We asked them if they had cross-sex friendships. Victor replied that he doesn't because friendships are not easy to develop due to his high standards. "For the most part it is so much safer and more fun to spend time with Yvonne." Yvonne, on the other hand, finds a male perspective helpful. Although we found in our study that cross-sex friendships tend to decrease with age, Yvonne, a woman in her mid-50s, offers a perspective on how her friendships help her marriage to Victor.

> I appreciate male friends I have had in the past because there are times I don't understand Victor, and I can call them up and [it] helps me understand a male perspective and can set me right about some things. They can say things to me about Victor that maybe Victor already said to me, and not hurt my feelings. "Just be quiet and give the man a break. You are on his back all the time." So it has been very healthy in our relationships to be able to talk to a man about what I am feeling and get a man's perspective.

As the interview progressed, Victor and Yvonne shared additional information about why making couple friends posed problems for them in the past. They are very well-educated and sent their children to private schools but live in a neighborhood with many vacant houses that some people are reluctant to visit. What this physical environment means to Yvonne is that "we have not had a community here." Yvonne stayed home with their children when they were young and the couple depended on Victor's income. He was unemployed for a period and they struggled financially. As Yvonne says, "We were just trying to get the tuition paid, the basics, so we didn't have money for the social piece and to try and raise kids so they did not feel they were poor." When her elderly parents needed help, they moved two blocks away so Yvonne could be their caregiver. Their children are grown, Yvonne's parents have died, and their financial worries are over. With more time and the desire to do so, developing new couples friendships is proving difficult.

Yvonne and Victor illustrate the problems that some couples have in making new couples friends when children have finally left the home. For this couple these difficulties seem due to a combination of several factors: a lack of parental role models, a neighborhood not conducive to inviting friends to their home, earlier financial struggles that made socializing difficult, multiple family demands, and their self-described high standards for couple friends. Only approximately one-quarter of couples in our sample reported that their parents had a few or no couples friends. Similarly relatively few individuals in our study viewed themselves (24%) or their partners (16%) as "very picky" when making couples friends. So Yvonne and Victor are unlike most of the couples in our study in two ways: They lack role models for forming couple friends and have very high standards for such friendships. This combination seems to have contributed to their difficulty in developing friendships with other couples. As Victor summarized earlier in observing the difficulty his parents had in making couple friends, he would like meaningful couples friendships but doesn't know how to develop them.

CONCLUSION

Couples in the middle stage of marriage are often in the midst of a complex balancing act. During this stage, many couples raise and then launch children. Some couples assume responsibility for the needs of aging parents. One or increasingly both members of the couple are trying to advance in their careers, so the need to prioritize and balance competing demands is very high. One couple featured in this chapter find that, at this point in their lives, they have little time for couple friendships as they feel caught between the competing demands of complex work schedules and raising children. Two of the couples have managed to weave couple friendships into a central place in their lives and find these relationships enriching. The remaining couple illustrate that time alone is not the only factor in getting together with couple friends; finding a "good fit" where all four people are friends is also an important consideration.

As we look at couples in the later years of marriage in the next chapter, we will see how retirement, physical changes, grandparenthood, and the death of one member of a couple can affect friendships between couples. Couples who have been together for a long time offer examples of how friendships change and the accommodations that couples choose to make or not make to maintain these friendships. These long-married couples can also take an extended view on how such friendships have affected their own marriage.

5

Older Couples and Their Couple Friendships

Ken and Leah have lived in the same city their entire married life, 60 plus years. They married shortly after World War II, have three grown children and seven grandchildren scattered across the United States. In his late 80s, he is still able to drive (and at night!), making him a hit with many of their friends. The difficult part for many of the older couples is that they have few couple friends where both partners are still alive. "I think friends are terribly important," Ken told us. "In fact, we are losing them at our age, and this is the thing that makes us very sad. I'd say in our married life we've had 15 to 20 couples we feel very close to and only one or two of those that are left are couples. Most singles that are left are women."

This final of three chapters that look at couples at different life stages will focus on couples ranging in age from their 60s to their early 90s. As can be imagined, this last stage of married life is very different from the first stage. No longer are there careers to be built. Financial situations have usually stabilized, although the recent recession has forced younger couples in this age range to either forestall retirement or come out of retirement when their savings took a battering. If the couple has children, they are probably grown and may be taking care of their parents. These couples span the beginning of the Baby Boomer generation to the middle of what has been called the silent generation, those who grew up before and during World War II. Most are "wired in" to computers, the Internet, and cell phones. Although they use electronics to stay in touch with friends, they are unlikely, according to the Pew Research Center,[1] to text each other, have social networking Web sites up and running, or sleep near their cell phones.

Approximately one in eight people (13%) in the couples' surveys are 61 years old and older, with 12% of the couples having a total age of 120 years or more. One couple's total age is 185 (their second marriage)! This age group of over 60s, the smallest of the three age groups we look at, comprises the widest age range—61 to 95. Two-thirds of this group is 61 to 70 and the other third, or 4% of the total sample, are 71 or older. All but one of these older couples is married (the one who is not is partnered), and slightly more than one-third have been married more than once. The marriages or commitments range from 1 year to over 60 years, with those in their first marriage averaging slightly more than 40 years of marriage. All but one of the couples in this 35-year age range have children; those children range in age from 17 to 68.

OLDER COUPLES' EXPERIENCES

If we use 1970 as a marker, a time when many of these couples were in their early 20s to mid-30s, we could almost divide these couples into two separate generations because their experiences are so different. In addition, this whole age group's experiences vary from the younger couples we describe in the previous two chapters. The couples at the younger end of this older group were just exiting college and/or entering the workforce in 1970. They were a part of, or at least strongly affected by, the Woodstock generation, the civil rights movement, the Vietnam War, and the slayings of Malcolm X, Martin Luther King Jr., and John and Robert Kennedy. Sex, drugs, and rock and roll were in the air. Those born 10 or more years earlier, and in their 30s or older by 1970, were members of the over 30 generation who were not to be trusted. They danced to other music and worried more about drinking too much than smoking too much. They may have been immigrants themselves or first generation Americans. They grew up during World War II, Korea, and, in some cases, the Great Depression. Their personalities and even their marriages were stabilized before the eruptions of the 1960s. Women's liberation had not reached its 20th-century apex. As a result of the more distant time in which they grew up and married, their couple friendships probably looked less like the friendships of those who came of age in the 1960s and certainly less like those of couples who are now in their 30s. Roles were more traditional.

That is not all that separates generations and even people born 10 years apart. People over 60 have completed less education than the younger generations,[2] as is true for those in our sample. In 1970 only 4% of wives outearned their husbands. By 2007, 22% of wives in the 30- to 44-year-old range were outearning husbands.[3] Women have also, since 1970, caught up with men in terms of education completed.[4] These shifts have been gradual over the past 40 years and may have had varying effects on the couples in our study. In this chapter, we discuss the differences both within this age group and between this age group and those in Chapters 3 and 4. And although some of these shifts result in gender-related adjustments for individual couples, other couples, like Ken and Leah whose story begins the chapter, are settled. Their primary concern is not about roles; rather, it is finding couple friends to go out with where the men are still alive.

Children and grandchildren are both a joy and a concern for older c꒑ The couples whom we interviewed are the top layer of the sandwich generation, a term coined for the younger generation who are caught between taking care of their children and their parents. Some of these couples are being assisted by their adult children and others are actively involved in helping to raise grandchildren. Grandchildren can give older couples meaning in their retirement years. As we will hear from Oscar and Paula, both in their 80s, they pick up one of their grand-children after school every day and help him with his homework. He has autism and this assistance is vitally important to their grandson's well-being as well as to his parents' ability to work. One finding from our study is that older couples were more likely than younger couples to say that extended family members impede their ability to make couple friends. We believe this is because older couples have more family responsibilities—to their children and grandchildren—than do cou-ples who are just starting out and trying to find their way as a couple.

Sometimes these family responsibilities can become complicated, as older couples are also more likely than younger couples to be in second marriages, which may, in turn, involve stepchildren. For example, the oldest couple inter-viewed for this study—he is 95 years old and she is 90 years old—are remarried and, at the time of the interview, have been together for 36 years. They have three stepchildren (two of his and one of hers), all in their 60s. "We have difficulties with our children," they reported. "Unfortunately there have been problems with the opposite's children. We have been trying to resolve this, but it's not easy. That's one difficulty about having been married before."

TRADITION

The way these couple friendships operate could be related to how men and women were socialized when roles were more narrowly defined than they are today. In a brief recap of what we discuss in the first chapter, differences exist between older women's and older men's friendship-making and friendship-maintaining styles as well as between older and younger women and older and younger men.

For example, at midlife, according to sociologists Carolyn Liebler and Gary Sandefur, women are more likely than men to give and receive emotional sup-port. Using data from the Wisconsin Longitudinal Study, Liebler and Sandefur grouped adults into four patterns of social support exchange: (1) "low exchang-ers" are not much involved in supportive exchanges with friends, co-workers, and neighbors; (2) "emotional support exchangers" give and get emotional sup-port; (3) "give all, get emotional support exchangers" give both emotional and concrete support but receive only emotional support; (4) "high exchangers" give and receive emotional and concrete support.[5] The men were more likely to be low exchangers, although 10% of the women and men were high exchangers.

This is the result of a lifetime of women being socialized to be more emotionally connected to others.

In addition, women, regardless of age, have more people they call friend than do men[6] and are more emotionally and physically expressive with those friends. Close friendships between women are more often characterized by self-disclosure and an increased range of strategies for coping with difficult situations than are men's close friendships, according to one group of researchers studying health in women.[7] With old age and the onset of spousal illness, women have more friends to call on for help and are less likely to "go it alone." Betty Kramer, a social work professor at the University of Wisconsin, found that older men are more isolated when it comes to taking care of their spouses than are older women.[8] The men have fewer friends to call on.

Despite differences between women and men across the life span, men's behaviors become more similar to women's as we age. Older men, according to author Gail Sheehy in her book on men's passages, have more time for leisure activities and for friends than do younger men and thus more opportunity to become close with them. Men at midlife value their friendships more highly and are able to speak about them in greater depth than are younger men.[9] Those friendships may become more satisfying, according to psychologists from the United States and Canada, because as men know their friends longer, they can share more personal information.[10]

Tolerance of friends and family generally also increases with age for both men and women, and people make greater attempts to resolve differences as they age.[11] In our study we found support for this—there was greater tolerance by both older men and older women for spending time with a couple when they disliked one of the partners than we found in younger couples.

With older age for men comes some (but not all) of the emotional expressiveness that women possess earlier. For the older men and women in our sample, the older they become the less likely they are to say that they "have enough friends and don't want any more." They are more likely to say that they "have enough friends yet want more" or that they "do not have enough individual friends." This holds true for couple friends, too. The older the couple is, the more likely they are to say they do not have enough couple friends.

With age also comes increased compatibility for many couples. When the couples in our research were asked if they agree about the amount of time to spend with couple friends, the older they are, the more likely they are to agree with each other. In addition, younger couples struggle more with how to include individual friends. When single, they invested more in individual friendships and may still be working to balance single and couple friends.

Another consideration in making friends is that people over 50 have been found to be happier. A Gallup poll found that people are more content at 85 than 18. It is not clear if this is due to chemical changes in the brain or life perspective that allows us to let go of insignificant or even major annoyances.[12] Maggie Scarf writes in *September Songs* about one couple she had interviewed twice over a 20-year period. At the second interview, this over-50 couple were much happier than they were when younger. An increase in happiness with age could affect how people view their relationships with their significant others as well as their friends. In fact, when we asked couples to identify a couple who were friends and rate that couple's relationship, older couples have a more favorable view of their friends' relationship than do younger couples.

When older men and women enjoy their friendships with couples, they are applying their friendship skills acquired over a lifetime of socialization. Many couple friendships are formed in youth and maintained over generations. When we asked couples to name a couple with whom they are close and answer questions about them, we asked how long they had known the couple they were about to describe. The average length of friendship for the older couples was 26 years, approximately twice the length of the friendships of couples in the middle age group. In addition, the older couples are more apt than the younger couples to say that their couple friendships are formed mutually rather than as the result of one member of the couple.

We found older couples to be generally more relaxed than younger couples about their own marriage and their friendships with other couples. Life is less intense. Awareness of the sometimes ephemeral nature of friendships is brought into sharp relief as couples retire, friends move away, and people die. In a conversation between a newly partnered couple and the young woman's 91-year-old grandmother, the couple asked for advice about whom to invite to a small party they were hosting. The younger couple was concerned that some of their friends might not get along. The grandmother's advice? "Let the couples worry about that."

A COUPLE IN THEIR 60S

Michael is a 68-year-old architect living outside of Washington, D.C., where he shares an office with his wife, Nadine, 66 years old, who helps with interior designs. Both work full-time and are white. They have a 29-year-old son who is married and lives within an hour's drive. They have no grandchildren but are hopeful. Their house, as would be expected, is well decorated with a variety of interesting curios from their extensive travel and professionally honed tastes. It feels comfortable and reflects a casualness the couple maintain in their activities. They have lived in the neighborhood and this house for many years and have deep roots in the community.

Michael and Nadine are highly social, the epitome of *Seeker* couples who like to go out with other couples. They are *Seekers* as individuals and as a couple and will meet couples at parties and become instant friends. Whereas they have one or two close individual friends, they have numerous couple friends. Unlike interviews with older couples in this chapter, Michael and Nadine never mentioned the challenges of age, illness, and death. They have not reached the age where these three life equalizers have begun to take their toll on relationships.

Defining Friendships

In their definition of couple friendships, first Nadine and then Michael talks about the importance of equality among the four friends. Equality, along with caring and gaining insight from interacting with a couple, is one of the definitions that emotion sharers use in describing couple friendships.

> Couple friendships are people we go out to dinner with. We like both the individuals and the couple. We like being with and talking with them. The most important ones are where we like them as couples and as individuals.
> We may not call them up individually; we may not have an individual friendship. We tend to interact as couples. For example, we enjoy being around Dick and Helen, and we went out to dinner with them Thursday night and I can't imagine us interacting with them other than as couples, though I would be thrilled to get together with either of them alone, but we also value our relationship as couples. We have a lot of chemistry and we always have fun.

Nadine adds, "I could go out with Helen. It's just sometime you don't have enough time, and she especially does not."

This exchange suggests that busy couples who value socializing make plans because they can then spend what free time they have with the other couple. By contrast, a *Nester* couple with little free time is more apt to spend it with family or alone.

A central characteristic for *Seeker* couples is that couple friendships are important as they are for Nadine and Michael. It is also a characteristic of older couples in our sample. Michael describes what attracts them to other couples. We also learn from Michael and Nadine throughout their interview how good couple friends enhance their own relationship.

> One of the things that characterizes the people we enjoy being with is that they always bring something new to the party. We are very socially active and a lot of people will want to go to dinner with us and we are pushing them off, not because we don't like them but we are trying to budget our time, since we are out a lot. Many of our couples are very interesting separately and are interesting together. Robert and Colleen are both attorneys; he's a successful guy and his wife is also good company, and it's fun to be around people like that because it is a learning experience. You are engaged in talking about things you would never have a chance to explore with anyone else, and it is a mind-expanding evening with people you really like.

Their observation that Robert and Colleen bring new ideas and energy to their interactions is consistent with Slatcher's ideas about the role of novelty in enhancing friendships.[13] We noted that they explained how couples can be interesting as individuals and even more stimulating as a couple.

Nadine explains,

> I don't know these people on their own, and Robert is Michael's friend from the Naval Academy. Robert is the more dominant personality and he is funny, so he turns me on and gets me going, and Colleen plays to him and is not in competition. We have never really been alone with them, the four of us; it is always a party here and at parties he is on. But she's not intimidated by him and he's not malicious to her. That is just who they are and they appreciate each other.

Competition in Couples

We asked Nadine to say more about what she meant by competition between them. We were curious because we asked in the study about the nature of competition between a couple when they socialize with another couple. The sample was asked their level of agreement or disagreement with the statement: "I feel my spouse/partner is competing with me when we are out with couples." A small percentage, 4%, indicated they agreed with this statement, and another 8% neither agreed nor disagreed. But, as might be expected, people who said there was competition or were neutral rarely described their partners as very happy in the marriage.

After Nadine responded, Michael added his impressions. What emerges is a window on their friends' relationship.

"He is who he is and he's doing his own thing and not trying to lord it over her or embarrass her."

"When he talks, she listens. It is not a break in the conversation. He's making a contribution to her conversation," Michael adds.

"He is very respectful of her," Nadine chimes in.

Michael says,

> Another old Naval Academy friend of mine, his wife died and he remarried and they are both incredibly interesting. We enjoy them more together because she has a more outgoing personality, very engaging. He is a bright guy but more reserved, so they are the reverse of the other couple. When he talks, she is respectful. There is no dominance at all, and I think we like that because Nadine and I, in our ways, are dominant individuals and we like to see people who stand for something, have something to say and it is fun if you see it in a relationship. We don't see that balance frequently, and it is the fact that they love and respect each other."

With their active social life, we were surprised when we learned they do not feel they have many friends. One of the reasons, as Nadine offers, is that her own family history makes her uncomfortable with certain types of people and couple interactions.

I don't think we have a huge number. Closest people are ones you enjoy being with. They are not abusive to each other. I find abusive people to be tedious and I hate it. All the people we have described respect each other. If there is some sort of undercurrent that is personal or alcohol related, I don't enjoy that and I don't want to be around them. I am funny about the way that people talk to each other. It may be the way I grew up. I may be too sensitive about it. Also there is an alcohol issue in my family. And when some people drink they get mean and I don't like it, and it turns me right off. When I have to be with them, I cringe and get through it as quickly as possible.

Nadine's response touches on two findings from our study. The first centers on the issue of liking one member of the couple and not the other. Most of the couples have experienced this, and their way of handling it, according to their responses, is similar to Nadine's: They deal with it and keep seeing the couple. The second most common strategy is to see the couple less, and the third approach is for the two closest friends to see each other and avoid socializing as a couple.

The other finding that Nadine's response raises is the possibility that the couple (wherein there is an abuse or a drinking problem) gets dumped altogether by Nadine and Michael so that even the individual friendships end. Most couples have not experienced dumping a couple or being dumped by another couple. We discuss this in depth in the next chapter.

Starting and Ending Friendships

The majority of the couple friendships in our study were started by one individual in the couple. As couples age, the couple friendships are more likely to be initiated by a couple meeting couples together. Nadine told us that their couple friendships were a combination of Michael's friends and people they met through their son or their work. An example of how they meet couples together is provided by Michael.

"We went to a party Saturday night and met two couples we both had fun with. We are going to try and figure out some way of getting together with them again. It was loud, there was a band, but I know if we had a party we would include them."

"The magic was there," Nadine added. "They were interesting on their own and nice to each other. They weren't crawling all over each other, weren't dominant, and it just fit all the criteria."

"I think it is the old thing—we look for the content of their character. How smart, bright, articulate, how they look at things. You can always tell if someone is kind. These were very nice people."

Nadine and Michael have experienced the divorce of a couple with whom they were friends. Having friends divorce is more common among older than younger couples in our study. Although it did not have an impact on their marriage (we found that older couples are less apt to be affected by their friends breaking up), they did lose one member of the couple as a friend and held on to the older individual friendship, typical of what happens after friends divorce (see Chapter 7).

"You can't keep them both," Nadine laughed.

"When they broke up, she was almost an abusive partner," Michael added.

"And we aren't talking out of school. That was exactly the type of couple, as I mentioned before, where I did not like to go out with them. They were not fun to be around. She had a terrible childhood and there is only so much understanding I can give, but at some point, I am not going to put up with it. He would drink a little too much, too, and could get into it. He was there first so we stayed friends with him."

Nadine elaborated further. "If both parties cannot tolerate the other couple, it won't work. Both have to like both members separately and together. I don't like being around people who have subterranean problems. I have old friends who have problems, and I accept them though I don't always like being around them."

"So are there times then when one of you is interested in being friends with another couple but your partner is not?" we asked.

"I am sure there are times when I feel I could divide a couple up. But if Michael is not interested and I am, I will just see the woman."

If they like one member of the couple and not the other, they both agreed that they would work it out. They answered almost in unison that they do not have to go out as a couple all the time and would see the friend individually. As Michael clarifies for us, by definition, those are not "couple" friendships. They have singles and widows and divorcées who are friends.

Michael explains further how it works for them. Essentially, he tolerates the other couple if the magic is lacking. He also offers a broader perspective on how some couple friendships can be maintained—at a bit of a distance.

A lot of times you don't connect at a couple level but [at] an individual level, and then you have to get both spouses to sign up sight unseen. After the individual connection happens, you might try and figure out in the group sense if the couple magic is there. It may or may not be. I think we are not locked in. A couple relationship does not mean you have to talk to them every day; it just means that you enjoy being together and you include them in your plans at some point.

When we asked if they had ever lost any couple friends, Nadine was quick to joke. But, as they talk more, she reveals that her spontaneous personality can sometimes rub people the wrong way. Michael supports her by giving her leeway with her behavior. If push came to shove, she would rein herself in.

"Have we lost couple friends? Yeah. Go through the phone book," she laughs.

"I remember, and Nadine will totally reject this, when we were much younger, Nadine can become the life of the party, particularly among the men, a little outlandish. Just making fun and whatever. The wives used to get terribly threatened. Individuals who we would enjoy getting together with, their wives would push [us] away."

"I cleaned up my act. I think if I did something and they rejected us, I think you [turning to Michael] would go along with me and not get bent out of shape. And if Michael would object, I would clean up my act."

"I don't believe in feeding others' insecurities," Michael adds. "And it really speaks to those insecurities that a woman who is threatened by that is not someone who I want as a friend."

"I like to be funny and to be comfortable with people and if I thought I had embarrassed somebody or hurt someone, I would feel awful and apologize. My intention is never to hurt someone else. There was an instance where my medication was off and I became manic and I made a comment and woke up not remembering and I was upset with myself. My intent was never to hurt anyone."

Friends as Reflections of the Couple

Their couple friendships have deepened with time, as they have more to share with their friends—children, marriage, and other transitions. Nadine said that the more that is shared, the closer the relationships become.[14] But their friendships are not necessarily a reflection of them. About three-quarters of the sample, when asked if their friends were a reflection of them, said they were, in that they shared similar values, interests, and life experiences. Couples also said their friends held similar personalities, education, and economic status to theirs. Michael, when asked if their friends were a reflection of them, redirected the question and pointed out that he was not seeking similarities.

"I tend to seek differences in people because if they are like me, I get bored. I enjoy people for what they bring to the party and what I can learn from them."

After a back-and-forth with Nadine about the question, Michael adds, without necessarily changing his answer to the question, "If there is a similarity, it can be good. Those I feel most comfortable with are those I share values with. It is not that we agree on everything, but we have set boundaries on the way we deal with ourselves and our relationships. The values have to be similar, but there can be a lot inside the envelope and from there it gets interesting."

Being with other couples whom they like is their ultimate goal as a couple, and we hear again how time spent with another couple enhances their own relationship. As Nadine put it, "It makes us happy. We enjoy being with them and we enjoy being happy."

Nadine and Michael, married 35 years, understand and respect each other. They are both *Seekers,* willing to engage new couples in friendships while still having time for their current friends. From their descriptions of past issues with friends, it is clear they are keenly aware of what they are willing to tolerate in others. Individual friends are accepted regardless of their warts, and they will tolerate, to a point, an old friend's partner. That can lead, as Nadine admitted, to tense times although those times appear to be in past. They live in the moment and are not thinking about slowing down or about potential losses related to illness or death. Those issues never come up as they seek the next fun couple with whom they can engage and grow.

A COUPLE IN THEIR 70s

Sometimes interviewing one member of a couple without the other offers a slightly different perspective—the interviewee may feel freer about commenting on the other partner. Roberta is 74, retired, and married for 54 years with two children in their 50s. She and her husband, Quincy (both are white), moved to their current location, after 10 years of marriage, when they were 30 and 32. He found work in management and she in a local school district. They did not grow up where they have lived most of their lives. She is tall and thin with short curly hair and looks younger than her age would suggest. The interview took place in her suburban home. From interviewing Roberta alone, we get an impression of Quincy as being the more reticent of the two. Unlike Michael and Nadine, who are both *Seekers,* this couple would put themselves into different categories from each other. We also learn from Roberta what happens when a couple who is part of a long-standing group of friends gets divorced: The couple gets dropped. Contrast this to being single around Diane and Charlie in Chapter 3 who almost purposefully incorporate single friends into their circle. Is it because times have changed, the couples are in different life stages, or is it the idiosyncratic nature of these couples? We suspect it is some combination.

The Benefits of Couple Friendships

For Roberta, couple friendships present the opportunity to do things with her husband.

> All four of you have to be friends. For single friends, you don't have to like each other's friends. Couples friends mean that my husband and I do more things together; we socialize together. It's nice because, in my case, my husband doesn't go out, go out looking for friends. He's not sociable. I don't know how to word it. Most of his friends are through me now since we've been married. He brought friends into our relationship because we met in college and he had friends who are still our friends. But after we married, it changed. He's rather shy. He doesn't hear well.

Roberta is convinced that, without the opportunity to socialize with her, her husband would not go out much. She estimates he sees his old male friends no more than once a year and has made few male friends in 55 years. He is a *Nester* and she is a *Seeker*.

We asked if they had lost any couple friendships through divorce and learned that among their close couple friends, when a couple divorced, they dropped out of a group who has been meeting for 50 years.

> There was one couple we traveled with who broke up. They were in our group from college who traveled to Vermont together. When they got divorced, they were asked to leave our group. The guy kept wanting to come to the weekends but the organizer, the one who put the group together told him, 'no,' he wasn't welcome any more and I thought that was great. We didn't see him after the divorce.

As will be seen in the chapter on divorce and the chapter in which we report on interviewing a group that has been meeting for years, this outcome is common. A couple gets divorced and relationships with other couples end. In our study, about two-thirds of the couples had couple friends who had broken up.

Roberta describes herself as the more open of the couple, which is typical for most couples. When she and Quincy are out with another couple, she has no trepidation about sharing information about their own lives because she does not have much to share (or much to be embarrassed about sharing). Part of her openness she chalks up to gender and age.

> I think women talk about things that men don't because I'll say to my husband, 'What did so and so say about that?' and I'll come back with all this news from the same couple and he will not have any. Women talk more. We don't have any secrets. I think our friends are all the same kind of people. We're not over the top. We come from the same generation that is sensible. I can't even think of something so dramatic in our lives that we wouldn't talk about.

Roberta gave one example of how they accommodated liking one member of a couple and not the other. As is sadly typical for many older couples, when one member of the couple dies, if he or she was the more likeable member of the couple, socializing can end for the survivor.

"We all liked the husband better. Unfortunately, he passed away. If everyone hadn't liked him better, we wouldn't have been friends at all with the wife. We felt bad for him. We thought she was selfish and thought, 'oh, you poor guy.'"

We wanted to know if they dumped them because of her behavior. Like many couples, they took the bitter with the sweet.

> No [we didn't drop them], but they would come over to dinner 45 minutes late because she was putting on makeup. And it got so, at one neighbor's house, we just ate without them because they were so late. When she arrived, she made light of it, and we felt bad for him because he was so embarrassed. She was incorrigible, someone I would not want to be friends with. He was a neat guy, so we made do.

Traditional Roles

Roberta describes herself as the social secretary in her marriage. She describes herself as better at making friends and that their couple friendships revolve more around her than him. As would be expected from Roberta's descriptions of her and Quincy's different personalities, she feels that she carries most of the weight when they socialize.

In our study, no significant trends emerged for age or gender about who carries the weight when the couple socializes. The response was more idiosyncratic to the couples and, as in the case of Roberta and Quincy, she is the more social and thus carries the weight. But, to a slightly different question, there were significant differences in responses to the statement, "My spouse/partner calls the shots when we socialize." Bottom line: Men and women agree that women call the shots with socializing although what actually happens when couples are out together (whether someone carries more of the weight) may not be as predictably gender based.

Roberta believes women and men follow traditional roles in leaving friendship maintenance to women. She would be open to new individual and couple friends and thinks her husband would say he has enough friends. With the couple friends they have, Roberta describes them as similar in terms of their spirit of adventure, being nonjudgmental, and being interesting to be around. As with other couples the same age as Roberta and Quincy, certain topics, like sex and money, are off limits.

With the exception of the one male friend who has died, Roberta does not offer a comment on the aging process. Her friends are actively engaged in socializing and in many enjoyable aspects of life. Of the other couples in their 70s who were interviewed, illness, aging, and death are mentioned by some but not all. It is on the radar for most in this age group and becomes a more universal topic for those over 80. At that age, it has a definite impact on couple friendships.

TWO COUPLES IN THEIR 80s

Ken and Leah, whom we highlighted at the beginning of this chapter, have been married more than 60 years and are 88 and 83 years old, respectively. They are white, have three grown children, and seven grandchildren scattered from the East to the West Coast. Ken was a manager of a large store until his retirement. Leah stayed home and was deeply involved in charity work. They grew up in the same city and began dating shortly after Ken returned from service in World War II. Their parents were acquaintances, so the marriage was comfortable for both families. They still live in an attractively decorated two-story house. Two of their three children live nearby but are not involved in caretaking as Ken and Leah are both fully capable of managing and until recently, when their youngest grandchild became old enough not to need child care, they would babysit. We interviewed them in their home. This couple, like the next couple, Oscar and Paula, who are the same age, are healthy, are highly astute, and have not lost a step with the years.

Most informative about these interviews is how the nature of couple friendships changes over time due to age, illness, geographic relocation, and death.

"I think couple friendships are important to your life because you get other people's points of view. You travel with people, often because it is more fun and to see some place new," Leah told us, emphasizing how such friends enrich a marriage. She then adds, "They have education that is different from yours, and sometimes their work is different. You learn from other people."

Ken chimes in with a slightly wistful tone and emphasizes losses that occur. "I think friends are terribly important. In fact, we are losing them at our age, and this is the thing that makes us very sad. I'd say in our married life we've had 15 to 20 couples we feel very close to, and only one or two of those are left. Most singles who are left are women."

Ken mentions how connections from childhood build closeness in adulthood (even if there is a geographic move) in ways he believes may not exist today.

> I had good friends in D.C. and, by coincidence, the girls Leah grew up with married the boys I grew up with. As a result we became very good friends. When we moved to Richmond, we ran into a group of people who were just getting married at that time, and we were able to join with them for three reasons: They were getting married just when we were, we were all the same religion, and a number of their parents knew my parents.

Their best friends were built from this group, and it became a habit to go out with a group of couples on Saturday nights and on New Year's Eve. They had started a family by this time and, if they could find a sitter, that was how the weekend was spent.

Leah says that, although they were highly social and could be categorized as *Seekers,* they also had another side to their relationship where they were quite comfortable with just each other. "We liked doing things by ourselves, and some of those things we didn't have friends who were interested in doing. I like to watch modern dance, and Ken was nice enough to go along with me to those performances, so we would go alone. We would go to the symphony with another couple who we were somewhat close with but Ken knew the guy from college."

"He married the first cousin of another roommate from college and that's how these things get intertwined and we became pretty close with them," Ken explains. "A lot of these friendships lasted 50 years."

We wondered if these friendships strengthened their marriage. This was not something they had considered.

"I never thought about it that way." Leah responded.

"I didn't either," Ken said. "I can say there is nothing that could pull us closer together. From the day I laid eyes on Leah, I never had another date and we've never had a disagreement. I guess if I had my first choice it would be to spend it alone with her, but we recognize we can't do that. Therefore, friends become very important. But I don't feel any different about our marriage being out with other couples."

But, we interjected, you did say it adds something.

"Definitely," Leah answers and again reflects on the value-added notion of couple friends.

> They have different interests and you learn from them. Or they have personalities and they clash with someone else. Sometimes they have friends who are peripheral to you who become your friends. We are having people over for dinner tonight and the number kept growing because one guest had children who were friends with another guest, so they were added at the last minute and that meant adding that set of children, so we started with 8 and soon got to 16. That is all because of friendships.

Ken is on the same page:

> I think friendships enrich your lives and going out with another couple, sure we feel better when we come home, and we feel better if we've been to a good movie. All these things add to your enjoyment of life. And sometimes you meet people through them whom you like a lot. You hope it works in the other direction, too. A lot of people we know well we know because of someone else.

Giving, Receiving, and Being Caught Between Two Couples After an Affair

We asked if they give and receive emotional support when they are with these other couples and learned that Leah, like most women, is more open about talking with friends about their children.

"I think that is a part of friendships," she told us. "Close friends know our children very well and we know their children very well and the problems that have ensued. Sometimes you can help and be helped."

Ken is more circumspect about revealing too much. "We may only have half a dozen couples at the most where I would feel close enough to talk about the troubles of our children. And we can't even say couples anymore because we have very few couples where both are still alive. We have neighbors whom we go out to dinner with but they are just friends, not close friends."

One of the standard questions is whether a couple has ever lost another couple as friends from some incident. Older couples in our study were more apt to have had that experience than younger ones because more years have passed. Leah and

Ken are no exception. In fact, they smile at each other simultaneously when we ask the question.

> We did lose one couple, and not permanently [Ken relates]. This is one of our closest couples with whom we traveled. We used to travel with a group of four couples, and one of the men in one couple had an affair with one of the women in the other couple. Both couples stayed together, but we had to choose which couple to travel with. We knew both couples for many years so it was not a matter of choosing the couple that came first, as they were both very old friends.

Leah explains what happened next and how it shaped the future friendships of all the couples.

> The wife of the man who had the affair knew that her husband liked women but never thought he would have a dalliance with someone so close to them. The men are now dead and the two women who are left will not go out together. We lost the friendship of one of those couples for 3 or 4 years until we became close with them again, but never again were we together as a group of four couples. It was awkward, and it is still awkward as we try and decide which of the widows to see each New Year's.

In their deciding which couple to stay close with, they chose the couple where the wife was not sexually involved. They described her as the "injured party," although they could have decided the other husband was the injured party. The affair had no impact on Ken and Leah's own marriage. Ken joked that he has hugged Leah at night and told her how happy he was to not be married to either of the two women.

With such a strong marriage, we anticipated that they would not need to discuss in advance what to share and not to share with their friends, that their sense of intuition would guide them. However, when we asked this question, we heard a slightly different answer, first from Ken and then from Leah, indicating they were not necessarily on the same page about how much to share. Ken keeps more to himself while Leah is helped by sharing. This is one of the differences between men and women at all ages that we discussed earlier in the chapter.

"Leah tends to share more than I do anyway by nature."

"I think that is more a feminine trait," she responds. "You have strong friends who are not going to blab around and may give you good advice. We may be the fulcrum in that we see a lot of pain in other people. We had a friend who died recently who had significant problems that we knew about."

"We've had our share of pain," Ken adds quietly.

Notice how their styles of sharing personal information are different, yet the marriage is strong. Strong marriages do not inure a couple from experiencing life's ups and downs, but strong marriages do help couples find a way to manage what comes along.

Maintaining Friendships

As for the question about how to handle couple friendships in which you like one partner and not the other, the older couples in our study tend to "deal with it"—it bothers them less than it does younger couples, who have less tolerance for spending time with a member of a couple they don't like. Ken and Leah are typical of older couples in their responses. It is essentially no big deal.

"Everyone has a few boring friends, but if they are nice people, we go out. We try and accommodate each other's wishes in going out with other people," Leah said.

Consistent with what we described in the first chapter, that men construct side-by-side friendships and women construct face-to-face friendships, Ken answers that he would be content going out with couples where he did not know or wasn't especially fond of the man if there was something to do.

"Leah has a book group of five women. She is friendlier with the women than I am with their husbands. Would we go out with any of them? Sure, to the ball game or the theater. We will go out once or twice a year. But Leah and I probably agree that men don't need to keep their friendships as ongoing as do women."

Over time and with advancing years, their friends have become less accessible because of difficulties in traveling to see each other. Also, as noted earlier, many friends have died, leaving a cadre of single women.

When we asked if their friends are a reflection of them, Leah explains, "On the whole, we think they have the same values: a loving family, interesting people who like to go places and see things."

Ken's answer is indicative of the importance placed by this couple on maintaining old ties. Other research has shown that time spent with old friends often centers on reminiscing and, with such memories, the old friends feel youthful once again. Ken and Leah have friends from almost 70 years ago they see once a year.

"When I came out of college, I had three close friends," Ken tells us. One was killed in the war, one is this fellow in the South who we try and see, and the third is in Philadelphia and we see him once a year."

Consistent with other older couples we interviewed, Leah and Ken are comfortable talking about any issue, with the exception of sex. When we asked whether they ever discussed sex with other couples, they indicated it was not a topic that was shared. They are extremely happy together and, although they can point out characteristics in other marriages that they admire, as Ken put it, "I don't wish our marriage was more like anyone else's."

Roberta, Nadine, and Michael do not focus on illness and death. Ken and Leah are painfully aware of the changes that come with advanced age.

My friends, and it makes me so sad, have died, [Ken laments]. Practically all our couple friends are now left as widows. We often try to take the widows out for dinner but more often Leah will take the widows out to lunch, which is a change in the relationship. We don't want to take two of them out to dinner because then it becomes a widows' dinner and that does not feel right.

Going out with the widows (or widowers) is a reminder of what has been lost. As we learn from the next couple, who are Ken and Leah's age, no couple at this stage of life is immune.

Oscar and Paula

Oscar and Paula, both white, are both retired. They owned a liquor store in Philadelphia for many years. The type of business one runs can affect friendships. For them, the liquor business meant they were never free to socialize on New Year's Eve—it was their biggest day of the year. Oscar, like Ken, served in World War II. He met Paula in 1946 after coming home from overseas. He was driving through the park in a convertible with a friend one spring day, and she was bicycling with a group of her friends. It was strong attraction at first sight. Coincidentally, their mothers knew each other from working in a department store and were hoping to fix them up. On the first date, he took her dancing and drinking, two activities with which she had little experience. She feared that because of her naiveté in both areas, he would not call her again. After a few weeks of silence, he showed up at her door and began actively pursuing her. They married a year later.

This interview, which took place in their ranch-style suburban home, highlights the difference between family and friends for some couples, as well as the apparent fragility of friendships if there is a social slight. Just as Ken and Leah are aware of the loss of friends, Paula and Oscar find they, too, have a dwindling number of men friends with whom they can socialize. Their life is active and, during the interview, we were frequently interrupted by incoming phone calls. Oscar answered the calls, usually about plans to get together with family or friends. A grandfather clock that chimed on the half hour seemed perfect for the setting and the themes raised during the interview. Chimes announce the end of one time period and the beginning of the next. Grandfather clocks were not seen in the homes of younger people we interviewed.

Paula and Oscar's first couple friends were made through a local club they joined soon after they were married. Over the years, many of those original friends drifted away or moved south and west to warmer climates. Others died. Like Ken, Oscar is often the only male over 85 years old left in the room. Their perspective on couple friends is, nonetheless, that they are extremely important.

Family Versus Friends and the Role of Women

What is the proper balance to strike between friendships with family members and friendships outside of the family? Some people we interviewed, including Diane in an earlier chapter, feel much closer to siblings and cousins than to friends and believe that family members understand them better. Others, like Oscar and Paula, may have had more complicated relations with family members and have purposefully sought out confidants outside the family.

"Friends are more important than relatives. It is a different life with friends than with relatives. I found you can disclose more innermost secrets with friends than with family. Our relationship with friends was very strong in our marriage. You travel with them; you don't travel with relatives."

Paula, from a large family, has a similar view.

Most of my family have died over the years. My father was one of nine, and the oldest. I will try to see the survivors and the children. I see the cousins on occasion. With friends we talk to them very often about our children and grandchildren. There is openness with friends. We are somewhat close with family but not very close. We ask how they are but we are not close like friends.

We wanted to pursue this difference and asked them to talk more about the difference between friends and family. In their answer, they describe themselves as an emotion sharing couple.

When I call, family rarely asks about our children, but our friends ask. Our son is a doctor in Alabama and he got divorced, and all our friends ask about his children and the divorce. Our other son has a child with autism and our friends ask about that. We take care of him during the week—pick him up at school and take him to his lessons. Our friends know all the intimate details. Our families do not. Oscar and I just don't talk to them and they don't seem interested.

"We are attracted to our friends because of their openness and caring," Oscar agrees. "Friends, we can say whatever we want to and we won't hurt their feelings. Friends I can call a dummy or whatever and it doesn't mean anything. With the relatives, unfortunately, they take it more personally."

"Oscar's relatives don't live close by so unless it is a special occasion, we don't see them."

Paula and Oscar believe that women in couples are more apt to make and maintain couple friendships. This view is consistent with that of other older couples in our study. Young couples are more apt to say that the responsibility for friendships is a shared prospect.

Like Ken and Leah, Oscar and Paula have been affected by the death of the men in their couple friends. They make an effort to include widows, to be inclusive, but in doing so, Oscar ends up feeling excluded.

> There were couples that we would get together with every weekend. We would have cocktails before going out; we'd celebrate birthdays together. But now a lot of them are gone. We still get together with some of them, but we are not as friendly as we were before. Occasionally they will go to dinner with us, but it is not the same as when their husbands were alive. We went to a party recently, and there were 12 women and 2 men. When there is a widow, although we don't, other people avoid them like the plague, which is unfortunate [Oscar lamented]. We are more compassionate. We will include, what's her name, once in a while though not as much as we did when her husband was alive. It's awkward with a number of women and just me. The conversation turns to things that don't include me. We like to go out to a movie with friends, and we will look for couples and either go out to dinner before or afterward with them. And now one of our best friends has pneumonia, so we don't go out with them and have to look for other people. If they drive, all the better because I don't drive at night. We ended up calling other people recently to go with them to a movie festival. We reached out to them.

As their ability to maneuver on their own is restricted, they shift their friendship styles and reach out more to others for assistance. Whereas in the past they could have waited for people to approach them, now they, as *Seekers,* reach out more to others.

In a similar vein to what Leah and Ken reported, when with old friends, annoying characteristics in one partner might be overlooked. Oscar's view is that friendships trump a lot of indiscretions. He told us, "If you are friends, you are friends." But then, and in a direct contradiction, we learned from Paula how fragile friendships can be, even for an 88-year-old man, and how easily he can get hurt. This emerged when we asked them if they had ever dumped another couple or been dumped by another couple.

> There have been occasions where Oscar will say, 'I don't want to go with them because I saw him at the golf club and he ignored me after I went over to him.' Oscar tapped him on the shoulder and said hi and the man never turned around. That happened last month. He came home and said he didn't want to go out with them anymore. They called and asked us out to dinner, and he said he didn't want to go.

Without directly disagreeing, Oscar did not seem to remember this had happened to him. He held on to the belief that friendship trumps most behaviors by citing a similar set of behaviors in others.

"I know of other friendships where the men get into a fight, and they don't want to go out with them anymore. That has never happened to us that we lost a friend over bad feelings, but there are friends of ours where that has happened after years. It was over a golf game."

"Or a drinking problem with one and now they avoid each other," Paula explains. "The wives are still friends, but the guys do not get together. It can be awkward because they may get invited to parties together. If they get invited, they would come but just not talk to each other. I never want to get in the middle of that, and no one ever said how it started and I didn't ask the wives."

Oscar offered us a lifetime perspective on friendships and how, just as there are seasons to people's lives, there are seasons, in his view, to couple friendships. This is in contrast to some of what is believed about individual friendships. For individual friendship, some men, for example, believe they can only be true friends with people they have known since they were young.[15] Aristotle offered a similar view. Such friendships would become fewer and farther between with advancing age. But here we see a man who thinks that couple friendships can follow cycles.

"Our friends from when we first got married 60 some years ago are gone. Now we make new friends every 20 years. We have made friends who are very close to us within the last 20 years."

Paula partially shares this view, although she appears to have a stronger preference for older individual friends. "One year we went to Florida and stayed 3 days with three different couples. We still talk with them on the phone. Different things happen and you make different friends over time. With the old friends we get together and talk about our times when we were young. Now with people we have met, it is just different."

Paula feels young again when she is with friends from childhood or from earlier days. In contrast to Paula, Oscar has few such friends left. By necessity, perhaps, he has stayed open to meeting new couple friends at a time when so few men are still around.

CONCLUSIONS

For the couples over 70 highlighted in this chapter, and consistent with Liebler and Sandefur's research, the women are more social. They also take responsibility for setting up relationships and are more interested in couple friends than are men. By this stage of life, and for the oldest couples, the number of couples available as friends has diminished and couple friendships are mostly a memory. Yet the two oldest couples featured here are open to potential additions to their lives. While acknowledging losses, they are interested in new experiences with couples and individuals. They look forward to every day, are grateful that they can still live independently in reasonably good health, and seek others for companionship.

In thinking about the couples we have interviewed and reported on in Chapters 3, 4, and 5, we see how interest in and time for couple friends shift across the life span. The younger couples are struggling with connecting with each other as well as with friends and family. The middle years' couples have figured out what they want to do with friends and to what extent to incorporate them into their lives. In some ways, the older couples have returned comfortably to their earlier years. When couples are just starting out, they often try to balance socializing with individual friends with a desire to be with couple friends. Once again, many of their friends (nearly all women) are single. Decades later, this friend-making stage of life has returned. It is ironic that what may have been one of the first challenges for a newly formed couple in relation to friendships may return as a naturally occurring event. And we also see that across the life span, friendships remain a vitally important component of their lives.

6

When Couples Have Been Dumped (or Dump); Like Her and Hate Him (or Vice Versa)

I kind of blame my husband for it. But he was also responsible for beginning the relationship so maybe it comes out even. Dick and Sally live in Texas and had been friends with us for over 25 years. Over the years, they visited us in Michigan and we visited them. The most recent visit to Texas did not go well. Sally is a control freak and that bothers my husband. My husband wanted to borrow their car; they said no. Then a day later there was a disagreement about what to do that day and my husband blew up. He criticized Sally and was rude. I felt like he overreacted because he wasn't allowed to be in control. It calmed down. We stayed the rest of the visit and we thought it had been ironed out. But after that, they never answered our letters or returned our phone calls no matter how much my husband tried to fix the situation.

The end to a friendship can be traumatic. Preschoolers often tearfully lament to their parents that Billy or Susie does not want to play with them anymore. In middle school and high school, tweens and teens are devastated when they are excluded from parties. In college, once close freshman roommates can join different fraternities or sororities, embark on parallel and separate social paths and grow more distant. And in young adulthood, as people begin seriously dating, friends may find they no longer have time for old friends, especially if the new love interest does not feel comfortable around them. Our guess is just about everyone has been dropped by a friend or has ended a friendship at some point in his or her life.

Sometimes friendships wither on the vine as people grow up and grow apart, move away to college, pursue career opportunities, or develop interest in activities. Other times friendships end because of something more significant: a fight between the friends, a destructive act that violates a friend's understanding of their relationship, or a misunderstanding in communication. These are signal events that can result in individuals breaking up their friendships or curtailing their interest in spending time with each other.

This chapter looks at friendships that have ended between couples. During our interviews, we asked if the couple had ever been dumped by another couple or had themselves ended a friendship with another couple. Almost one-third of the couples we interviewed said a couple friendship had ended; twice as many said they had dumped the other couple as had been dumped themselves. It is not surprising that people more often see themselves as the ones doing the dumping, rather than the ones being dumped: Who wants to admit to being dropped as a friend? In this chapter we also look at what happens with the more subtle and less dramatic changes in couple relationships, when couples slowly push themselves away from another couple because they do not like one member of that couple. It is important to note that some couple friendships never get off the ground and should not be considered true friendships. We will be focusing here on those friendships that end after a personal investment has been made and the other couple is considered to be friends.

COMMITMENT TO FRIENDSHIP

Some people would never consider dropping a friendship believing "once a friend, always a friend." Others are willing, based on the context, to put a stop to one when it turns sour. One way to consider friendships is through a philosophical lens. Diane Jeske, a professor of philosophy at the University of Iowa, frames her discussion of friendship by contrasting Immanuel Kant and Aristotle. Kant believed that friendships exist to serve a purpose and that the utility or value of a friendship varies with the context. Aristotle believed that having the capacity for a friendship is a sign of virtue and that friendship is marked by a high level of caring for another even above caring for oneself. For Aristotle, a true friendship can only be with a virtuous person and one must be virtuous in turn to have such a friendship. Jeske writes, "The virtuous are worthy or deserving of concern. We are justified in becoming friends with the virtuous because they are appropriate objects of the attitudes that are partly constitutive of friendship."[1] Friends are cared about for their own sake. Contrast this with the Kantian view where friends are valued, in part, for what they provide us and for what we can get from friends.

Why consider these two competing philosophies? Because our reactions to friends are driven by our beliefs. In the Kantian view, we may drop friends when they no longer are worth the work it takes or when the friendship no longer serves our purpose. In the Aristotelian view, we may work hard to maintain friends even when they do something upsetting. Jeske proposes that concern for a friend when he or she acts poorly may drive a person to a closer, rather than a more distant, friendship. "Discovery of faults, even serious moral flaws, in persons we have come to care about should lead us to help them to overcome those flaws, not abandon them to their own devices."[2] Jeske does not believe that we have to be friends with evil people; there is a limit to standing by friends when they act reprehensibly. Her message, with a nod to Aristotle, is that we should not abandon a friendship when conflict arises or people disagree over minor indiscretions. This is similar to the "once a friend, always a friend" approach that we have heard regarding how individuals approach friendships.

WHY INDIVIDUAL FRIENDSHIPS END

Making and maintaining individual friends is hard enough for individuals. In research on same-sex friendships, 80% to 85% of adult women and men said they had lost a friend at some point during their life. Between 20% and 30% said friends had drifted away from them with time.[3] Women noted that sometimes same-sex friendships end because they are "draining" or are no longer reciprocal; that is, they thought they were putting more into them than they were getting out of them.[4] More common were friendships ending because of some event that occurred between the friends.[5] These events usually involved disputes about boyfriends or girlfriends, ex-spouses, money, or children. Many times they involved trust being betrayed. Friends did not respect confidences they were asked to keep. They shared information with others that was told them in secret. One 21-year-old white college student told us that she dropped one of her friends after the friend told another young woman one of the 21-year-old's secrets. She never confronted her friend about it but instead maintained a pseudo relationship with her where they remained in contact but close confidences were never again shared. Loyalty, trust, dependability, and conveying understanding are all important components of individual friendships.[6] When those have been erased, the end of the relationship may be near.

Men tend to be more comfortable with friendships ending than women. Women will work harder to find out why they ended and will try harder to resolve them when they do end. Men are more likely to let them drop without pursuing the reasons. This is consistent with many men's lack of comfort in processing emotional events.[7]

While people grow up and move on, the extent to which this process occurs has changed. With Facebook and other social networking aids, it is easier to reconnect with old friends than ever before, even if the reconnecting only involves e-mail contact. Thirty years ago one would have to first locate an old friend and then write (time consuming) or make a long-distance call (expensive). Today, those impediments no longer exist, replaced by search engines and free e-mail. People use these search engines to locate and reconnect with old classmates, teammates, and camp friends. Even so, many once close friends drift off and are never seen or heard from again.

Sociologist Sarah Matthews, in her study of friendships across the life span, writes about friendships that "peter out" and "fade away" as well those that "ended in a more active way."[8] She refers to friends who have "disqualified themselves by doing something that betrayed the friendship, or changed an informant's evaluation of the person."[9] Her examples of disqualification and betrayal include two from men, one whose friend became "rotten" and went AWOL from the army and the other whose friend stole a car that was jointly owned. In both cases, the behavior was sufficiently unacceptable that the men did not want to see their friend anymore. Certainly these two examples may test even the closest of friendships.

Matthews interviewed people who were dumped as friends. In most examples, those dumped did not understand why they were dropped and they ended up characterizing the ex-friend as "disturbed" or "strange." Matthews concluded that none of the supposed reasons for termination of the friendship seemed justified to the interviewees.

Ambiguous events can drive a wedge between friends. Slights may be perceived that may have been intended or unintended. Words that are expressed between friends are parsed either at the time they were said or on later reflection. Robert Louis Stevenson wrote in 1881 of how tenuous friendships can be. "A man who has a few friends, or one who has a dozen (if there be any one so wealthy on this earth), cannot forget on how precarious a base his happiness reposes; and how by a stroke or two of fate—a death, a few light words, a piece of stamped paper, a woman's bright eyes—he may be left, in a month, destitute of all."[10]

Note Stevenson's reference to "a few light words." Matthews recounts one instance where a woman dropped another woman as a friend because her words were insensitive. If, for example, a friend is perceived as not being supportive of the good fortune of another friend, the fortunate friend has to decide if it is jealousy, lack of support, or a misunderstanding. Remember how hurt Jenny in Chapter 3 was when her friend could not take joy in her new house? She dropped the couple because she felt unsupported by her female friend.

When someone is ignored in a social gathering, is it intentional or a fleeting lapse? Remember how hurt Oscar in Chapter 5 was when he was ignored at the club by his friend? His 88 years of life did not inure him from the knee-jerk reaction of dropping the friend. He needed his wife to calm him down before he would agree to socialize with the couple again.

So we have the typical developmental reasons of growing up, graduating, and moving on that end friendships as well as a lack of support, insensitivity, or misinterpretation that can break up friendships. Whereas these reasons are often part of normal change and may be due to an unintended word or reaction, significant events also can abruptly end friendships. Boyfriends or wives are seduced, money is stolen, someone is cheated by a friend, a trust is broken, or a friend's behavior is so egregious that it cannot be forgiven. These events can be in and of themselves convincing reasons for long-time friends to end friendships.

WHY COUPLE FRIENDSHIPS END

What then leads a couple to end a friendship with both members of another couple? Loyalty to, or a lifelong friendship with, one of the members of the couple would certainly be a reason to hold on to the couple. The majority of couple friendships in our research are based on one member of the couple having a prior friendship with one member of the other couple (high school buddies who grow up and marry and add their spouses to the friendship is a typical example) while a small number of couples said their friendships started mutually when all four met each other for the first time (through children or a religious setting).

The reasons for dropping another couple are varied, and the reasons that a couple is dropped are often unfathomable to those who are dropped. As suggested in the passage on philosophy, a couple may agonize before they drop friends because they may have a long-standing commitment to them. It is a normal part of growing up and moving on that friends drift apart and the friendship withers. When a friendship ends for these reasons, it is often more a statement about the healthy circumstances (growing up) that pull the people away than about the flawed nature of the people.

Jeske would argue that conflict and differences are normal in friendships and should be worked out. When couples are involved, there are twice as many permutations that can end their friendship. Only one of the four has to be offended, hurt, or disrespected for that person to want to pull the plug on the relationship. In fact, those who have been dumped are more likely to describe themselves and their spouses as being very picky when it comes to friends than those who said they were not dumped.[11] The majority of those we interviewed said they had not been dumped and had not dumped another couple; people are much more likely to say their individual friendships have ended.

Why might couples be less apt to dump friendships or be dumped than individuals? Unlike one-on-one relationships, the spouse or partner of the hurt or offended person may help that spouse or partner work it through in the service of trying to maintain the relationship. Sometimes talking things out with a trusted partner can help people change their mind about a perceived event. The spouse or partner may be especially interested in processing what has happened if the spouse or partner is invested in maintaining the couple friendship.

We think of these friendships, when compared to individual ones, as a regression to the mean. Two people as a couple are less likely to have an extreme reaction and risk the chance of getting hurt than are individuals who operate on their own and do not have a sounding board (their partner) to help process what has happened. Imagine the scenario when one partner complains to her spouse about the woman in the other couple with whom they have just eaten dinner. The woman is upset about what the other woman said to the waiter. If the couple can talk about it and her husband has a different interpretation about the comment or has a more laissez-faire attitude, it may lead to saving the relationship.

On the other hand, if the husband agrees with what his wife heard, it may reinforce the desire to end the relationship with the other couple altogether or just end the relationship with the four of them; he may continue the relationship with his guy friend. As mentioned, it may take only one person out of the four to nix the relationship; this can make maintaining it more tenuous. Based on the responses we received, the tendency is for a couple to modulate their response rather than terminate the friendship. The couple may also tend toward not ending the relationship in a definitive fashion, for example, calling them and telling them they do not want to be friends with them anymore, but rather letting it wither on the vine. Letting it fade away rather than confronting the other couple may be easier to manage interpersonally, especially if both partners are not in agreement about whether and how to end it.[12]

Of course, part of being friends with another couple is accepting their ups and downs, their lack of returning calls quickly enough, or their always wanting to include another couple when socializing. Being friends also means sharing them with other couple friends—they may be telling their most private secrets to another couple or taking them to a special concert when free tickets fall into their hands. Couples with a lot of friends have less time for any one couple. The wider that couple's social network is, the less likely any one couple is to be included in their intimate plans.

Sometimes the determination about whom to drop from one's own network can be considered, in the terms of Immanuel Kant, as a sizing up of options. Couples get dropped because they are never available or are known to be closer friends with another couple. On the other hand, a couple may decide that if Jeremy and Stella are dropped as friends, the couple will not get invited to their great parties where they meet wonderful people. Maybe keeping Jeremy and Stella as friends has its advantages even if the couples are not that close.

We return to the initial question that frames this chapter: What happens between couples that ends a friendship?

SOME STORIES AND COMMON REASONS FOR DUMPING TO OCCUR

We looked at the reasons couples gave for being dumped or for dumping another couple. Some of these stories came to us through the interviews and some from their written questionnaire responses. Although a few couples we interviewed described outward tension or confrontation with another couple as part of a breakup, this is rare. One example of a confrontation was given by Harry, a 75-year-old white radiologist. He and his wife had been long-term friends with another couple. The husband in that couple became ill, and the wife was feeling under great stress because of the illness. The couple's daughter was getting married in a small town, a 4-hour drive away from Harry's home. Harry and his wife were invited to the wedding, which included many family members and friends. Harry had no interest in driving 8 hours for a wedding in which he would play a minor role. He also wanted to play golf and tennis that weekend. He declined the invitation, and his wife was unwilling to drive herself. The mother of the bride was so hurt by his refusal to attend that she never wants to see Harry again, though she is still willing to see his wife. They are no longer couple friends.

More common are the circumstances where people either stop calling or let the relationship fade away. Sometimes a couple is left unsure why the friendship ended; this was not the case with Harry.

A Couple Loses Friends After Divorce

Divorce is a significant reason for why couple friendships end—there is no longer a couple with whom to be friends. Usually, someone gets dropped, as we see in the next chapter on the aftermath of divorce. In our examples provided here, the sands shifted in the relationships and communication stopped; couples picked sides and it was difficult to maintain separate relationships.

One African American couple in their late 20s, she a therapist and he a stay-at-home father, told us about their experience with a divorcing couple. The women had been friends initially from school but, after the breakup, the couple came to like the classmate's husband more. As a result, perhaps of the favoritism shown him, her original friend dropped her.

> I was her maid of honor, and when she got married the guys got acquainted. Now that their relationship is not going to work out, I have a stronger relationship with the guy. It feels strange to me though because I hope I have both of them as friends when it is over. I do the calling and the e-mailing, and she is not responding. She is supposed to be my really good friend, and I feel dumped because of the breakup.

A 60-year-old white social work administrator was also the one who got dumped, he told us.

> When my first marriage broke up, there was a couple that we were both friends with, and the husband from that couple told me that my wife was telling them that they couldn't be friends with both of us. So, I told him to choose to be my ex-wife's friends because she needed more friends than I did. He was really happy because his wife wanted to remain friends with my estranged wife. It was sort of both of our decisions. And his wife has never talked to me again.

A Couple Dumps Another Couple Because They Do
Not Like One Member of the Couple

This takes two forms. In the most common scenario, couples conclude they do not like at least one member of the couple and drop them. Usually it is because the member is boring or obnoxious, rather than she or he has done or said something reprehensible. The couple gets fed up dealing with the member, or the member has done something in another venue that makes the obnoxious behavior more intolerable. Take the example of a man who has been annoying, but his wife is a gem. At some point, his treatment of her starts to get worse, or his behavior on the basketball court with his friends becomes too much to take. His behavior over time tips the relationship over the edge and the couple is dropped.

The "obnoxious" situation was the case with this couple in their 20s. Both white, she's a police officer and he is an engineer. Money, often an issue in some form or another, was involved. Tiffany told us, "I am the one who didn't like the other member. Mike's a little nicer than I am," she laughs. "It was one of his work friend's wives, and she was so negative about everything, nothing in her life was ever good. It irritated me because her husband makes almost six figures and she was talking about having no money. I dealt with her by never talking to her when we were out. It finally started irritating Mike too, so we sort of agreed not to go out with them."

From this 27-year-old white man we hear this tale that is probably more typical of the 20-somethings in our research than older couples.

> There was a girl in my wife's circle. One time I kind of called her out. It wasn't inappropriate. She said she was a better traveler than anyone because when she went to a resort she would ask if the phone calls were free. That made her the best traveler, she said, because she could get something for nothing. Man, when I said something to her, it was like the world had ended. Food flew. Personality conflicts. She was able to manipulate every one in the entire group. The group ostracized my wife for my behavior. My wife called up the woman to talk about it, but then things escalated and my wife stood up for herself and put up boundaries. The friend rejected that and ostracized her, so my wife said to just forget it.

In the other form in which couples get dropped, people say or do things that are reprehensible and they are not forgiven. A 31-year-old white lawyer had this experience. "Amy's friend from college is some sort of law enforcement officer and so is her husband. They said some messed-up racist things and we dumped them. I was upset and didn't want to eat with them any more. Her time was limited even before she married. She was a weak friend and needed to be weeded. We haven't seen them since. I was irate."

Here the relationship started with two female friends, grew to include the men, and then ended. Perhaps the key descriptor is that this was a "weak friend."

We do not know what would have happened if the friend had been a close friend. According to the philosophy professor, Diane Jeske, she might have stuck by her. Here the racism was raised in the partner of the friend. To what extent does someone maintain a close friendship with the couple when the partner is the difficult member of the couple? We return to this shortly.

The Relationship With the Friends Poses a Threat to the Couple

People attempt to become friends, and then they find out they feel uncomfortable with the other couple. This next story came from a white couple in their 40s who were in the technology field. "We dropped them because one of them has demons that they can't resolve. We just avoided them and told them we were busy. Once I said to my wife that this person was really bad for her and I can't take them. If they call, we say we are busy."

Couples can pull back when they get pulled into partnership problems. A couple may each be friends with the other members of the couple and are hearing conflicting stories about marital problems. They also may be invited to take sides. Couples can also pull back when they see themselves in the problems their friends are having. A couple's marriage may not be strong enough for them to feel comfortable being with a couple that is having problems similar to theirs. As noted earlier, couples often see the other couple as a reflection of themselves and when that couple is in trouble, it consciously or unconsciously brings the weaknesses of the relationship to the fore. A white couple, married for 25 years, told us simply, "They were having a lot of marital discord, and we felt it was affecting our relationship."

Children Get in the Way

Couple friendships are often formed through children's shared activities. Couples meet each other at back-to-school nights, violin lessons, or sporting events. There are risks with some of these friendships if things get too competitive. One father may coach a soccer team with a friend's child on it and, if the friend's child sits on the bench or is coached in a way the parents do not like, the friendship can end. In this instance, the reason for the breakup would be clear, but sometimes parents are left in the dark, as with this next couple.

A white couple in their 50s, a government worker and real estate contractor, experienced friction with another couple when both had younger children. They tried to resolve it and were rebuffed. The wife told us, "We were dumped over child relationships. Taking up for your children. It was years ago. I knew it was over when I called repeatedly and made an effort to get together and finally got the message that they were not going to go out with us anymore." The couple never did find out what happened.

Finally, the birth of a child can cause a relationship to end. A couple in their early 30s told us, "The dynamics changed with some couple friends following our marriage and our news that we are expecting. The level of closeness has changed with these couples due to what could be attributed to resentment or jealousy."

A Couple Realizes the Friendship Is Not Working and Ends It, Either Because There Is No Chemistry or Because They Are Growing Apart

Along with people moving away from each other, a friendship that is no longer working is the most common reason for friendships to end. These may not have been significant friendships in the first place, but if they were, it may be that each couple has grown up, started down different tracks, and lost interest in the other couple.

A 37-year-old mixed-race student married to an African American hospital worker gave us her view of this occurrence

> My husband does not notice what I notice and maybe it's just a guy thing. I'll be like, "Hmmm. Did you realize this and that about them?" He's like, "I didn't see it." I have my thoughts and he has his, but I am usually the problem one. Sometimes I will think, "Oh, Lord, would my husband stop talking so we can end this (friendship)?" I pretend everything is fine.
>
> With this one couple, things just kept going that way and are obvious now. Everyone is keeping their distance, but I knew this was not going to work. You try each time and it gets worse and you know it's not working as a friendship. They got the picture so now they are minding their own business.

As mentioned, couples are not always certain why they are dropped. They may attempt to schedule a "date" and not get return calls. One Latino newlywed couple in their 20s—she is in the military and he is in insurance sales—told us, "They just stopped talking to us. The last time we hung out, we went bowling, couples against couples. I don't know if that got in the way. We talk now but not as often. They never call."

From this white retired couple in their 80s, we get a sense of how couples grow apart, even at a later stage in life. "We were friends with a couple who didn't like to travel anywhere. When I retired, we wanted to travel and they didn't want to come, so we found others to travel with. I think it hurt them, but we felt it was our time in our life to travel." Another white couple reported being the ones getting dumped in a similar situation when couples' interests changed. "We lost a couple as friends because Hermie could no longer play golf, and the relationship was based on that. He had no use for him after that. If we didn't play golf with them as a couple, they had nothing to do with us."

Siblings Form a Bond That Does Not Include a Sibling

One white man described how he and his wife were closed out of friendships with his siblings. He wanted to be closer with them, but they were not reciprocating. Although not actually dumped, he nonetheless felt the loss of a relationship he wanted to nurture. He adapted, but it was not a choice he would have made. In his early 60s and retired from teaching, he told us, "I was frozen out of my two siblings' and their wives' close relationship with each other. It wasn't that they actively pushed me out; they were just very close with each other, and I felt there was no place for me. We sought out other couples to compensate for this."

It is difficult to know with siblings to what extent this was a pattern that was repeated from childhood. They may have always closed him out.

Boundary Crossing (Too Much Information and Flirting)

We know that friends can cross boundaries and act inappropriately when they are with others. A few couples reported that their friends revealed too much personal information and they became uncomfortable. They dealt with it by distancing themselves from the overly revelatory couple.

Sometimes a display of too much affection can make one or both members of another couple uncomfortable. We asked couples how affectionate their close couple friends are with each other. Two-thirds said their couple friends are usually or sometimes affectionate, and one-third said their friends were rarely or never affectionate. Couples often have a reaction to the level of affection witnessed (whether there is too much or too little) and, when too much affection is showed, some couples want to distance themselves from the friendship. It falls under the heading of "too much information."

Flirting has been part of some marriages and divorces we encountered in our research. When flirting becomes too intense between couples, it can end a couple friendship. One 31-year-old told us about her experience. "I felt a guy in one of our couple friendships was giving me more attention than I wanted and that he was crossing boundaries that you just don't do and I called him on it. It's like the friendship has broken up, but when we see each other we are cordial and civil but we don't hang out together as a couple like we would have."

Like Her, Hate Him (or Vice Versa)

What happens in couples when he is liked and she is not? Take this example: He's an old college buddy who married the demanding and self-centered woman that everyone was hoping he would never marry. When socializing with them in different venues, she pulls the air out of the room. What does a couple do? Or what happens when one member of a couple who was once tolerated becomes more boorish or difficult as he ages? In these situations, the couple does not get "dumped" as a couple, but some social maneuvering becomes necessary.

Over three-quarters of those we interviewed said they have had the experience of liking one member of the couple and not the other. When that happens, couples typically adopt one of three strategies. The majority stay with the couple relationship. Essentially, they, to quote one respondent, "suck it up." They make the best of it and tell each other that they like the other member of the couple enough to still spend time with both of them. They may feel loyalty to one of the members and maintain the friendship out of that sense of obligation. The couple works around the more disliked member. In one-third of the couples where they have not liked one member, they maintain contact but socialize with them less as a couple. They have not dumped them, but they see them less. The remaining couples stop socializing as a foursome, and one member of the couple socializes with the member of the other couple who is better liked.

As mentioned in Chapter 5, the older the couple is, the more likely they are to exercise the first option; that is, they "suck it up" and maintain the couple friendship. We also found that younger couples were more likely than older couples to have the experience of not liking one member of the other couple.[13] Older couples, by definition, are going to have friendships and loyalties of longer standing and may be more reluctant to let those go.

With long-standing friendships, there may be good reasons to accept a friend in a couple despite annoying behavior. As a 73-year-old white man who has been married for 50 years told us, when asked if he and his wife had experienced liking one person and not the other,

> That reminds me of a quote. "There is no such thing as an ugly woman, but some women are more beautiful than others." We think of our friendships like that. If you look for good things in someone, you find them. We do that for the partner of the person we like. We are willing to put energy into the relationship with our friends and this means the partner, too.

This man then placed the experience in a broader context. Yes, he and his wife find the woman abrasive, he said. Sometimes she can be annoying. "But when it comes down to it, which is more important, the fact that this friend is overly critical of things or that she visited my wife every day in the hospital when she went in for surgery?"

He is reflecting a philosophical belief akin to that posited by Diane Jeske: One hangs in there with friends, regardless of most of their behavior.

Not all couples have experienced disliking one member of another couple. Couples who are in this category tend to rate couple friendships as less important than other couples and to have not experienced the loss of a couple friendship. How do we interpret this? We believe that if the couple views couple friendships as important, they are going to have them on their radar, have a greater emotional investment in them, and be more aware of when these friendships are not working, that is, when they don't like one member of the other couple.[14]

What About When One Member of the Couple Is Reluctant to Socialize With a Couple?

We have examined when a couple friendship has ended and when a couple does not like one member of a couple. What about when one member of the couple is interested in making friends with another couple, but his or her partner is reluctant? One out of 10 couples asked this question said reluctance on the part of one member of the couple to socialize with another couple was a frequent occurrence, 2 out of 10 said it was an occasional occurrence, and 7 out of 10 said it rarely occurred. This indicates to us a fairly high level of agreement concerning with whom to socialize.

One example of what may happen when one member of a couple is reluctant to socialize with another member of a couple is provided by Philip Galanes, who writes a column for the *New York Times* on etiquette-related matters. A letter writer poses to Galanes the problem of her husband no longer wanting to socialize with his male friend after that friend told the husband he was having an affair. But this is a couple friendship, and now the letter-writing wife does not know what to tell the wife of the unfaithful man about why they do not want to socialize with them anymore.[15] While part of the advice was getting the letter writer's husband to consider the Aristotelian nature of their friendship (i.e., the man should stick by his friend), this portrays how friendships between couples can shift when one member finds another one distasteful.

If we think about Marks's three-corner model,[16] agreeing to socialize with mutual friends is an example of the potential benefits to a marriage when a couple jointly shares a "third corner." Shared experiences of socializing with friends can strengthen a couple's sense of themselves as a couple while providing energy and new interests to enliven their marriage. On the other hand, couples who rarely agree about socializing with another couple might have more separate than shared "third-corner" interests.

When we looked further at those couples in which one member was frequently reluctant to socialize, we found that these couples had fewer couple friends than other couples. This connection makes sense given one member's reluctance to socialize.

Her Time, His Time, or Their Time?

Finally, to explore how couples include or exclude other couples in their lives, couples were asked whether they agree on the amount of time they should spend with other couples versus spending time alone with each other. If a couple can negotiate their time with other couples easily, they may have an easier time negotiating which friends to keep and how to incorporate those friends into their lives. The responses were similar to those for the previous question: Of the couples we interviewed, 7 out of 10 said they frequently agree about the about of time to spend with each other versus with other couples; 2 out of 10 said they occasionally agree; and only a handful, less than 1 in 10, said they disagree.

Those couples who agree about how to spend time with other couples can teach us something about couple relationships. They tend to be the couples where there is no reluctance on one member's part to socialize with another couple.

And women in these couples tend to have fewer individual friends than women who are not members of these couples (possibly because they have more shared friends with whom they spend time). No such trend appeared for the men and their men friends. Further, we note that when members of couples agree on how to spend their time, they are more likely to describe their spouses as very happy in the marriage. Of those who said they frequently agree on the amount of time to spend with other couples, 71% believe their spouse or partner is very happy. By comparison, of those who said they never, rarely, or only occasionally agree ont the amount of time to spend with other couples, 36% believe their spouse or partner is very happy with the marriage or relationship.

This last discussion helps us draw a more complete picture of the factors that may be related to how couple relationships operate. Couples who have rough spots in their relationship may have trouble agreeing on how to spend their time and may have one member who is reluctant to socialize on occasion with other couples. They then may have fewer couple friends and fewer opportunities to develop the friendships they have, which may contribute to their sense that these friendships are not important.

CONCLUSIONS

Couple friendships end when people grow up, grow apart, and move away. They also end when there are misunderstandings, boundary crossings, harsh words spoken, trusts broken, divorces, and disputes involving children.

The loss of a couple friendship, no matter the reason, is often difficult and can cause a couple to reevaluate their own philosophical views about friendship, loyalty, and tolerance. Each couple has to determine to what extent an action, a perceived injustice or a hurt has pushed the limits of what they can accept from one or both members of the other couple and still maintain the friendship. The ability of the couple to deal with this third corner of their relationship requires negotiation. We see that couples that have difficulty agreeing on when to spend time together may also be those experiencing more stress in their marriage.

More common than the loss of a couple friendship due to some dramatic event is when couples have a friendship where they do not enjoy being around one member of the couple. When this happens, most couples manage by trying to preserve the couple friendship. Loyalty to one or both members of the couple may be the motivating force here. Maintaining friendships when possible is the tendency of most of the couples interviewed. Ultimately through their daily interactions, each couple is constantly deciding whom they keep close and how they manage that closeness.

7

The Impact of Divorce on Couple Friendships

Dan, a 53-year-old white business consultant, has been married and divorced twice. He shares custody of his 12-year-old son with his second wife who lives nearby. Over coffee in a small bakery he tells us that whereas he is very social, a *Seeker* in fact, neither of his first two wives was comfortable around other couples. He had to make all the plans if they were going to socialize with other couples. When Dan and his second wife broke up, the little social life he had together with couples ended. "No one wants to go out with just me," he said. Dan makes efforts to see his individual friends, but they usually squeeze him in during the week when they are free. On weekend nights, when he would like company to go to a movie or dinner, his friends are out with their spouses.

Divorce is a common event in the lives of many Americans and has been for decades.[1] In 2008 there was almost a 2:1 ratio of marriages to divorces,[2] a ratio that has fluctuated over the past few generations and now shows signs of declining. A recent U.S. Census Bureau report indicates that as people wait longer to marry, those who do marry are less likely to divorce.[3] We may be at the beginning of a period of fewer divorces; as people marry later, there is some indication that they are more likely to stay married. It is doubtful that anyone reading this book does not know someone who is separated or divorced. The emotional, social, and economic disruptions that accompany divorce are often felt by friends and family of the divorced and include feelings of loss and sadness, anger, anxiety, and depression. Cutoffs from friends and in-laws are common, particularly if the breakup has been highly acrimonious and friends take sides. The breakup also takes a financial toll on the couple if the cost of maintaining living space comes to include another home.

These disruptions can leave the newly separated and divorced uncertain about social relationships. Not only are they likely to feel sad and unsure of themselves, but they worry what others think of them. It is common to wonder of a friend or friends: Does she think I am to blame for the breakup? Does he think I am a vic-tim? Why hasn't she called to see how I am doing? Is he (or are they) seeing more of my ex-spouse than me? Are they going to side with my ex-spouse?

This chapter examines what happens specifically to couple friendships when a couple divorces. People who had divorced were asked what their experiences were with their couple friends both before and since the breakup. In earlier chap-ters we heard from married couples who lost friends after the divorce. Here we wanted to hear from those people who went through a divorce about how divorce affected their couple friendships. We also looked at individual friendships believing that such friendships are often related to couple friendships and may help people compensate for losing couple friends. We will look at the responses from the sample in two time frames: before the breakup (we are using the terms *divorce, separation,* and *breakup* interchangeably here) and since the breakup.[4]

We want to stress that, as in the earlier chapters, great variation exists in the experiences of those interviewed. No single case captures the range of reactions that people have. The cases we offer are illustrative but not all inclusive. With this caveat, some key findings emerged about how couples friendships can change before and after divorce. First, our interviews suggest that many couples begin to withdraw from other couples as their marriage starts to unravel. (We realize that some people are blindsided by the breakup and are not necessarily withdraw-ing from friends.) As couples withdraw, they may begin to seek out individual friends as a way to prepare for the breakup. They may also simultaneously be less willing to spend time with couple friends for various reasons, such as feeling uncomfortable about exposing the problems in their own marriage or not liking one member of the other couple and being unwilling to put up with him or her any longer. Second, after the breakup, many couple friends fall by the wayside and individual friends become more important. Maintaining a couple friendship when one is newly single may be challenging not only for the divorced person but also for the couple who may feel uncomfortable choosing sides in the divorce or socializing with only one person.

ONE DIVORCE LAWYER'S VIEW

To get a better understanding of how divorce affects couple friendships, we inter-viewed Baltimore-based divorce lawyer and mediator Richard Jacobs. Jacobs, at the peak of his career, occupies a comfortably decorated suite of offices that includes photographs from his travels as well as posters from famous movies with divorce themes (think Kate Hudson and Naomi Watts in the 2008 movie, *Le Divorce*).

At the outset of the interview, we did not want to assume that friendships with other couples was a common topic with a divorce lawyer, so we asked. It is. "We try and get to know the people we represent. I would guess about 85% of the clients will bring up their friendships with couples within our first few meetings," Jacobs told us. "What happens is that the person who perceives him or herself as the victim tries to get all their friends into their camp. They try and take possession of the friends. They do it for comfort, or they may do it to try and paint the divorce as a black and white situation. Sometimes they tell their friends that if they remain friends with their ex they are being disloyal."

In our study of married couples, women tend to maintain and take responsibility for initiating couple friendships more than the men. Jacobs said that was his experience, too. "Men may not know how to socialize as well as the women. Sometimes the men may not be interested in keeping their friends. They may want to reinvent themselves with the end of their marriage."

We wondered what part friends play in the marriage and whether they help or hurt the couples he sees in his practice. "Sometimes friends can hold a marriage together for a while. They serve as a buffer." What he means by this is that a couple surrounds themselves with distractions, like friends, so they don't have to deal with their own unhappiness. This is a different picture of a troubled marriage than one in which couples isolate themselves because it is too painful to be around couples who are happily married.

The other side of the coin is that "friends can also withdraw from the couple that is divorcing and drop them. The divorcing couple is seen as a threat to their own marriage." When this happens, it is often the woman in the couple that finds the divorce to be upsetting and so will push the divorcing friends away, Jacobs tells us.

We wondered if, in his experience, divorces more often occurred because of people falling in love with close couple friends, with people at work, or in some other sphere. "You have to have access to the person to fall in love with them, so it can happen in many circumstances. In one case I know, a husband was getting together with his wife's friend to plan a 25th anniversary party. While planning the party, they had an affair."

He then told us about a highly publicized case with more tragic consequences. In another situation where two couples were close friends, the man in one couple began having an affair with the woman in the other. When his wife found out her husband was having an affair with her close friend, she took her own life. The man and the woman who were having the affair eventually married.

WHAT HAPPENS WITH DIVORCE

Marriages often end for multiple reasons. One survey of divorcing men and women suggests that breakups usually occur because spouses grow apart and cannot meet each other's emotional needs, are bored with the marriage, have lifestyle differences, and/or have an acrimonious and demeaning relationship.[5] Common reasons for couples to grow apart often revolve around sex, money, and children.

Whether infidelity causes couples to grow apart or couples grow apart and then become unfaithful is difficult to pinpoint. Recent research suggests that sex outside of marriage is not uncommon: Twenty-eight percent of men over 60 and 15% of women over 60 have been unfaithful at some point during their married lives, according to one study.[6]

Essayist Lisa del Rosso writes about her own experience about growing apart and then becoming unfaithful.

> On beautiful Sunday afternoons I'd ask him to go for walks with me in Riverside Park and he'd always decline, saying he had work to do. Hours later I would return to find that nothing had been done. ... We had no social life, because in addition to the troubles that took up his spare time, we worked opposite schedules. ... My lonely walks got longer and longer, and the sunshine ceased making me happy. So I began having affairs.[7]

Whatever the reason or reasons for any couple's breaking up, a rough period of adjustment can follow, particularly if blame is thrown around, custody is contested, and money is poured out for legal fees.

The breakup can be rough also because, with marriage, the family and friend networks that each spouse has brought into the marriage begin to merge. Researchers Jill Kearns and Kenneth Leonard tracked 347 couples through the late stages of courtship and early stages of marriage and documented the sharing of networks that developed. The more interplay there is between the networks, the happier the marriage is in the early years.[8] With a divorce, friends that the couple shared in common may not hold together.

Clearly some people emerge from divorce more wounded than others and are less capable or interested in maintaining friends. Sociologists Hongyu Wang and Paul Amato, in studying what predicts adjustment after divorce, note that having a higher income, dating one person rather than dating around, and having a positive attitude about divorce help adjustment significantly. They also cite the importance of friends. "Although divorce is often followed by a decline in social network size, individuals who maintain their friendships or who form new social ties are likely to receive valuable social support."[9] What they do not mention specifically are couple friends after divorce.

Social psychologist Marylyn Rands interviewed 20 divorced women and 20 divorced men and tracked what happened to their social networks. An average of 8 months post-separation, those interviewed reported only about 60% of their network remained. At the 2-year mark, only 51% remained. Relatives were more likely to remain in the network than friends, particularly one's own relatives in comparison with the spouse's relatives. Same-sex friendships were more stable than opposite-sex friendships, as were friendships the respondent established rather than those the ex-spouse established. Finally, she found men seemed to bounce back from the separation sooner than women.[10] There is a common phrase: Women mourn; men replace. In our sample, half the men have remarried and only one-third of the women, lending credence to this adage. And, again, we see in Rands's work how the number of friendships diminishes with divorce.

While friendship networks diminish with time, time can also be a friend when it comes to adapting. Jay Lebow, a professor of psychology at Northwestern University and an expert in couple therapy, characterizes the literature on divorce as unambiguous in showing that the short-term consequences are negative.[11] With time, perhaps up to 2 years, adults and family members adapt and look similar to non-divorced adults on a variety of measures related to well-being. Lebow cautions that some of the comparisons that have been made by researchers are often between divorcing families and happy families, not between divorcing families and unhappy families that are staying together. When children are involved, the impact on them also varies. In violent marriages and those where there is great conflict about custody and visitation, property and money, children fare worse. The economic resources of both partners and the children, as mentioned earlier, usually diminish, which adds further pressure to the family members. Such pressure can spill over into the support a divorcing person needs from friends. If the network shrinks, the support is likely to be reduced.

Divorce usually (though not always) follows a period of unhappiness on one or both partners' parts. They may have tried individual therapy, couple therapy, or group therapy in an attempt to save their marriage or to make their divorce more amicable. They may have gone for mediation. Lebow suggests that although most divorced adults turn out okay after the unhappy times preceding and immediately following the breakup, painful memories may persist.

We believe those memories may not only center on the ex-spouse, they may also center on the way friends and family react. When a primary relationship like a marriage ends, people often need to attach more strongly to their friends and family and are highly sensitive to losses. The importance of both individual and couple friends may increase to help fill an emotional void left by the loss of the spouse. Friends and family are needed for reassurance that the divorced person still has worth and will be liked without the other spouse's presence. Sometimes spouses feel their main social value is through their spouse and that the spouse is viewed by friends as the more enjoyable person with whom to spend time. Spouses also may hear for years within the confines of a crumbling marriage how unlikable or unlovable they are. Eventually they may wonder if others feel the same way. This is when the need for and reassurance from friends may be strongest.

INTERVIEWS WITH DIVORCED PEOPLE ABOUT THEIR COUPLE FRIENDS

About two-thirds of the couples we interviewed reported that at least one couple with whom they were friends broke up or divorced. These couples reported usually staying friends with the person they knew the longest or with whom one or both partners felt the closest and reducing or stopping contact with the other partner. Some couples successfully maintained friendships with both partners that were separate and equally fulfilling, but that was rare. Here we wanted to know what happened with friendships with couples from the other perspective, that of the divorced person. Of the 58 people interviewed for this chapter, almost two-thirds (38) were women. The sample was married an average of 10 years and was divorced (or separated) an average of 10 years at the time of the interview. Some were recently separated, within the last 6 months. For others, more than 30 years had elapsed. Slightly more than one-third of these 58 had remarried.

We first introduce Selma and Sol to provide two very different snapshots of what happens with divorce and couple friends. Selma, a 56-year-old white woman who works in business and is the mother of two children in their 20s, has been separated for 5 years now, following 20 years of marriage. For the last 10 years she and her husband were together, they slept in separate bedrooms. She was by far the more social of the two—their couple friendships revolved around her planning and maintaining them. She described her husband as a "loner." Their breakup was not easy and came after a great deal of planning and prayer, as both the church community and her religion were important to her. She describes her husband as nonsupportive and a flirt when they went out together, making her decision to leave him easier. Her friends witnessed his behavior. It took the support of a close female friend to get Selma to consider freeing herself from the marriage.

> This woman was so worried about (my marriage) that she helped me with a 2-year plan to separate and then divorce because I was nervous all the time that my whole intestinal system felt so bad I was sure I was dying of cancer from unhappiness. So the first year of the plan—I didn't feel as though God had relieved me. It doesn't matter to me what other people think, but it does matter what God thinks about the commitment I had made to the marriage. I was so unhappy, but I still needed God's permission and I didn't feel I had it at that point. The first year of the plan was to just make sure I was happy and make steps toward divorce that may or may not happen. The second year was to make sure all the financials were in order, and my goal was that we would not be in debt. Our last car payment was made in July and in September I planned to leave. I took my kids on a camping trip and, when they went to bed in the tent, I sat outside and stared at the stars and suddenly felt God gave me permission. He said, "This is enough and you need to get out of this."

We asked what happened with their couple friends after the breakup.

They are still my friends, pretty much. We did not have that many because he tended to be less social. But most of my friends just kept with me. If they have to see him—unfortunately he moved only a little way away in the neighborhood and that hasn't been easy for me (because we are not on good terms)—people are polite to him, but they are really my friends because I cultivate friendships.

Part of the transition to being single has not been difficult. She felt so alone for so many years that not having her husband around does not make much of a difference. But another part of the transition has been a struggle. She and her husband were part of a larger church community of couple and individual friends. Although that involvement provided support for her, she first felt awkward. The differences in feeling are a reflection of the difference between the personal loss associated with divorce and the social losses that have to do with how the community views the divorce.

My husband and I had gone to church together, and divorce in the Christian arena is difficult. At the time, we were attending one church and then we moved to another. I think there is always some sort of little change in—maybe not even from Christian friends—but there's some difference that I can't explain. You feel like you are regarded differently. In the church family, it is not like people are unkind to you, but there is still some stigma. My good friends and those at the church where I am going now were very loving people for the most part. There are always a few bad apples wherever you go, but my close friends were very nice."

Selma provides a good portrait of what Jay Lebow described. Initially, there is discomfort but with time (for Selma it has been 5 years) and with the help of friends, people adjust after a breakup to their new situation.

Whereas Selma reached out to others, Sol, 41 years old, isolated himself when he first separated. Married for less than 2 years in his 20s and now remarried for 16 years, he is the father of two teens. He and his first wife had a number of couple friends that each had brought individually into the marriage from their school days. None of these couple friendships was highly satisfying.

We had couples who were friends but none of them were balanced where all four of us got along. Either me and the husband were friends and the wives just dealt with each other or the wives were friends and the boys just dealt with each other. All these friendships broke down (after the breakup) based upon who were friends (originally).

With the breakup, Sol pulled away from people, repeating a pattern of interaction he experienced in the marriage.

I had just graduated from grad school, so I moved away from all my friends and returned to this area but distanced myself from folks around here. ... It was my self-preservation kicking in. I wouldn't let anyone close enough again to hurt me like that. See, the marriage was falling apart. It was very rough. I wouldn't have said I'd be surprised if it failed, but I hadn't given up. I came home one day to find her gone, having emptied the house with movers, emptied the bank accounts 2 weeks earlier. Very planned. Very much forethought placed into the abandonment. That is why trust is killed.

Sol believes he drove most of his couple and individual friends away and has not maintained any from that period of his life. Today, he and his wife have couples friends, many of whom they have met through their children. He only has one good male friend. He wishes he had more. The painful memory of his first marriage still is operating (as Lebow suggests it might) when he thinks about his abilities to make friends with couples in the future. He told us, "Divorce tends to be unhappy at the least, nasty more likely. A couple friendship is drawn into the mess. It might seem that they are friends with both equally, but I don't see that as real."

THE IMPORTANCE OF COUPLE FRIENDSHIPS

The divorced sample tends to define couple friendships with the same themes that the married individuals we interviewed defined them. The majority in both samples sees couple friends as people to hang out with, have fun with, and with whom a couple has common interests. Couple friends are viewed as people with whom they can have an enjoyable time without necessarily discussing emotionally important content. On the other hand, about one-third of the people we interviewed, regardless of whether they were single or married, use more emotionally laden terms: "Couple friends are people with whom we can share anything," and "we feel close to them emotionally." They also use terms indicating that they are balanced relationships where all four people are friends with each other. They are not referring then to couple friendships where one spouse drags the other along. Terms that were used were: "We are all equal in the relationship and each enjoys the others." These are more than just fun sharing relationships.

Although the groups are similar in their definitions of couple friendship, we clearly see a marked difference between the value placed on couple friendships. When the divorced sample was asked how important couple friendships were to the *couple* during the marriage, 16% said they were very important. By comparison, 41% (more than 2½ times) of the people in married and partnered couples indicated couple friendships were very important to them as a couple.[12]

We looked more closely at people who said couple friendships were very important during the marriage. As might be expected, they tend to have more close couple friends. Of those who said their couple friends were very important, *everyone* had three or more close couple friends during the last year of marriage. By comparison, the majority of those who said they were not very important had fewer close couple friends (2 or less). In this chicken-or-egg situation, it is hard to know what comes first: Do couples who put a high value on couple friends have more of them, or do people with a lot of couple friends value them more? Whichever it is, couple friends are generally valued less by couples who are divorcing than by those who are staying together.

One reason to devalue them could be that maintaining couple friends is difficult when a marriage is in trouble. One couple therapist we interviewed for the book told us that couples who come for therapy are struggling to keep their own relationship together. They do not have time to work on maintaining couple friendships, too. This makes sense to us. Couples also separate themselves from other couples because being with them can be painful. Consider the following scenario: Frank and Ali were having marital problems centered on Frank's running around and drinking. One of Frank's buddies and his wife was a couple with whom Frank and Ali socialized. Ali, in her late 20s at the time, put an end to it. "We avoided them because the husband was an alcoholic and cheating on his spouse. I didn't enjoy being around the husband, and I didn't think I should have to be around someone like that. The husband worked with my spouse, and clearly they had a lot in common. Maybe that's why I didn't want to be around another man like my spouse."

While the definitions of couple friendships are similar, it also makes sense to us that the divorced sample feels they are less important. As couples like Frank and Ali start to pull away from other couples, they make a cognitive shift and begin to value them less. According to Marks's theory, the couple shares less in their third corner. Why value something that may be a bone of contention and may not be as comfortable as it once was? We also see, as we discuss later, that after the breakup, couples friends are lost in most cases. Couple friendships may have been on the wane as the marriage was winding down.

Part of what happens is that couples who may have been sources of support are no longer used in the same way. Some couples do not feel comfortable talking about their marital problems, even with close couple friends. We asked people who had divorced how comfortable they were during their marriage discussing a range of topics with a couple to whom they felt close. The topic that was the least comfortable for this group was their plan to divorce, cited by 45%. In addition, 37% were uncomfortable discussing the quality of their marriage. For this group of people, their discomfort in talking with close couple friends about problems in their marriage meant that they were unable to use these friends as a source of support.

Two cases illustrate issues with another couple that can arise when discussing problems in a marriage. Nell, a biracial (Latina and Native American) woman in her 30s, was married for 5 years and divorced for 3 years when she was interviewed. She talked to us about her level of comfort in discussing these issues. She normalizes her feelings about talking about some personal issues except when it comes to the state of her marriage. In that realm she was acutely aware of what was different for her.

> I think it would be easy to talk about the child problems. Everybody has issues with their kids. I don't know so much about sexual issues because it's kind of a delicate topic and someone has to be kind of close to you to be able to talk to them about [it], so I think I would be very uncomfortable talking to one of those couples. Money issues, ehh, everybody's having them, we're in a recession, so I don't think that would be an issue. The quality of my marriage would have been uncomfortable because when you're with those couples, you are trying to put forth one face, like everything is good. We're on a double date, and it is almost like you're in competition with the other couple. It's tremendous pressure to be more romantic than them or whatever so … to admit that your marriage isn't all it's cracked up to be, that's tough. Plans to divorce or separate, likewise.

Sue, a 27-year-old Asian woman who is in graduate school and separated from her husband for 4 years after a 3-year marriage, also talks about not wanting to put on a bad face in front of friends by talking about troubles in the marriage. "It is very personal when your marriage is falling apart or it was never together in the first place. People don't want to show their bad side or that things are not going well. Everyone wants to feel like they're doing good, and everyone wants people to think that about them."

Of course, and unfortunately, as a result of such feelings, couples withdraw. They then often end up not getting the support they need from friends.

We believe that couple friends are lost, as the marriage weakens, for four reasons. As our therapist friend said, the couple does not have the energy to socialize with others. Second, friends do not want to spend time with a couple that is having marital troubles (as we heard from married and partnered couples). Third, couples who are having difficulties with each other may feel uncomfortable going out with other couples (as we heard from Nell and Sue) and may isolate themselves or seek out individual friends instead. If they do go out with another couple, they may do it in the service of seeking fun and escape and not to have what some might consider a "high maintenance" evening, during which significant feelings are shared. Some people share those types of feelings only rarely and, if they do share them, it might be only with a close individual friend. Fourth, they begin to seek out individual friends for solace. Seeking out individual friends, as we heard from Selma, may be a desirable step toward establishing an individual identity and support system outside of the marriage. Thus, not only do divorced people lose couple friends after they break up (as we will show), they may also be in the process of losing them prior to breaking up.

In fact, one other factor for couples to consider is that their social network may already have shrunk from what it was when they were single. According to the dyadic withdrawal hypothesis, networks shrink when people get married as the newlyweds get involved with each other and have less time for friends. The shift that occurs in the family network is not as clear.[13] As a result, divorcing couples may have even more work to do if they want to reinvest with their old friends.

Impact of Another Couple Breaking Up

Couples do not operate in a vacuum. We know from other research that friends and family can affect a couple that is newly forming and assist them in staying together or encourage them to break up.[14] As the couples that divorced were struggling, they may have been influenced by couple friends who were also breaking up. When a marriage is in trouble, it can affect another marriage. A friend leaving an unhappy marriage can open up that possibility for another friend who thinks, "If he can do it and survive, maybe I can, too." About one-third of those who knew another couple that broke up reported it had an impact on their marriage, sometimes for the worse. For example, Sol told us that his then wife began hanging out with another woman who had just divorced, which may have helped edge his divorce to fruition. "There was the potential that the girlfriend saw my ex as a compadre, someone to share in the misery they were both experiencing."

Breakups of couple friends do not have only a negative impact on a couple. Sometimes others' woes can, in a healthy way, cause a couple to want to examine their relationship to make it work, as we heard from the married couples. We also heard this from people in the divorced sample. Jon, recently divorced after a 3-year marriage, is a 27-year-old Latino naval officer. He and his then wife knew of another couple that was breaking up and that compelled them to work harder although they ultimately broke up, also. "My ex and I talked more about where our relationship was going and how we would not end up splitting up. We talked about how we were different and tried to discuss any problems we had."

We asked a number of other questions targeting the last year of the marriage. By this time in the relationship, couple friendships often have dropped off in number. The median number of close couples friends was two; 14% reported having no couple friends whatsoever. We compared this with the married and partnered people from almost 250 couples who were interviewed about the number of their couple friends. Only one couple reported no current couple friends while the median number of couple friends for married and partnered couples was five.

Socializing remained important for people in their last year of marriage, but 19% agreed that they would be content not socializing with other couples.[15] This is a higher percentage than we found with the married individuals we interviewed: Only 8% of those married answered they would be content not socializing. In general, this is a picture of people that may be uncomfortable talking about their marital difficulties, may have fewer couple friends than their married or partnered counterparts, and may be more content not socializing with other couples.

Behaviors That Can Hurt a Marriage When With Other Couples

We tried to capture the prevalence of certain negative behaviors between the couple during the last year of the marriage that might be evident in front of other couples. Such behaviors may have made being with the couple less comfortable and could have contributed to the divorcing couple withdrawing from friends. We learned the following:

> Almost one-third thought their spouse was flirting when they were out with another couple.
>
> Slightly more than one-quarter thought the spouse was not supportive of them in front of other couples.
>
> Almost one-quarter thought their spouse was competing with them when they went out with another couple.
>
> One-quarter believed that alcohol got in the way of their having fun when they socialized with other couples.

Many of these behaviors were evident in the same couples. The married and partnered sample was much less likely to indicate these as an issue.[16] Carrie, a 55-year-old white human services consultant who is now married for the third time, offers an example of how drinking ended her second marriage. In telling her story, this mother and stepmother of four children explains the important role her friends played in dealing with that husband's behavior.

> Everyone was so wonderfully supportive and people tried to be supportive of both of us, but he wouldn't let them be supportive of him. He dumped all our friends, and people eventually gave up trying. He was also kind of going off the deep end. He was an alcoholic. But my friends were fantastic, and they listened to me but helped me keep from getting bitter and angry. I think that my keeping closer to our mutual friends helped me from being bitter. We were always respectful and hoped he'd be happy. We only ended up separating because he was an alcoholic and wouldn't give up drinking. We even (did) an intervention. They didn't blame me for insisting that he stop drinking, so they were supportive when I decided to end the relationship.

For Carrie, alcohol got in the way of socializing and also irreparably damaged her marriage. Problems were clearly recognized by many couples prior to the breakup. Therapy was attempted by a majority of these couples. Fifty-seven percent were in couple therapy, 40% were in individual therapy when they were having trouble in their marriage, and 33% were in both couple and individual therapy.

Couple Friends After the Breakup

Both women and men were likely to lose couple friends with the breakup. When the divorced group was asked on the questionnaire if they lost couple friends within the first year of the divorce or separation, 69% indicated that happened frequently or occasionally. The rest, less than one-third, said that happened rarely. During the face-to-face interviews, the picture painted was not rosy either, and couples friends were again likely to be described as falling by the wayside. A majority (59%) told us they lost some or all of their couple friends, with 39% saying they lost all their couple friends. Fewer than 21% said they kept all their couple friends, and the rest indicated they stayed close with their oldest friend in the couple or with the same-sex friend in the couple.

In her study of 40 divorced men and women, Marylyn Rands found at the 8-month mark post-divorce that 60% of the social network remained and that at 2 years 51% remained. We did not ask for a percentage of the network, but clearly both studies show that something significant happens with friends. In our study, unlike all others, we specifically asked about couple friends—in many cases, they fade away.

Slightly less than half (47%) said they were very satisfied with the number of couple friends they kept after divorce. A slightly smaller number (41%) were somewhat satisfied, and 12% of the divorced sample said they were "not at all satisfied" with the number of couple friends they kept after divorce. It may be that people did not want to keep couple friends or did not have a lot of couple friends to begin with. In fact, the people who indicated they were not at all satisfied tended to count more couples as their friends during the marriage. They also were more apt to say that couple friends were very important to them as individuals (as opposed to as a couple) than the rest of the sample. These findings suggest that those most dissatisfied with their current number of couple friends had valued them highly and may have had more couple friends to lose.

Nell, whom we just quoted, talks eloquently about the transition her social life went through when she initially separated. She describes how the friendships that existed before the marriage continued whereas the ones that started with her husband ground to a halt.

> The couple that I brought into the relationship, my experience with them was that they were supportive. They didn't say, "He's an idiot" … they just listened to me talk, *ad nauseam,* and they are still my friends today. The couples that we met together, I don't hang out with any of them. I don't know if he does either. It just totally broke apart. It was like our whole friendship was based on the fact that we were couples and so it was really weird. And even stuff like church and stuff that we did together with other couples, all of a sudden I wasn't invited because I wasn't a couple anymore … so all of a sudden I just didn't have those friends. I don't know if that's like something everyone deals with in relationships. I know people deal

with it when it comes to death that it works that way, too. I think people are more empathetic when a spouse dies and it's like, "Oh, we don't want you to be alone even though you are not a couple," whereas if you are getting a divorce, you are not invited.

Another woman, Nancy, a 42-year-old white teacher who had been divorced for 5 years when she was interviewed told us about the angst she felt with one couple with whom she was friends. First she describes how she distanced herself from her couple friends because she felt they would not understand what she was going through.

> Basically my closest friends I kind of shut down. I didn't want to talk about what was going on. It was very difficult for me. I didn't talk about it and that put a little strain on our friendship. It was embarrassing. I didn't think they would understand because the couples we were friends with have such solid relationships that I don't think that they would understand what I am dealing with … What made them solid was that they always had a mutual respect for each other. Their arguments were never harsh the way Hiram's and mine were.

As the interview continued, Nancy described how she worked through some of the difficulties with one couple. They did not seem to understand what she was going through as a result of her husband's behavior, and that kept their relationship superficial. But then they were able, with time, to reconcile and become closer.

> The first year or so was very strange. We were just talking about everyday things like the regular kind of BS, not getting into anything heavy or deep. I wouldn't share what was going on with me. And, you know, the police were involved and the harassment and craziness. I didn't tell them anything until, I think, they realized it themselves. Hiram was calling the guy in the other couple and after a while he realized that Hiram was not well. I didn't say much of anything to them about it. Everything is perfectly fine now and with our friendship. It is like nothing has changed … It got rectified when they realized that Hiram was crazy, off the wall. I think they viewed it like he was acting out because I left him and they could not sympathize with that. They thought I didn't try hard enough and that I left too soon. [The man in the other couple and Hiram were very close. In addition, Hiram was close with that couple's children.] But when they realized it wasn't me leaving him, it was just Hiram not being able to deal with life, and endangering my son, they saw that it wasn't my fault.

While Nancy kept this couple as friends, there were other couples where the results were mixed. She held on to one couple whom she described as always on her side, though she chose to never share anything with them about her problems with Hiram. Another couple she lost as friends because she "shut herself off" from them.

Couples friends can be difficult to hang on to because of the intricacies of relationships. Initially, the man in the couple sided with Hiram. The children liked Hiram. The couple blamed Nancy, and Nancy shut herself off from them by her own admission. All of these factors could make a person who was not as interested in maintaining the friendship as Nancy was decide to turn off the friendship spigot.

Thus we have a clear picture, first painted by the couples we interviewed and now painted by the divorced sample, that couple friendships frequently end with the breakup. Now that we have both sides of the picture, we see that the end of couple relationships can follow different scenarios.

Scenario 1: The divorced person loses both friends in the couple. When this happens, it is often because the couple had an older established friendship with the ex-spouse and is choosing that spouse. But the couple could also make a more active choice to side with the ex-spouse based on their reservations about what happened in the marriage. Note how this happened with Deacon, whom you will read about below.

Scenario 2: The married or partnered couple drifts away, choosing to spend time with other couples and not with the now single person. There may be an initial socialization period so that the couple is showing the newly divorced that he or she is still their friend, but with time they stop choosing to socialize with just one person. The divorced person may have wished for continued contact. Note how this happened with Dan.

Scenario 3: The divorced person actively drops all couple friends because he feels uncomfortable socializing with them as a single person. This can occur because of his own feelings about the breakup and being the odd man out or because he picks up a vibe from the couple that makes it less comfortable to be with them. Note how this happened with Nancy.

Scenario 4: The divorced person moves out of the area and loses contact with old friends. This, of course, happens with many people and their friends, regardless of marital status.

Individual Friends After the Breakup

Individual friends take a different course after the breakup. Although our focus is on couple friendships in the book, it is difficult to discuss one and not the other because of the overlap between the two (individual friends often become couple friends when the old friend gets married) and because people often weigh their friendships with individuals against their friendships with couples. Sociologist Diane Felmlee describes in her study of the social networks of 290 university students the importance that friends and family can play in helping to keep a couple together. They also can help to break a couple apart if they disapprove. Felmlee offers that if friends and family can serve as an alternative source of companionship for a weak intimate relationship, they lessen the need for such a relationship.[17] We also believe in this "alternative companionship theory," that individual friends can compensate for the demise of couple friends or family support.

We asked the divorced sample how many individual friends they currently have. Men had a median number of 3 male and 3 female friends, and divorced women had a median number of 3 male friends and 7 female friends.[18] For those married or partnered whom we interviewed, men have a median number of 5 male friends and 2 female friends and women have a median number of 5 female friends and 2 male friends. Why does the number of opposite-sex friends increase with divorce? It may be that because opposite-sex friends sometimes pose a threat in marriages, married people have more trouble maintaining them. Divorced people do not have to worry about the impact of opposite-sex friends on their partner. And why do men have fewer same-sex friends when they are divorced while women have more? It may be that women, who often think more about friendship maintenance than men, are concerned about whether their husbands or partners have enough friends and help them make friends.[19] Women may in turn have fewer friends when married because they have less time to devote to them. We had cited earlier research (on marriage work) about women having friends when they are married that are very important to them and to whom they go with personal issues, rather than to their husbands. We do believe that married women's friendships are very important to them; it just may be that they have fewer of them because of time.

We should not conclude that once people get divorced and drop their couple friends that they feel they lack friendships. Over 90% said they have enough friends, and almost everyone said that among their friends was someone they could call in the event of an emergency. Divorced people have more time for friends, as they are not also trying to balance time with their spouse. With more time to pursue friendships, they may feel that the number they have is enough. Those trying to balance a primary relationship and friends may feel that they do not have enough friends even though the total number they identify as friends may be greater.

Most of the men and women (60%) said during the interviews that their individual friends were supportive and stayed with them after the divorce. A few (18%) said that they became even closer with their individual friends and spent more time with them than before. In only 10% of the cases were individual friends lost. A few examples illustrate some of the different outcomes with friends.

Jon, the 27-year-old Navy employee who we introduced earlier, provides a typical response.

My friendships with my individual friends got a lot closer, especially with a few of my closest friends. I stopped going out as much and just hung around a few of my close friends. I was just trying to figure stuff out. The only individual friend that I lost was my ex's best friend, who I also went to high school with. Both my ex and I were originally invited to her wedding and once I got divorced, I was no longer invited.

Because he is in the military, Jon believes that even the couple friends he and his ex used to be close with would be available. As he explains, the relationships formed in the military where everyone has everyone else's back: "There is a bond that forms and you either sink or swim. I would call up any of the couples my ex and I were friends with. There are no bitter feelings."

Mary, a 30-year-old white receptionist who married young and has now been divorced for 7 years, told us simply how "valuable" her friends were to her. "My relationship with my friends remained relaxed and fun. They became the happy times for me. We go bowling together, to the movies and dinner." She also stayed friends with many of her couple friends "if they were mature enough" to not put themselves in the middle of her relationship with her ex-husband.

Gloria, a 39-year-old African American social worker who was married for 10 years and divorced for 5 years, described how her friends picked her up when she was down.

My friends are ride-or-die kind of chicks. They are down for whatever and thought my ex deserved what I did to him. [She admitted to having an affair with her best friend's spouse.] They cracked a lot of jokes with me and helped me to keep it moving. My friends are very important, and they are still my friends to this day. We were crazy and young and made jokes about everything we could think of ... his size, his financial status, his credit score, stuff like that ... They did not allow me to feel depressed, sad, or anything.

Other people, a minority of those interviewed, described a more mixed picture about what happened with individual friends. Similar themes emerged about the loss of some couple friends: (1) Those divorcing did not think their friends understood what they were going through, (2) those divorcing believed they were dropped and their ex-spouse was not, and (3) those divorcing withdrew from their friends because they had a hard time dealing with their own situation. These next two examples illustrate the first two themes while Sol's story, with his withdrawal, illustrates the third theme of self-withdrawal.

Sue, the 27-year-old Asian woman whom we quoted earlier said,

My friends varied. Some were as supportive as they could be. A lot of people didn't know what to say. They didn't know what was going on. It was hard. Nobody understood because I didn't have any friends at that time who had been through anything like this. There was no way they could understand it. They were not as close as we used to be. It was irreparable damage and I felt I couldn't trust anyone because they weren't there when I needed them. I had to go out and make new friends and they turned out to be better.

Deacon, a 41-year-old white firefighter and father of three, has been separated for 2 years after 9 years of marriage. He believes he was dropped in favor of his ex. "I had some friends remain very close or become closer after my divorce but had more friends who became strained or who chose to remain better friends with my ex-wife. Generally, I had a net loss of friends."

Deacon had the same result with couple friends. His impression as to why people chose his ex-wife over him carries a bitter tone and is based on the belief that his friends made no attempt to understand his experiences.

> People sided with her because she kept the kids with her for the majority of the time. That made her the martyr single mom, left by her husband, struggling while the husband goes away to live his own life. Most of the couples that sided with her just never talked much to me or cared to find out both sides of the issues. I think the couple and individual friends I still have were the ones that were solid to begin with.

Part of understanding couple friendships after divorce is whether friends have taken sides, as Deacon recounted. Selma describes how their couple friends stuck with her—she was the more socially active of the two. Sol took the opposite approach and lost friends. We don't know if his ex-wife kept the couple friends. Friends are often given one side of the story and do not know if that story is true unless they have witnessed too much drinking, flirting, or demeaning behavior by one spouse toward the other. Short of a "smoking gun," friends will tend to stick with their oldest friend in the couple.

The Role of Family

Family can play a vital point in helping out in a crisis. As cited in earlier research, divorced people are more apt to lose their friend network than their larger social network that includes family.[20] Sheila, a 52-year-old white woman who works as a cashier, reflects back on a 7-year marriage that broke up at the same time her now 26-year-old child was born. Her tale shows the role that family can play in picking up the pieces.

> I became closer to my sisters and my family. They were my support system as well as one friend was there for me a lot. I was depressed and antisocial at the time due to postpartum depression. I was really depressed and had to deal with my ex and the baby so I wasn't social for 6 months, and then I felt better a year later and I went back to work and started having more of a social life and connected more with individual friends. I drifted apart from my individual friends because I was just focused on my child and moving out of my mom's house. Some of my friends weren't married and could not understand what I was going through.

The in-law family connection can also end with divorce. In fact, the family of the ex-spouse may be the first friendships to go as well as all the friends established through the ex-spouse's family. Sheila told us,

> A lot of our couple friends were on his side of the family. A lot of his cousins were married and we used to go out with them a lot, and it wasn't that I wasn't friendly with them but I just didn't feel comfortable going out with his family. … The people he introduced me to I stopped talking to and the ones I introduced him to stopped talking to him, so it became awkward for everyone. I lost all my couples friends until I met someone else and we started having couple friends again.

IS THERE A WOMAN'S AND A MAN'S POSTDIVORCE EXPERIENCE WITH COUPLE FRIENDS?

Although the size of the sample makes it difficult to calculate whether there are any statistically significant differences between women and men, some intriguing possible trends emerge from the responses. During the marriage, while 53% of the women said couple friendships were very important or somewhat important to the couple, 85% of the men gave that level of importance to couple friendships. Looked at another way, only 15% of the men said couple friendships were slightly or not at all important during the marriage as compared with 47% of the women.

Why the discrepancy between how women value couple friendship for the couple? Are women slightly more likely to want time alone with their husband as the marriage unravels and thus pull away from couples? Do women have a more accurate perception of the importance of couple friendships to the couple? Do women believe that their spouses did not find couple friendship important? We believe all three hypotheses are possible and suspect the last hypothesis is the most likely. When we asked the women how important they felt couple friendships were to them (and not to the couple), the percentage considering them very important doubled to 32%. In other words, women believed the couple friendships to be more important to them than to their husbands and them as a couple.

Were men also more apt to think couple friendships were more important to them than to the couple? No. Twenty-five percent of the men said couple friendships were slightly or not at all important to them as compared with 15% who said they were slightly or not at all important to the couple. This could indicate that some men thought their wives valued the couple friendships more than the men did. Such a valuing of friendships is consistent with the literature about men's and women's orientation to friendships wherein women value them more and spend more time pursuing them. The men do not care about them as much for themselves—their value raises when they consider how their wives perceive them.

Some other differences between men and women during the marriage include the following:

1. Women were more likely to view their spouse as flirting when they were out with other couples—42% of the women held that view as compared with 10% of the men.
2. Women were more likely to believe that alcohol got in the way of their having fun when they were out with another couple—37% of the women held that perception as compared with 5% of the men.
3. Men were more likely to believe their spouse was better at making friends than they were—30% of the men held that view as compared with 13% of the women.

Whereas some slight differences appear between men and women before the breakup, almost no differences emerged in the questionnaire or interview responses in the experiences of the men and women with their couple friends after the breakup. We were surprised by this. We would have thought that men, who often carry more social cachet on the dating scene, would have been sought out more and would have remained closer with couple friends who may have been interested in introducing them to single friends. On the other hand, divorced men were less sure of the support they were receiving. Half of the men thought couple friends sided with them after the breakup while almost three-quarters of the women believed friends sided with them.

SEEKERS, KEEPERS, NESTERS, AND LESSONS LEARNED

We believe that couples, as the marriage falters, often begin to look like *Nesters* as they withdraw from other couples. Selma and her husband were *Nesters* during the marriage because he was not social. But once she was free of him, she began to cultivate friendships, to seek out others on her own. Sol went from having couple friends in his first marriage (though he lamented the quality of them) to withdrawing as the marriage deteriorated. He continued isolating himself from friends after the divorce. In his second marriage, he renewed his interest in couple friendships. Whereas couple friends from his first marriage were brought in initially as individual friends, in his second marriage couple friendships were built through his children. These friendship-making categories appear to be the most dynamic in relation to divorce as couples experience great shifts in their couple relationships.

And what did those who divorced take from their experiences that they will bring to their next relationship if they remarry or find a partner? What are the lessons learned? The most frequently given answer is one that we view to be about self-protection. We heard responses like "Have a lot of friends," "Keep your own friends," and "Don't air your dirty laundry" (the implication being that self-revelations can be harmful). Sue, who was introduced earlier in the chapter offers her perspective on this.

> It is good to have people with similar interests and backgrounds as you do, but it is also good to not just restrict yourself to people who are similar. Then you can't grow. It is good to have a variety of relationships with other couples, some older so you can learn from them, and also younger couples. It is important to have balance in just about everything there is in life.

People also recommended better communication with their next spouse or partner about the meaning of friendships. People suggested talking to their partner about the role that couple friendships could play in the relationship and how they felt about such friendships. The sense was there was a need to get on the same page in relation to friends in the relationship. Forming strong bonds with each member of the new couple is also a lesson learned. That allows the couple friendship to be balanced.

From one 60-year-old man, who has been divorced 25 years and has maintained couple friends, we hear this piece of advice: "Friends are priceless. You try and keep as many as possible and realize those that are special to you and you to them. Build on that continually."

ADVICE FOR KEEPING COUPLE FRIENDS

Finally, we asked the divorced persons we interviewed if they had suggestions for how others going through a divorce could keep their couple friendships after the breakup. A few people were disinterested in keeping couple friends and told us they used the divorce as a way to end friendships and make a "fresh start." Carmelita, a 51-year-old Latina psychologist who was married for 11 years and divorced 6 years ago, took this position. She explains what happened after her separation,

> Our couples friends tried to give me a lot of support. I was the one who decided to separate from them because originally they were my husband's friends first. The reason I decided to take distance was because I was in a process of self discovery, trying to adjust to my new life and I thought it was the best decision for my sanity. Also I took that decision because my ex-husband got married very soon after our divorce, and he started to introduce his new wife to these friends and that was very uncomfortable.

When people did give advice, it was either suggestions of things to avoid or proactive steps to take to maintain a friendship with a couple. Belinda, a 50-year-old white teacher who was divorced 15 years ago following a marriage that lasted 14 years, concentrated on things to avoid. She explained that she and her husband had only a few couple friends during their marriage and lost them all following the divorce.

It's hard because you are no longer a couple. It's really hard. You have to be really conscious of the fact that your friends, the couple, generally really care for both of you. So you wouldn't want to have conversations with them that would make them take a side or have to feel negatively toward your spouse or ex-spouse because they really were friends with both of you. It puts them in a very bad spot.

Other advice focused on ways a divorced person could be proactive in trying to maintain couple friendships, including directly asking the couple if they can remain friends, providing friends with information about what is happening in the separation or divorce, and telling couples how much you value their friendship. Nell, who was introduced earlier in this chapter, explains the benefits of reaching out to couple friends despite feeling awkward.

Both parties feel weird about calling you because you're going through the divorce, and you feel weird about talking to them because you're going through the divorce, and you kinda expect them to reach out to you and they're probably like "Well, we don't want to pry," so then no one ends up doing anything. So I guess my advice would be reach out to them. And if you reach out to them you might end up actually keeping the couple after your [breakup].

George, a white 57-year old government employee who divorced 20 years ago and has since remarried, recognizes in retrospect his hesitation to stay in contact with couple friends after his divorce.

I don't know whether I was reluctant to [contact former friends] because I knew that most of them were my ex-wife's friends. I just didn't want to get into that. I didn't want to create a situation where they needed to pick or decide who they wanted to support because for the most part it was an amicable breakup. [Reflecting on how he might have taken more initiative, he adds] You may need to make the contact yourself because they feel reluctant. You may have to feel out the situation. If they feel uncomfortable getting together with you, then you may back off. But I think I lost some friendships for no other reason than lack of action on my part.

CONCLUSIONS

What may happen to couples friendships with divorce? Although there is no single reaction, some common themes have emerged from the interviews. If the marriage goes through a period of unhappiness prior to the breakup, it may be marked by the couple withdrawing from couple friends and not feeling comfortable sharing their difficulties with other couples. The other couple may no longer be a source of support. The divorcing couple may value couple friendships less as the members in the couple seek out support from their individual friends.

When a couple divorces, each spouse in the couple is likely to lose some or all of the couple friendships. Couple friends may take sides either individually or as a couple with one or the other member of the divorcing couple. Couple friends may also distance themselves from both members of the divorcing couple, not wanting to be drawn into the potential conflict. While couple friends are withdrawing, individual friendships may become stronger and more meaningful for two reasons: They are needed more and the time that was spent by the partners in the divorcing couple tending to the marriage may now be turned toward the friendships. One of the lessons learned from those who have divorced is to maintain individual friendships so that in case of a future breakup, friends will be there.

Richard Jacobs, the lawyer who was interviewed in the beginning of the chapter, gives couples who are divorcing advice on how to maintain their friends after the breakup. Jacobs recommends asking friends to not pick sides but to try and be friends with both partners. If someone picks a side and the couple gets back together, the friendship is out the door. He also recommends that the newly divorced should not take a new boyfriend or girlfriend out with couple friends too soon. It can get sticky given the range of topics that cannot be discussed, he says. In the best of circumstances, and Jacobs knows of many, partners who divorce can each maintain friendships with their old couple friends. But they are going to have to want those friendships and work hard to adapt to each other.

8

When Two Couples Get It Right
An Interview About 38 Years of Couple Friendship

Much of what we have offered has centered on couples or partners whom we interviewed alone. While these interviews provide a key lens through which to view couple friendships, another way of understanding how couple relationships work is to interview couples together so they can bounce ideas and reactions off each other. The next chapter describes an interview with a couples group where seven couples discuss their friendships with each other as a group. This chapter focuses on two white couples who describe a deeply satisfying and nourishing couple friendship that they have maintained since the early 1970s. As we asked them to articulate the genesis of their friendship and how it works, we are reminded of a high-wire act that has been perfected over years of balancing and trusting. Each of the four partners builds on the others, helping each to soar higher while also offering a safety net when needed. Part vaudeville act, part therapy session, the interview contains moments of entertainment interspersed with discussions about loneliness, difficult patches in marriages, and struggles with children. These two couples have been there for each other, watched each other, learned from each other, and now want to grow old together.

In the transition from being single to being married, the need to define themselves as a "married couple" to solidify their newlywed status attracted them to each other. They each had something the other dyad needed: a chance to be a "couple" with another couple. Then they made conscious choices that have held the relationship together over the years. They have raised seven children, often with the help of the other couple. Now, as they age into their 60s, they cannot imagine a future without each other nearby.

The interview took place in a 2-hour stretch in one couple's home in a small college town in Ohio.[1] It is a pretty clapboard house with two floors, four bedrooms, two baths, and a large wraparound deck. The house is warm and informal and has been honored by Mick in a song he wrote about its quirky characteristics. The door is often left unlocked as befits the trusting atmosphere in the neighborhood. The men became friends in college. Shortly after Mick's marriage to Bianca and Jerry's marriage to Linda, Jerry and Linda rented the upstairs in Mick and Bianca's house before moving into their own home across the street a year later. Mick and Bianca, in whose house the interview took place, work in the school system, though Mick is recently retired from full-time teaching. Linda is a counselor in the city schools and Jerry is retired from his own construction business. All have been involved in their churches and are well respected in the community. After graduation, they were so enamored with the small town environment the community provided along with the job possibilities, they elected to stay and raise their children; the children all left town as young adults.

Before starting the interview, we give a questionnaire that asks basic questions about friendships and orients the couples to the topic. Linda pounced on one of the questions, which asked if a couple has enough friends. She liked the fact that one of the possible responses on the questionnaire was "We have enough friends and do not want anymore." "That so describes me," she said. "I think there comes a point where you don't have enough quality time to maintain a good relationship and I am at a point in my life where I am not seeking out other friendships and sometimes I feel like I am being a snob. I am very happy—we have a lot of couple friends. I am not looking for anymore." She has deftly described some of the characteristics of our category of *Keepers*. She loves her friends, has many, and is not seeking more. Her husband Jerry nods. He is on the same page and offers two other dimensions of couple friendships: They change over time and they change as a couple has more free time.

"It would be okay to have more when people come along, but I am not actively seeking them. I feel like I get enough from the friends that I have. That's changed over the last few years. I've been able to spend more quality time with the friends that I have since being retired and a couple of them are retired. That's made a huge difference."

Mick picks up the theme of how one's age and stage of life have a critical impact on friendships. "Bianca and I were talking earlier today that it could be because we are older and a lot of stuff that mattered to me when I was younger does not matter to me at all now. At the same time, I *appreciate* everything we do have a million times more and that changes *everything*. I am older and not the same person I used to be. My whole perspective has changed."

Linda, playing on her skills as a counselor, probes Mick a little more. Her abilities as a professional listener, as well as the other three's abilities as listeners, will surface as a linchpin for these couples. The brief exchange between Linda and Mick is emblematic of the way the friendship operates. It is spot-on and we see how growth-promoting this couple friendship can be.

"When did that happen? With your parents? With you retiring?" she asks Mick.

Mick answers,

It could be that our parents are really old. It could be being retired or being smart enough to realize things I didn't realize before. I also, with being physically older, don't feel competitive about things any more. When men are younger they feel competitive. [Jerry nods in agreement.] You can't escape that in our culture and it may be true of guys all across the planet. All of that tension is gone and that is a luxury.

Is there a link between competition, or the diminution in it, and friendships, we ask?

"It is a link to appreciating friendships and could be a piece of making new friendships because if you are not competitive you are not threatening. It doesn't bring out that head-butting reaction I got into when I was younger," Mick again responds.

How does that help to maintain friendships, we ask?

"I appreciate everything. We have a wonderful set of guys in the neighborhood and we're all the same age and when we get together we have a good time and it is very noncompetitive. I appreciate that experience and when we get together as couples,"

The question then arose as to whether male competition affects couple competition. In essence, yes—with less male competition, couples relationships are more likely to flow more smoothly. Jerry gets to this in a slightly roundabout manner.

"It's a male thing and I agree with Mick that we are now in a different place in life with our age and it allows guys to have closer relationships because we don't have that competition. There is always a sense for me of a little standoffishness. I've got to keep my guard up, even with a good friend. At this point it is too late to impress anybody (laughs). We can be more relaxed."

Mick jumps at the chance to support Jerry. "I can be really comfortable communicating really deep things to you man, totally."

Bianca, who has been silent to this point, picks up the theme of communication between close couple friends and she and Linda talk for a while, mirroring what has just happened between Mick and Jerry.

"I don't feel I can share everything with everybody but with these guys (referring to Jerry and Linda), there is no limit to what I would discuss with them."

Linda picks up the thread of both conversations.

I think because of the level of honesty that we have with the four of us, the competition is out of there because we have seen each other at our worst and we love each other anyway and so "what's the problem?" That has been unique in our relationship, the four of us. It's huge because I am sure there is not another couple I feel that candid with, except maybe my family.

So how is this different than family, we ask?

The women respond, Linda first, and then Bianca.

"I don't see these guys as being different from my family ..."

"They are like family."

"… and we talked about how lucky we are," Linda continues. "Our kids are friends; they used to run in and out of each other's homes. That's still the case. There are other couples we are friends with but the level of candidness here is closer."

So how do they define couple friendship? Linda speaks for the group and offers one of the definitions that we found in our sample of couples who are comfortable sharing emotions: equality between members.

"For me, couples friendships are when all four people are friends with all four and it is not just me taking Jerry along for the ride to be with another couple whom I like. It is more that we each feel we could have as good a conversation with one member of the couple as the other."

FIRST DATING AS COUPLES

Mick and then Bianca describe how the couples first began to "date" each other as couples 38 years ago.

"I think back to when we first got together. There was a sense then that this is something we need to do as a couple. This was a deliberate move being made by a couple, not just one person. It was, 'Okay, let's do this.'"

> We were very intentional in trying to get to know each other. We were at a baseball game at college and Mick and Jerry knew each other from college and we were looking for a new apartment and I knew Linda's brother and that was the beginning. We thought it would be fun to try and get to know them. So we'd have them over for dinner and they'd have us over for dinner and we were doing that early couple thing.

Tell us about the "early couple thing," we ask.

"When you intentionally invite someone you'd like to get to know better and hope it works out. I was not choosing one of them or the other. I wanted this couple relationship. It seemed very grown up to do this. We were just in our early marrieds and it seemed like what early marrieds do," Bianca explains.

"You invite people over, and you eat dinner, and you listen to music and you play cards instead of the college thing, which was sit around and get sloppy drunk or high or whatever it is you do. It was like we had moved to another level." Linda chimed in. "My parents did that a lot. Not get high," Linda laughed. "My parents had a lot of dinners and they had friends whom they went through a lot with. For me, that was an important thing that you do, to have couples that are friends so that you could do stuff together."

DEFINING THEMSELVES AS A COUPLE

Part of the attraction was that this was what couples do as they become adults, a model of couple friendships Linda had in her head. It was also what newlyweds do so they can have time together as a couple and start to separate from their single friends.

Jerry's take was slightly different regarding what he was seeking initially, but he reached a similar conclusion. "I did not see it as (and Jerry holds up his fingers to indicate quotation marks) 'now we are grown up.' For me it was, okay, now that we are married, let's find things that Linda and I can do together, which meant getting together with another couple rather than Mick and I just getting together. We need to get together with other couples so we can do things as a couple."

This is what couples do to define themselves as a couple and why couple friendships can be so important: They cement a marriage or partnership by helping the unit achieve identity by being with another couple.[2]

Bianca, though, had another reason for wanting to find couple friends: She felt she was an appendage to Mick's career as a musician and wanted to form her own identity with Mick.

> I agree with what Jerry said (about getting together with other couples) because I did not have friends in college like Mick did and I was very lonely in many ways. We didn't have couples friends as a dating couple. I was the fifth wheel in the band and I spent a lot of time with guys who were Mick's friends. I was the tag along. They were always very nice, but it wasn't about mutuality. My needs were not being mutually affirmed. I think, for me, although it seemed like a more mature thing, as Linda was saying, making friends was about doing something on a level of equality where my needs, his needs, and our getting together (referring to Mick, Bianca, Linda, and Jerry), as opposed to my tagging along with him, which happened a lot at college and when we were first married. My best girlfriend had left and I was lonely and it made me happy to think that we could get together with a couple.

With Bianca's admission about being lonely, we also see how the one partner's situation could drive the need for couple friendships. In our interviews with couples, 12% responded they did not have enough individual friends. Lack of friends here is a motivating factor in trying to establish couple friendships. Mick believes he was sensitive to what Bianca was experiencing.

"My sense of things back then was if we were going to be successful as a couple it was to our advantage to spend time with other couples. At some point I had a sense that being with couples would be healthy."

MARRIAGE ENRICHMENT

Listening to Bianca and Mick's discussion about how couple friendships were central in defining themselves as a couple, Linda turns to Jerry. She asks him about their initiation in a marriage support group.

"In retrospect, needing to be with other couples was very true for us though I am not sure that was a conscious thought at the time. What got us to marriage support? There must have been some sense of needing support or needing to be with other couples."

Jerry laughs at the notion that he was the initiator. "The first weekend we went, you took me. I had no clue as to what it was all about but once I saw what was going on, it really hooked me. And then I went to another meeting and that is where we decided to start our own group."

We ask Jerry about the link between a marriage enrichment group and couple friendships. (This group, which continued for a decade, turned out to be central to both couples in the positive impact it had on their marriages.)

> So much of what we did in our marriage support was small group work, which was two couples talking to each other, the men together and the women together, or the whole group. So much sharing happened [and] you discovered that everyone has the same issues that you have and you become close and willing to share and those couples can become close friends very quickly. Otherwise it won't work as a marriage support group. If you get the right mix of people who are willing to share everything with other couples, it will become very easy to become close friends.

And that reinforces the marriage, we ask?

"Big time," everyone chimes in.

"The way it works," Bianca explains, "is that if you go to marriage support and get healthier, you bring a healthier relationship to the couple friendships. I wouldn't be friends with a couple that bickers. If we are healthy, we are more fun for them to be with. We are someone who another couple wants to be with and we want to be with them."

Bianca goes on to point out that there are other couples who work quite well as group members though she would not want to be friends with them outside of the group. "Marriage support is not an automatic friendship builder between couples."

"What I got from marriage enrichment," Mick explains,

> is that you are experiencing exactly what all the other guys in this room are experiencing and to find out that they are doing the same things, feeling the same things, having the same strengths and weaknesses. All of a sudden, I am not a mutant. When we are having a conversation about something, an issue Bianca and I are struggling with, I don't bring this sense that I am the only one. It is, "Okay, we can do this. Everyone is doing this; we can solve this," and that makes me a very

different person with whom to interact. It makes me a lot more comfortable with where I am, too.

This is the power of getting together both with one couple to whom you are close as well as with a group of couples. Group experiences enable people to learn that what they are experiencing is not unique to them. Groups normalize experiences for people and, if they are healthy groups, offer adaptive ways to solve or cope with problems.

THE IMPACT OF OTHER COUPLES BREAKING UP

We know from others interviewed for this book that when close friends break up, reverberations can be felt by the couple. It can make them question their own relationship, recalibrate it if needed, and also pull them closer to each other. Linda and Jerry describe what happened with them when a couple in their marriage support group broke up. It surprised them and, even though they knew how strong their best friends' marriage was, they wondered for a moment if they too could split up.

"Ultimately, I think it made us closer. I can remember us talking about how Jerry and I and Mick and Bianca were beating the odds. We're the mutants now, the odd ones out, that we have maintained this relationship with our spouses and it was like, 'Oh God (looking at Mick and Bianca), don't you guys break up, too.'"

The threat of a marriage breaking up heightened the importance of the friendship between the two couples.

"It is true that I find Linda and Jerry to be a touchstone," Bianca replies. She continues:

> There is grounding between us. I find that if I'm feeling freaked out by something like that, I come to Linda for grounding because we agree, for the most part, on what really matters and we live what really matters and I go to her as my touchstone. So when things get freaked out, like a couple breaking up, it intensifies it between all of us. I felt the divorce of others made us closer because we needed each other more and that was a new chapter in closeness.

Mick expands on the notion that tough times pull couples together with their couple friends. Linda then picks up on that theme.

"I feel that way about every big deal that rolls down the road at us. It isn't just divorce, it is everything that comes our way ..."

"When either of us has gone through tough times, they are the touchstone—I have to go across the street. Get the wine out!"

"... and how lucky we are," Mick asserts.

So are there boundaries between these couples; is there anything that is off limits to share? Bianca answers first: "I honestly can't think of anything."

Linda supports this statement. "For the most part, difficult situations for me personally, for Jerry and me, or that have gone on in our family, we have shared with Bianca and Mick. They know everything whether they wanted to or not."

In fact, each other's children would often use the other couple as a sounding board, which thrilled both couples because it provided an extended network of helpers for their children when crises arose. This level of openness between the couples and their children does not mean that the couples are closed off to others. They both are nested in wide and varied friendships with other couples and individuals, including family members. They even travel with other couples. But, as Bianca shares, they get lonely for each other if they are away for too long.

PROXIMITY MAKES IT EASIER, AS DOES LIVING IN A SMALL TOWN

For these two couples, living physically close to each other has made a significant difference in their lives. The ability to be 30 seconds away from each other and the permission to drop in any time have not only worn a straight line in the street between the two homes, it has sustained them. Jerry remarks on this when he talks about his relationship with his own family and how this friendship is more significant.

> I think we (referring to the two couples) are much closer than I am with my family. A lot of that is proximity. I don't see my sisters that often, as they live far from here. We have phone conversations and that's not the same. And the things that Linda and I have been through, they have not been part of. You guys know me far better than they do even though I am pretty close with one of them. We have had our lives together. We have been on this street together through all the same stuff.

"I think the word *proximity* is a good one," Bianca adds. "When you guys talked about moving out to another house a few miles from here, it would not have been that far but I freaked. I really panicked because I think proximity was huge, and it was huge for our kids to just go across the street whether they were little or big."

"If proximity wasn't big, Linda and I would have moved out of that house a long time ago. We stayed selfishly. We look at one another and say how can we move away from this, being able to walk across the street if I need to cry or laugh or jump up and down and celebrate. Thank God we did not move."

And what about living in a small town? Could neighbors in a large metropolitan area construct this type of relationship?

Mick answers first and says that it is not only the size of the town but the luck of being in a supportive smaller community even within a small town.

"This is a good street out of Norman Rockwell and that's helped. Having terrific neighbors, folks who modeled for us how to live in a community; that really matters. Be a contributing member of a community is what we learned."

"I think it is neighborhood versus small town, big town. You can have a neighborhood anywhere," Bianca adds.

Jerry offers a different lens:

> If we were living in a larger town, we would find more diverse things to do maybe as couples and as individuals that we wouldn't share. Here, there are fewer things to do. In a larger city, there may be an infinite number of things to do. Youth group, church are here but in a large town, you have a thousand choices. Here you go to the same theater, the same restaurants and have more common and shared experiences.

Mick agrees. "Fewer choices make us more apt to share experiences with Linda and Jerry. Jerry talks about eating at a restaurant, and Bianca and I have probably eaten there, so we have that to share. You also will see each other more by chance than in a large city and that's cool."

LEARNING FROM EACH OTHER'S MARRIAGE

Couple friendships provide a window into another couple's marriage. These two couples have much to admire in each other's marriage. The following back and forth exchange affords insight into what they like about the relationships each has and how that has helped their own marriage. The women speak first and then Mick.

"I love the way that Mick looks at Bianca," Linda gushes. "I love the unabashed devotion and adoration he has for her. It is awe-inspiring."

"I love the way that even if Linda is upset with Jerry that when she sees him, she will still give him a kiss, even when she is mad, and say 'I love you.'"

"We have benefited from the fact that we all delight in life together and I think it has been a terrific blessing for us that Jerry and Linda have modeled that. You guys enjoy stuff and that fulfills the prophecy that you get in couples relationships because it will help your own relationship. That is what you guys have done."

Bianca speaks next. "I like the way you don't harp on each other. Linda does not sit around and complain; you work things out and deal with it in a respectful way. It is not that you don't get frustrated with each other but you work it out because you love each other."

"You're right. We don't fight very often," Linda affirms.

"We don't either, though we used to," Bianca reveals.

Both couples have helped each other by showing other ways of interacting, by focusing on the positive aspects of a relationship, and moving on when it is time to move on. When another couple can observe at close range how a couple negotiates their disputes successfully, a great deal of learning occurs.

"Being with another couple who bickers makes me uncomfortable. I know there are times when you each drive each other crazy, and so do we, but that's normal and, if addressed in a positive, healthy way, that can get resolved," Linda continues.

"I like that Mick and I are affectionate and walk hand-in-hand. And I think that you are wonderful parents and that makes you richer and makes us richer, too."

For Jerry the couple friendship works because of similar outlooks. For many of the couples interviewed in the study, having things in common was the *sine qua non* of a couple friendship.

> I think we agree on the way to live; we have so many things in common in the way we approach life, and that is what makes us so comfortable together because we have the same value system. When I am struggling with something between us, I am watching you and seeing how you guys are doing it. It's like, "Okay, I can do that." You see how the other couple treats each other.

Mick returns the compliment. "You guys can laugh at things, I need to see that model, because otherwise I take things too seriously, but I learn so much from you where you do something and take it nowhere near as seriously as I would. It reframes what is troubling me in a more lighthearted way."

FRIENDSHIPS THAT CHANGE OVER TIME

Reflecting further about how friendships like these grow deeper and more satisfying with time, Mick details how much they have been through together and how shared experiences like theirs have made them even closer. Aristotle described how close friendships need to be cultivated over time and must contain an element of "shared salt." By that Aristotle meant that people had to have difficult experiences with each other in order to form close bonds.

Bianca offers a view of the strength she derives from their friendship.

> I think of nourishment, a level of nourishment I get from being with you guys. Times when I need fun and I am not having much, I can look to you guys for let's go do something and have fun. That nourishes me. Or if I need a deep conversation or advice. It's the nourishment after having been together, I feel nourished and some of that is the effort I put into it and some of it is the effort each one of us puts into it. It's different than in the early days when we were goofing around and having fun, and it was fun, and nourishing, but I understand nourishment differently now.

Jerry and Linda rejected moving a few miles away a number of years ago. What does the future hold for their relationship? Will they be able to live across the street from each other forever? Linda answers for the four of them.

> Jerry and I talk about the future and I cannot imagine not living across the street from these guys so we have talked about getting into a retirement home or community someplace. Are we ever going to move away from here? I can't imagine it. I

know we are going to be 85 some day and not be able to go up and down stairs, but right now it is hard to envision not living near these guys. If you guys are leaving, we are leaving with you.

ADVICE FOR OTHER COUPLES

This conversation between the four of them can be a road map for couples who are wondering how such long-term, deep relationships work. We also ask for advice they would offer about how to make and maintain couple friendships. While Mick jokingly offers up the importance of being lucky in meeting the right people at the right time, the couples also give specifics that could carry over into individual friendships.

Being lucky helps. But you need to be deliberate. We have encouraged our (25-year-old) son to be deliberate about making friends. You can't wait for things to happen. It helps to deliberately say, "Okay, let's hook up with those two guys. We're going to get together with them Saturday night and make a date. We will call them up, make plans and follow through on this." If that works out, you will do it again and again, or you realize this couple is not a good fit for whatever reason.

Bianca adds,

When you get together you share experiences, and friendships are experiences shared. Conversation. What I like is that we have four really good listeners. If we are asking us all to listen, and each one of us listens in a different way, listening and having those conversations and creating that safe space is part of getting together. Once you have those shared experiences, you have good listening and you feel understood and heard, and feeling heard is so important, then you have safe space.

To paraphrase Bianca, safe space is where people feel comfortable being who they want to be in relation to someone else and to themselves. That provides fertile ground for growing a friendship that can develop into a more mature and nourished friendship. Bianca knows a space is not safe when "people interrupt, they don't affirm, they have judgments, are critical, bring out the heavy drugs, whatever that happens to be. You feel alarmed. I get vibes. I can feel things and walk into room and it either feels welcoming to me or feels neutral or hostile."

For Jerry it is not only the vibe that needs to be there, there have to be commonalities.

It has to be more than feeling safe and affirmed for me. You have to have outlooks that are similar, hobbies, that you are going to want to get together with those people and do things. You have to work at this. It takes time. I can remember [turning to Linda], where there are times that you have said I met this woman and I think you'll like her husband so let's try it. And we'll make a couple's date. Sometimes it works well and sometimes it does not.

"It took Jerry and me going on a trip with another couple to realize we could do that," Linda said. "We enjoy each other's company. I didn't think I knew the wife well enough to make sure it would work, but it ended up working. Jerry was friends with the husband. A young couples group can be a great way for couples to get together around marriage enrichment or something else. We spent years in marriage enrichment honing our skills. If the four of you aren't going to talk and listen, it won't work."

Marriage support turned out to be a seminal experience for the four of them. As they reported, it taught them the willingness to be open and to try things in marriage. It taught them to be willing to let people into their lives.

Finally, and perhaps most importantly, all four extol the virtue of generosity and giving. They talk about the giving of concrete things, like tools or the loan of a car if needed. But they also talk about generosity in terms of time. For instance, if friends cannot afford a ride to the airport, a lift would be given. They admire the friends who, when they are asked for a favor, will say yes even before they know what the favor might be. That is generosity and one of the hallmarks of a friendship.

CONCLUSIONS

All four agree that friendships are hard work and that when a couple is engaged in a good relationship with another couple, their marriage can be strengthened. But couple friendships do not happen out of thin air, they caution. They take effort and they require generosity of spirit and time. As Linda explains,

> There have been times when my kids have needed to come over and talk with these guys and it is in the evening after a long day at work and the last thing Mick and Bianca wanted to do was talk our son off his anger mountain but they would do it. And whatever they needed we were there. You don't just sit back and rest on your laurels—you have to be there when it's hard.

Their work together and separately in a marriage enrichment group has also helped them to learn from others about the normal ups and downs of relationships. As they separated from the larger group, they have their own two-couple group.

These are two couples who are sharing both the good times and the bad times with each other. They are fun sharing and emotion sharing and have seen each other at their best and at their worst. There is nothing to hide. Their experiences of how this has worked for them are supported by the literature that we reviewed.

In the beginning, their friendship with each other couple helped them form an identity as a married couple. As the four began to share other friends in common (those in the community and in their marriage group), their marriages strengthened.[3] And, over time, as they shared more with each other, they became even closer as couples.[4]

9

One Couples Group
A Possible Blueprint for Others

It is 6 p.m. on a Sunday evening in the fall when we drive up and park on a tree-lined street in a suburb of Washington, D.C. We have been invited to attend a quarterly gathering of a couples group that has been meeting with a changing cast of couples for nearly 25 years. The group's first iteration was as a class for couples who attended a mainline Protestant church and were interested in discussing the marriage bond. The group now meets outside of the church's purview and continues to explore marital and family relationships. A number of the couples in the group, including the couple hosting this meeting, have been members since the group's inception. The group is structured so that different couples take turns hosting the potluck dinners. After dinner, the host couple suggests the theme and format for the evening. For example, couples may be given a specific topic, asked to spend some time alone, and then return to the group to share their thoughts on the topic. Children are often present during the dinner and then find space to do their homework while the adults meet. This church has a number of such groups meeting in different formats throughout their community.

We believe that this particular group is typical of many groups that have formed based on shared religious and/or spiritual values. Couples groups meet for various reasons—from common tastes in fine wine and dining, to book discussions, to strengthening their understanding of their own relationships. The frequency of meetings varies also—some couples groups focusing on relationships hold occasional marathon weekend get-togethers whereas others meet monthly or quarterly. This group provides one snapshot of a couples group focusing on marriage and the types of bonds forged within the group. We include it in the book because it has a social function while focusing explicitly on couples' marriages. As such, it can be a template for other groups looking for information about what can occur in a group during its lifetime as well as a template for couples considering starting a group with a similar purpose.

THE CONTEXT

At tonight's meeting, held in a house that can accommodate cocktails in one room and dining for 16 in a former screened-in porch that is now walled in, all seven couples are present. They range in age from their 30s to their 70s. All have children. A few have been married for 40 years; at least one couple is in their second marriage and a few are interfaith marriages. Almost half of the group are "lifers," having belonged since the group began when our hosts first offered the church class. Two couples have joined within the last year after being invited in by the rest of the group. Why were they invited? Members of the group met them at church and thought they would be wonderful additions. All belonged to the church at one time, though one couple, members of the group for 10 years, recently left the church for another religious setting. They asked permission to remain with the group and were reassured that their presence was still welcome. Common topics of discussion are children, in-laws, vacations, aging parents, and money. Other conversations may grow out of these topics if a couple comes with a particular need to discuss an issue between them.

INTERVIEWING INDIVIDUAL COUPLES

We learned about the group from a mutual friend and approached the founding couple, who then received approval from the rest of the group for us to interview them. We believed we did not know anyone in the group, but at the meeting it turned out one of us had worked many years ago on a project with one of the group members.[1] Our plan was to interview the group together to learn how they collectively and individually viewed friendships that have evolved through their group experiences.

Because getting to know 14 people at once in a group can be daunting, we interviewed four couples alone before the group discussion began and touched bases with the other three during the social hour and dinner. In our private interviews with the four couples, we found each to be fascinating in their own right and wished that we had had more time with them. All had thought about the topic in advance. Due to time constraints and dinner awaiting us, we focused on their backgrounds and their views of couple friendships outside the group.[2] The partners in the couple did not always share each other's outlooks but tended to build on each other's responses rather than dispute them. This communication enhancement style is at the core of such groups. The groups are comprised of couples who are working on their relationship as a couple and wish to share their time with couples who have similar values. The partners listen well to each other (similar to Bianca, Mick, Linda, and Jerry in Chapter 8) while also feeling independent enough to state a differing opinion when it is strongly held.

Some Couples' Backgrounds

Many couples have been lifelong residents of their community. Some are on their second marriage. The first couple we interviewed alone has years of experience with couples groups. They were in marriage encounter groups in the late 1960s and have long-lived friendships as well as couple friends in this current group. They belong to another church-related group, for interfaith marriages, but they like the members of this group so much, they were eager to join it too. One difference between this and the interfaith group is that this group has children come to meetings and is more social. The other group, given its interfaith nature, is more focused on religion and meets monthly with occasional retreats. It is more intense given its meeting schedule.

When we ask this first couple how important couple friendships are, the husband expresses his perspective with a very clear statement. "As important as they are, my family always comes first and I mean my immediate family." His wife agrees. And when we ask how they define couple friendships, she tells us about the value of an emotionally healthy marriage. "Couple friendships are a relationship with both people that is very energetic and lively, especially if both couples are stable. It is not fun if one couple is falling apart. It is hard to keep going with both if that is happening." We also hear from them that when couples break up, staying friends is difficult. "We have lost single friends. At our stage, the single person, who is often divorced or widowed, is not so comfortable with the couple and may develop his or her own life as a single person." This is the same theme we heard from the divorced individuals we interviewed, who are profiled in Chapter 7: People often want to be with people with whom they share similar circumstances.

This couple identify themselves as a *Seeker* couple. When we asked them about the three categories, they recounted how they were considering inviting over younger couples from the church so that they could expand their friendship network.

The second couple, married 34 years, was one of the originators of the group, which was formed initially to explore the dimensions of marriage. "A couples group is the only place we have," we are told, "where we can talk about those issues as couples that were important to us. The couples we know outside the group, we only talk to very superficially." This couple sees the group in a reformulation phase now that it has added couples within the last year. "We don't have the sense of intimacy that we had with the original group where everyone had the original class together, but it has been very supportive. When we have had children issues, this has been a wonderful place to vent and get support."

This couple compartmentalizes their relationships and uses the group effectively to get their needs met. Their emotion sharing goes on in the group while their fun sharing friends tend to be outside of the group. They also have a different view of singles friendships than the first couple we interviewed, as they have maintained those friendships. "We have good relationships with a number of different individuals and couples outside of the group, but this is where we focus intentionally on this type of relationship. This is the only group we are in. Couples relationships are important to us, but we have a lot of friends who are not married, also."

The wife in the couple told us, "Couple friendships to me are being comfortable talking with a man and a woman. There is a presumption of commonality. There is no tension between men and women who are not together (as a couple). When we are with our couple friends, there is a relaxing and a comfortableness that I really like."

The husband adds further description. "I can think of two couples with whom we can sit down and emotionally undress. One has two kids, so we can explore everything and lament and rejoice. It's limited, but the couples whom we are friends with are very rewarding. And that's it. Maybe everyone else has 30 or more," he laughs. The few close couple friends they have might make them a *Nester* couple. Yet they are in a couples group of long-standing which might, by definition, make them a *Keeper* couple.

The third couple, married for over 20 years with one child still at home, is transitioning from a child-centric life to one where they have more time for themselves. They were *Keepers,* they told us, and now might be shifting to a *Seeker* category. The husband reports, "Couples friendships have meant people who have kids. We have some friends and we are satisfied with that, although now that the kids are getting out of the house, I am thinking about finding other friends. I am getting into music. We may be in transition, but we are consumed with work and don't always have the time."

The fourth couple, married 15 years and in their late 30s with young children, also said that couple friendships are very important. Highly active socially, they are members of another couples group while also maintaining couple friends outside of both groups. Whereas the first couple saw tonight's group as being more social, this couple sees it as being more focused and as an adjunct to other couple friendships. The husband explains, "This group has a purpose, not just to socialize but to get together to discuss a topic related to marriage. We started another group that flopped because people moved away or divorced. I think it is helpful to get out of your routine and focus on the topic of the night."

The wife shared their need for couple friendships both in and outside the group, especially given the distance that separates them from their families.

> We are at the busiest part of our lives right now. Our family does not live nearby so these friendships among these couples feel familial. I do not have to be nice or agree with everyone. If I have to wake up in the middle of the night, I could call them and they would be on the way. My best friend from college had been dating this guy for years and they were married before I knew Mike. We travel to see them for holidays and we have a lot of rituals and they feel like family and as if our

children are cousins. We have been through a lot of things together, including the death of one of their brothers.

The other group this couple belongs to is less structured than tonight's group, they tell us. Ultimately they see their group participation as reinforcing their own marriage. "There is something about coming together as a couple, as a unit, that is essential. If you are married, it is hard to have friendships over times that don't involve your family and it is a natural evolution to go with couples." This couple consider themselves *Keepers*. They have a few significant couple friends, are involved in two couple groups, and are not interested in building their friendship network.

INTERVIEWING THE WHOLE GROUP

Tracking 14 members of a group and describing each member's contributions is beyond the scope of this chapter.[3] Rather we focus here on comments made by group members without identifying them. When considering friendships in the group, it is important to remember the benefits of being in a support, self-help, or therapy group. Although this is not a therapy group, and some see it purely as a social gathering, some elements are similar. Irvin Yalom, the noted group psychotherapist and writer, has explained some of the benefits of group therapy (which he calls *curative factors*), which are present here. These benefits include catharsis (the expression of feelings), universality (the sense that what one member in the group is experiencing, others are also experiencing), imparting information (a couple shares how they successfully handled a situation similar to that being raised by another couple), interpersonal learning (a member learns more about herself or himself from the group interaction), and altruism (the positive feeling one gets from helping others). Yalom also wrote about the instillation of hope that can emerge from a group, meaning that a couple can come away from the group with the sense that the relationship issue they raised can be improved after the encounter they just had with other group members. As couples talk, we hear some of these curative factors echoed. One member says he comes to the group and hears that others are also struggling with a cantankerous teen (universality). Another says that she uses the group to vent (catharsis). A third states that although advice is not specifically given around an issue, people will talk about their own experiences with that issue (no one ever tells a couple they "should" do something), which leads the couple to draw their own conclusions about what steps to take (imparting information and interpersonal learning).

All groups, as with relationships, go through stages in development. Much has been written about the beginning, middle, and end stages of groups and how the emotional and educational content that those group members can handle varies by stage. For example, groups in existence for a while are able to handle more complex material than groups that are meeting for the first time. This particular group has been in existence for some members for nearly 25 years. New members have joined as recently as a year ago. Sometimes the arrival of new members can return old members to the beginning stage of interaction as they learn to trust each other. At the same time, new members may be struggling to be accepted by the old members and to learn the culture of the group. For example, new members may be unsure how much personal information to share and how vulnerable to be with others in the group.

Couples view the group differently depending, in part, on their history with the group, their experiences with other groups, and what they hope to gain from and contribute to the group. For example, whereas one couple finds the group fairly unstructured, another finds it structured.

Confidentiality in all matters is expected at this group and in all educational and support activities related to the church. What is said in the group stays in the group. This expectation doesn't need to be discussed; it is understood as a basic tenet of the group.

As mentioned, the group began as a church-based marriage course. It had a high bar: Couples were to pledge to put their marriage and their relationship with their spouse above their children. It was a spouse-first pledge. That first course met for six sessions and a weekend. During the weekend, one of the couples believe they conceived their second child. "By the end of the course," one of the early leaders said, "the group had become so bonded to each other they didn't want to end the class, so we decided to keep meeting. We felt if we kept meeting we would have to talk about deep, meaningful matters. So we all agreed and here we are 24 years later." Eventually, over many years, couples left and were replaced by three new waves of couples, one wave as recently as one year ago.

Marital Bumps in the Road

One couple divorced while they were in the group and, as would be imagined, it had an impact on the group. We know from interviews with couples in our study that a breakup of another couple can cause a reconsideration of one's own marriage. We asked what the effect was here. One member started to describe what happened and it ping-ponged to others. "[After the breakup] the group became a place where the woman came and complained." "Cried," another member inserted. "Cried," the first repeated, "and that did not end up being a proper thing for a couple's group to be doing. I told her to find a singles group. That was very poorly received by some of the people in the group at that time."

"There was an issue there," another member amplified. "We wanted to be supportive of her, but it was a couple's group by definition and this was not helpful to the rest of the couples."

She left the group. Deciding when to add members and when to ask them to leave is a central function of groups and, depending on how this is handled, can reverberate for months. Every member has to consider what the group would do to them if they were single and no longer wanted in the group. At the same time, it is an important way to recontract with the other group members about the purpose the group and can be a call for renewed focus in the group. People may reinvest in the group and its focus on couples after such an event occurs.

We asked, as we have of other couples whose friends divorced, whether that divorce was a threat to couples in the group. Although it threatened the functioning of the group, it did not threaten the couples. "We could see it coming almost from day one. The husband was a solid person and she was less so. But no, it did not have any impact," one member explained.

Marital troubles surfaced in another couple.

"A couple," one of the founding members told us, "who were an institution in the group eventually moved away. But they would go through enormous fights in the group, and some weeks one would come and the other would stay home."

"They would even come in separate cars, but they stayed in the group until they moved out of town," another member added.

"They would come and pick at each other but [their fights] never involved other members of the group. We weren't part of their drama."

When asked if they believed that the group had helped this couple with their marriage, there was a consensus that it had. One of the founding members of the group explained the role of the group members."We were there to listen, and we didn't judge who was right in any of the fights." Another member added, "And we talked about real issues and there are different dimensions to real issues."

From these two examples, we are left with the impression that the couples we interviewed maintain clear boundaries between themselves and other couples. Difficult times emerged with these two couples and, although they may have interfered with the maintenance of the group at the time, they did not shake the foundations of the marriages of couples in the group. Group members who knew both these couples felt the group was helpful to them in negotiating issues the couples brought with them. And, despite their problems, the couple who aired their conflicts in the group was viewed as contributing by helping define issues the group should be addressing.

Group Topics

As mentioned, the host couple selects the topic for the evening. One member explained,

> The couple chooses an issue or a tension inherent in the marriage—vacations, in-laws, children, children, and more children. As each child gets to a different developmental stage, the issue comes up. The host couple presents it in a way that each couple can look at it. First we have a social time before dinner and sometimes, if we have not met for a while, we just spend time catching up because we know what

have been issues regarding children and our own health over time so we are inter-ested in finding out what's been going on.

As mentioned, advice is rarely given. As one member said, "It is more, 'I felt like that before and I faced it this way.'"
One man revealed specifically how the other couples had helped him.

I'll say the group has been very supportive. We've had some things in the past year about one of our children which we could bring before the group. One of the mem-bers here taught our daughter in her Sunday school class and she told us that she had faith in her and that was really important. That is not support it was more, "Go with her. She knows what she needs. Trust her." It is very selective when advice is given because people are very respectful of where each of us is and what we need. If occasionally advice is given, it is done in a sensitive way.

Another member tempers this statement when she says, "The ethos of our church classes is that we don't give advice. It is more, 'I have been there before and this is something you can get through.' I feel very often when we have been in crisis with one of our children or an aging parent that the group has been there. Issues change over time."

As one of the newer members indicates, no group orientation is given or needed because they are all familiar with each other. "There is a shared reality of the common ways of thinking through the church. This we have in common. The reality of the ambiguity in life, and of not knowing the right answers, are all part of the culture of the church. So joining the group was not jumping into new waters, it was a continuation." Discussions around marriage provide thematic structure, but the members resist seeing this as marriage enrichment.

From our research, we know that money and sex are not often talked about between couples who are friends. We asked the group if and how these topics were approached. Money is a much more frequent topic than sex. Annually, the group will talk specifically about money and ask such questions as: Who is responsible for the checkbook? Who handles finances? Who makes sure the checks are paid? How does the couple work out these and other matters?

The fact that this group of couples talks openly about money is particularly noteworthy since most couples we interviewed avoid this topic. It appears that providing a space for couples to work on their relationship with each other, and the recognition that money is an issue in all marriages, makes this topic accept-able for group discussion.

Group Format

A typical format is that couples go off together to talk about the issue that is the theme of the evening and return after deciding how much they want to share with the group. One example is that each couple may be given an index card and discuss privately, "Five things I love about my spouse" or "Five things I might want to change about my spouse."

"The topic that is used," one woman explains, "can relate to whatever issue that is most relevant in your own marriage so you may get a wide range of responses from money to sex to something else. The question usually phrased with the topic is an inquiring stance of, 'What comes up for you?' and 'Where does that leave you?'"

One member cautions about the suggested topics for discussion, "We don't try and inflame relationships. We have respect for the fragility of relationships."

Hearing this, and acknowledging the fragility of relationships, one relative newcomer recounted that she joined this group after her old couples group dissolved following the divorce of many of the couples in that group. "We were the remainders," she joked.

Groups can be helpful when the world is fragile, another member reflected. In referring to American culture, which has many freedoms, he said, "In a culture where there are not as many rules defining behavior as there might once have been, the need for support results in people turning to each other, rather than to the law. So what you are seeing in subcultures that are not pledged to rules is the need for support of people who can share the experience."

During the group interview, the members differentiated this group from marriage enrichment and Imago Therapy groups. Marriage enrichment is often connected to a religious organization and is designed to improve marriage. Imago Therapy is a form of couple's work that is not specifically church based. It is geared toward enhancing marital relationships by teaching communication and listening skills that also aid self-understanding. This group is more centered on couple friendships with other couples. While marriage (or being a part of a couple) is the defining frame within which this occurs, there is no specific attempt through the meetings to enrich a marriage, though that often occurs as a by-product of being with other couples.

The members, while liking the fellowship of the group, do not always agree with how the time together is spent but are willing to acquiesce. "We joined the group solely to form friendships with other couples from the church," a member of one of the newest couples explains.

> We did not know that it grew out of a class at the church 25 years ago. We have always struggled with there being a topic that we discuss in the group. But this is a group made up of couples whom we would like to get to know better beyond the 3 minutes you get to talk to someone at church, and were anxious to join for that reason. We figured we would have to get over the fact that there is a specific topic each meeting.

This new couple joked about their attempt to steer the group away from a specific marriage-related topic by asking couples at their first hosting to share music that they loved with other couples. A second couple, who is also relatively new, agrees with this conceptualization of the group—that it is more about getting together with couples they like as friends than about marriage work.

Thinking About the Group Ahead of Time

We asked if there were times that a couple would talk at home before a group meeting about a certain family-related topic that would be off limits to the group. One member said he thought the opposite was true—that a couple would say to each other, "Let's take this to the group and get their feedback."

His wife expanded on how the group is used. "I think people are very brave and bold in taking an emotional risk and bringing their most tender and vulnerable issues to the group, and I think it is intentional on the part of the couple to say they think they can do this with the group. This makes the group tremendously meaningful."

Another woman further characterized the nature of the interactions. "I think there is a huge amount of trust among the people in the group. I think I would trust you guys with anything I need to talk to you about."

"We have empirical experience bringing our good, bad, and ugly here and being helped," one of the original members added.

A newer member, who is an organizational consultant, gave this thoughtful explanation:

> The value of information is dependent upon the nature and function of the group. So personal information in a work group of competitors for promotion is a riskier kind of exposure than in a group where there is no competition, no turf to protect. So it is a matter of the character of the people, and you make that decision when you join the group, that there are no hidden agendas or spitefulness between members and no need to take advantage of the vulnerability of the other members.

Church seems to provide a unique environment, another man opined. "There are so many areas of your life where things are competitive or you want the same thing as other people. A church, by its nature, does not have to be that way. It is like a free space, which is important in this world."

Using the distinction we described in Chapter 2, that couple friendships tend to emphasize fun sharing or emotion sharing, this group of couples operates as a space for sharing close personal information and emotion. Length of time in the group and individual personalities may influence how much each person shares. However, as the member quoted above states, the group invites and honors members "bringing their most tender and vulnerable issues to the group," which contributes to forming close and meaningful friendships.

Expectations Around Termination

One responsibility of being a member of any group is observing the rules about a couple leaving the group. Earlier we discussed how one newly separated wife was asked to leave the group. We also discussed how another couple left the church and openly approached the group about staying in the group. When a couple leaves the group, they are expected to meet with the group and explain why they are leaving.

Tension in the Group

Tensions in the group appear to be rare but have occurred when members have either divorced, have bickered openly in the group, or have left the group without saying goodbye. Within the last few years, one couple who was an integral part of the group stopped attending. This was a blow to some members because it was a loss of two people whom they liked. According to one long-standing group member, the couple "did not give a 'liturgy of departure' so to speak. We did not create an opportunity and they did not ask for an opportunity to really tell us their reason for leaving, and that was bothersome to me because part of our ethic is to be honest with each other when the time comes to leave, openly state our reason for it to happen, and for the group to process it. That did not happen." The couple stayed involved with the church but not the group. They have since left the church.

Their departure left people to guess the reasons. One member joked that she thought she was the reason they left. While intended as a joke, it is common in group settings for people to wonder if it was "something I said or did" when someone does not return to the group. She also said it made her sad that they left, "like a bomb" had been dropped. This couple's withdrawing without explaining why was also a blow to the tenets of the church that encourages people to speak their mind openly. A departure from the group that is not explained can unsettle the group. It also offers a chance for the group to redefine its contract and state its rules about leaving the group. Such discussions can cause people to recommit to the group.

CONCLUSIONS

A group experience with other couples does not appeal to everyone. Some people feel their lives are full without adding another commitment. Others are not comfortable talking in groups or sharing personal information outside of the company of one or two people. But for those who are drawn to others and like the notion of an occasional yet structured get-together, a couples group has tremendous benefits. Not only can it become a place for people to learn about themselves and others' relationships, it can help to strengthen the couple as a unit. We heard this from the members of this group, and we learned this from the two couples interviewed in the previous chapter who participated in a more formal marriage enrichment experience for 10 years.

This is not a therapy group. There is no professional leading it. Family-of-origin issues were never mentioned. Gender as an organizing societal theme was also not mentioned. It is a social gathering that includes a focus on how to strengthen the couple's relationship. For those wishing to know more about marriage enrichment, other resources are available.[4]

The long-term success of this group is due, we believe, to hard work and luck. The hard work is reflected in the time and thought people have put into their marriages, and their dedication to the values by which they live. The luck comes from the chemistry of the group. The members have great personal attraction for each. Whereas friendships have long been defined as fueled by a combination of common interests, proximity, and acceptance by the other person, chemistry also plays a part. And these couples genuinely like and admire each other from their experiences together in their church and the group.

How large this group looms in the life of each couple varies, as we heard. Some couples are in other groups and have many friends, whereas a few have a life more closely centered around this group and its members. Regardless of where each couple places this particular group in importance, the group members attest to the value that other couples play in their understanding of themselves as individuals and as a couple.

10

Building Couple Friendships for the Future

We learned a great deal about couple friendships from the couples we interviewed for this book. In the previous chapters we describe what couple friendships look like, how they change over time, and how couples navigate the joys and challenges of friendships that may grow over decades, fade, or even end abruptly. Many couples interviewed for this book mentioned that they have never given much thought to their couple friendships but, once asked, were eager to reflect on this aspect of their lives. In our final round of interviews we added the question, "Does the time you spend with other couples impact your own marriage/relationship in any way? If so, explain." We also invited couples to share suggestions for how other couples might develop or strengthen their couple friendships. Their responses to these two questions are the focus of this final chapter.

THE EFFECTS OF COUPLE FRIENDSHIPS ON MARRIAGE

We grouped couples' responses to the question about the impact of couple friendships on their marriage under four themes. Couples report that their couple friendships: (1) change the couple dynamics, (2) offer support and advice, (3) stimulate comparisons to their own marriage, and (4) provide opportunities for shared friendships. We illustrate each theme by quoting some of the couples we interviewed.

Changing the Couple Dynamics

One of the most common ways that couples report that their couple friendships impact their marriage is by adding something new or novel. Some couples report that spending too much time with their spouse can get boring and another couple adds fun. Several couples describe going out with another couple as a "double date," implying they view these events as special occasions. A few people we interviewed mention that observing their spouse interacting with other couples allows them to see the attributes of their spouse they like the best.

Gwen and Gerry are an African American couple, both 44 years old, and married for 16 years. Gwen is a computer technician and Gerry an engineer. Gwen good-naturedly explains how the need for interaction with couple friends has changed for her over time.

> Okay, so you get married and you think, oh my gosh, I want to spend all this time with this person. And then you realize, there's more time [laughs] … there's so much time … you really need to spend some time with other folks for a little bit. … So, you think you want to spend all the time, and you spend all this time, and things get old [laughs]. You want an outlet, you find that it's the same old, same old. It's like the kids with the toys—they continue to play and then they get bored with that.

Alicia is a 24-year-old white sales associate who was in a committed relationship with Arnie, a white pipefitter, for 4 years before they recently married. She does not describe herself as bored with Arnie, but she does identify a spark that occurs when she and Arnie get together with couple friends. "I think [couple friendships] help us stay closer together because they give us more interests. It gives us something to look forward to … the wider our friends are the more different things we do. … [Experiencing a new activity with each other] is better than just staying in the house and not doing anything."

One couple we interviewed revealed why their particular circumstances make couple friendships so meaningful to them. Barry, a 50-year-old unemployed white male, has been married for 9 years to Babs, age 48, also white, who serves as his caretaker. Barry is paralyzed from the waist down following a shooting accident. He fears that his disability "scares people off" and finds comfort in socializing with other couples where one member is handicapped because "they make me feel a little more normal because they have a disability too." As Barry explains,

> We play poker once a month when I am healthy. We call it the Gimp Games. The reason we call it that is because we play with another quadriplegic. And another is legally blind so we play with big cards. And another is a recovering alcoholic and another is a deadhead who smoked too much weed and he knows it [laughter]. Over the last 3 months, we have only gone out together once and it impacts me emotionally not seeing friends. … [Couples friendships] are very important. They give us a chance to get out and get away from what my position is. I think Babs feels the same way. She doesn't feel burdened with me at home when we are out and about with people.

Babs agrees. "I get to socialize with people outside of the house and not focus just on him."

Sandi and Stan are a white couple in their mid-50s who have been married for 30 years. She is a nutritionist, and he works as a customer service manager. They recognize that Sandi enjoys time spent with their couple friends more than Stan.

From Sandi's perspective, "Every once in a while it is nice to go out in couples, to dinner or something, with other people. [I enjoy most] the conversation and the interaction. It brings a different dynamic. Say, Stan and I go out to golf, we know what is going on. But if we go out with another couple, it is different and we have something to talk about later."

However, Stan experiences these occasions differently. As he explains, "At times [couple friendships] almost become a nuisance. I feel like I have to be an actor and carry on the conversation. For me, it feels like a task and I feel like I have to go ahead and carry it and I think Sandi just enjoys it much more."

Part of Sandi's reason for liking these occasions is her experience of how Stan acts when they are with couple friends. She explains, "I do think I enjoy it more. I get to see Stan behave in a different way. He is so charismatic. I know he feels like he is acting, but I like to see him be charismatic."

Sandi's positive view of Stan when they are among friends echoes that of 25-year-old Paul's view of his wife Carolyn, age 27, whom we introduced in Chapter 2. Carolyn, an attorney, describes herself as an extrovert and Paul, a software developer, as an introvert. Although she likes to stay longer than Paul at parties, she's learned to compromise to accommodate Paul's needs. As she explains, "I'm more sensitive to when he is getting tired and he tries to put in an extra effort to stay longer because he knows I want to. It probably also makes us a better couple because we are really happy with all of our friends and the community."

Paul agrees about the positives of "having that big circle of friends." But for him the enjoyment comes from seeing his extroverted wife in the middle of things. He explains, "When I see everyone, I get to see everything I love about Carolyn. And it brings it all into perspective for me."

When Sandi sees Stan being "charismatic" and Paul sees Carolyn being her delightful and extroverted self, they observe qualities they admire in their partner but are not always at play when they are alone as a couple. Seeing their partner "sparkle" with friends enhances the affection and admiration they feel for their partner.

Alice, a white 25-year-old graduate student was recently married to 28-year-old Aaron, also white, who works for the government. She sees a profound effect that their friendships with other couples have on their marriage:

> We often behave better or worse depending on where the other couple is. Couples who are happier together and loving impact us to be more loving and forgiving. … When we hang out with couples that are happy together it rubs off on us and we can't help but be impacted by it. Just like when we're around couples who are fighting—I think it's harder to be so lovey-dovey and all that.

Offering Support and Advice

Erik, a 39-year-old African American information technician has been married for 9 years to Joyce, age 37, also African American, who manages medical records. Consistent with Marks's[1] ideas that spouses need to find a balance between time spent with each other and time spent in individual pursuits, Erik mentions the positive aspects of spending time with couple friends but adds the importance of balancing time with Joyce.

> Couples friends help us to stay balanced and provide us with a good outlet from being closed up in the house all the time. … When we get around them, they help us get refreshed and renewed. We always have a good time, with good laughs, and it just enhances us. In the beginning, I think we spent too much time with our friends and not enough with each other, but now we have our date nights, and we are serious about those.

Both Erik and Joyce view their couple friendships as an important way to give and receive support and advice. As Erik says, "Real friends can tell the truth even when it hurts or doesn't feel good. In essence, if a friend couple is in the middle of an argument and the man is wrong, as a fellow husband I would tell him and hold him accountable to get it right."

Joyce agrees. "As the wife, I would tell her, too. Our friendship is more than just having fun; it's holding each other accountable to do the right thing."

Francesca is a 40-year-old Hispanic housekeeper who emigrated from South America with her husband, Miguel, age 46, who works as a water technician. They described their couple friendships in their native country as revolving around smoking, drinking, and dancing. After coming to the United States, they decided they wanted something different and converted to Christianity. As Francesca describes, "We prayed for a long time that God could give us friends with the same points of view as ours … new people who could help us grow and become better human beings."

Similar to Erik and Joyce, Francesca and Miguel view these new friends as an important source of help and support. From Francesca's perspective: "I think when you choose the correct people, they [couples] are a source of wisdom when you share experiences and learn from them." Miguel adds, "[Couple friendships] are more to feel that you count on them when you need them or they count on you. That when you are having problems you have someone to talk [with] better than having them just for going out or having a good time."

Mike, a sales representative, and Marlene, a homemaker, are a white couple in their early 20s. They have been married 1 year and were expecting their first child at the time of the interview. Mike drew a distinction between their couple friends and single friends. "People who aren't married don't understand [when you get into a tough relationship problem], so they don't have good advice about how to deal with the issues you have when you are married. You need to have a couple that you can talk to about things like that because they can relate and be like, 'Yeah, I've been there.'"

Marlene agrees. "To have another couple that is at the same relationship level of marriage as you makes it nice because nobody else understands that dynamic, which is why I think that having a married couple friendship is very important."

Stimulating Comparisons to Their Own Marriages

Another way that couple friendships affect a marriage occurs when one couple uses another as either a positive or negative model of marriage. Couples report discussing with each other what they've noticed about how their couple friends treat each other. They take note of positive interactions or comment on behavior they never want to see develop in their own marriage.

Greg is a 54-year-old African American investigator who has been married to Gloria, age 51, also African American, for 25 years. They help to run a marriage preparation program. Greg reflects on his experiences with their couple friends. "I know when I interact with couples I see certain things, and I think about those things in relation to my own relationship. So yes, [seeing other couples] does affect it, because since we have married friends sometimes they'll show me things and I'll think, that's a great idea or man, I would never say something like that to my wife."

Quentin, an archeologist and Rose, a librarian, are a white couple in their mid-30s who have been married for 11 years. Rose reflects on how couples friendships provide a mirror on her own marriage. "Spending time with others as a couple helps us see our own relationship in perspective. It lets us see each other through the eyes of others, blow off steam that may otherwise build negative feelings, and develop a sounding board to discuss issues in common."

Quentin adds how their marriage has been affected when couples with whom they were friends break up. "It makes us think each time about what went wrong for them and try and appreciate what we have because so many relationships end in divorce. It's important to learn from other people's mistakes and try not to repeat them."

Providing Opportunities for Shared Friendships

Jeanette, a law student and Jim, an accountant, both white, are in their mid-20s and have been in a committed relationship for 4 years. When asked how couple friendships affect their relationship, Jeannette echoes the two couples quoted above in how she and Jim examine things they both admire and dislike about a couple with whom they are close. "I'll compare, maybe see something I like that they do. ... We will also use [our friendship with this couple] as an educational tool cause I'll be like, 'Oh, look at how they fight or whatever. Let's try hard never, never to be like that.'"

As he reflected on the question, Jim added a new element: the opportunity that couple friendships provide to share time with your partner and your friends.

> I think that you get to see other couples more closely and you get to reflect on what you have and don't have. I think that couples may feed off each other because you know you're with your partner, but you're also with friends and it's just a way to combine everything. … What's good about a couple relationship is that you get your male bonding and your female bonding, but you also have someone of the opposite sex to have the relationship [with]. Couple relationships provide you with a lot of stuff you may not get normally.

Grant is a 63-year-old retired white man who married Helen, a 55-year-old white graphic artist, 5 years ago. Grant takes a position we rarely encountered in our interviews: that all friendships for married partners should be joint friendships. As he explains, "I would say that couples friendships are very important. When you get individual friendships, the spouse is normally sitting out on a limb doing nothing or feeling left out. I feel it's most important to have activities and friends that each member of the couple can take part in."

Grant goes on to explain how a friendship between two couples provides opportunities for connections to develop between all four people, not just between two women or two men. "I would say that couples friends are a pair of people where all four are interchangeably comfortable with each other. No one is left out. For instance when you sit down to talk … it's not like the two guys and two girls talk. What you do can vary widely, but it's the connection and conversation that is the real draw for the relationship."

Mary, a 49-year-old white homemaker married for 25 years to Marvin, a 52-year-old white physician, notes the pleasure that comes from spending time with another couple when all four people like each other. "I think that having all four people get along and like each other is very important because then you feel less like you need to entertain and be cautious and you can relax and be yourself."

WHAT IS UNIQUE ABOUT COUPLE FRIENDSHIPS?

Couples we interviewed describe benefits they derive from their couple friendships. They observe their couple friends for ideas about ways to make a marriage work. They enlist them as sources of advice and support. They experience their interactions with their couple friends as enlivening their own marriage by bringing new perspectives and the chance to see their spouse in a different light. Finally, couple friendships give them an opportunity to share a meaningful relationship as a couple with another couple they like and with whom they enjoy spending time.

In Chapter 2 we describe research on how individual friendships may affect a couple's marriage by providing opportunities to discuss marriage-related topics, gain additional support, and strengthen a sense of individual identity. The four themes we describe above provide a beginning understanding of the ways that couple friendships can affect a couple's marriage, distinct from the effects of individual friendships. What is unique about couple friendships is that the interpersonal exchanges are shared by both members of a couple. Using Marks's[2] three-corner model, couple friendships are an example of the dynamic relationship between a third corner that a couple share (their friendship with another couple) and their second corner (their own relationship). Because couple friendships provide shared experiences, couple-to-couple friendships appear to be distinct from any individual friendships (e.g., between the women or men in the two couples). When two couples are together, they exchange support, gain new perspectives, engage in enjoyable activities (fun sharing), and experience feeling close (emotion sharing) to each other. Similar to earlier research,[3] couples tell us of the positive effects of seeing qualities of their partner that they love or admire when with their couple friends. These shared experiences can strengthen the friendship between the two couples and affect both couples' marriages or partnerships. Even when a couple is alone together, their couple-to-couple friendships continue to influence their marriage. Couples we interviewed describe witnessing the ways that another couple relate to each other and discussing afterward how they would like to resolve conflict or show affection in a way that was similar to, or different from, their friends.

HOW TO IMPROVE COUPLE FRIENDSHIPS

We asked married and partnered men and women for suggestions on how couples might improve friendships with their couple friends. Although some had no advice to offer, many couples drew on their own experiences to offer suggestions. We, along with the couples we interviewed, offer some stepping stones to couples who may be looking for ways to develop or strengthen their couple friendships. Some of these suggestions apply to any friendship; others specifically address friendships between couples.

- Make time for couple friendships a priority.
  - Look for couples with whom you have things in common.
  - Be patient with the less-than-comfortable aspects of starting new friendships.
  - Look for activities that are fun to do with another couple.
  - Invite another couple to do things all four people enjoy.
    - At the same time, understand that time with another couple has to be balanced with time for your own relationship, your

own friends, and family. Striking this balance is one of the most important and difficult tasks in a marriage. Every relationship has to strike this balance. Our framework of *Seekers, Keepers,* and *Nesters,* along with our identification of couples as fun sharing or emotion sharing, offers a place for couples to begin a conversation about how to strike this balance.

- Be open to trying new things.
  - Remember the importance of introducing "novelty."
  - Try something new with old friends. Instead of having dinner with a couple you know well, try exploring a new place or activity together.
  - Be open to other perspectives.
- Communicate openly.
  - Get to know both members of the couple. Reach out to the person you do not know as well.
  - Listen carefully—this strengthens any relationship.
  - If differences arise between you and the other couple, try to resolve them openly.
  - Have clear lines of communication between you and your partner so you both know what is okay to discuss with the other couple. One of you may be uncomfortable talking about something that the other wants to discuss.
  - Have clear lines of communication between you and your partner about what you are supposed to know about the other couple. Sometimes, two women have shared information with each other and then they share that with their partners. The partners then share it when it was supposed to be kept secret.
  - In one experiment, when dating couples were asked to self-disclose to another dating couple they did not previously know, they felt closer to them a month later than did couples who were asked to only engage in small talk. Of note, the members of the self-disclosing couples also felt closer to their partner.[4] When couples feel ready, they should consider trying increasing levels of self-disclosure with other couples. That may enhance their own relationship, too.
  - If your couple friends divorce and you want to remain friends, have an open discussion with them about what kind of friendship they and you are seeking.
- Be a good friend yourself.
  - Be available to help and ask for help when you need it.
  - Show interest in what's happening in your friends' lives.
  - Understand that being a good friend often entails loyalty, trustworthiness, and dependability.

- Understand your own orientation to friendships.
  - Understand if you are a *Seeker, Keeper,* or *Nester* couple or a hybrid of these (taking the quiz in Appendix C can help frame this conversation).
  - Understand if you are more interested in fun sharing or emotion sharing with another couple.
  - Be aware that men and women often have different styles of friend making and that what men and women like to do and talk about often varies.
  - Be aware that friendships and people's time for them change with age and their stage in life.
  - Consider joining or starting a couples group if you are interested in a structured experience with other couples.
  - Be aware of the influence your own upbringing and what you learned about couple friendships from your parents have on how you are now forming couple friendships.
- Some Words of Caution:
  - Do not spend time with another couple as a favor. Do it because you want to.
  - Do not try to force a friendship.
  - Do not compare your spouse unfavorably to your friends.
  - If you are having trouble showing respect and understanding to your partner, it will be difficult to bring these qualities to your couple friendships.
  - If you are considering distancing yourself from another couple or a member of the couple who is difficult to be around, talk about it with your partner in advance. If you have been dropped by another couple, consider the reasons and explore if you need to work on some aspect of your own relationship.
  - If another couple is having a disagreement in your presence, tread softly around it. It is their disagreement, not yours.
  - Be wary about being pulled into another couple's battles. They may attempt to pull you in. In addition, be alert to such disputes because their battle may reflect a similar issue with which you are struggling.
  - Know your "soft spots" as a couple and discuss in advance if you think those soft spots are ones that may be touched during your time with another couple.

Appendix A: How We Conducted the Study and Implications for Future Research

Data for this book are drawn from three distinct mixed-methods studies and our own in-depth interviews with couples, partners in couples, and divorced individuals. A mixed-methods approach refers to a combination of quantitative and qualitative interview methods; in these cases the participants completed a written questionnaire and were interviewed by researchers asking open-ended questions. In addition, we conducted numerous in-depth interviews, which are highlighted in the chapters and which we use to clarify information gained from the studies and to pursue new ideas about couples as they emerged.

For the three studies, the research project was submitted to the authors' Institutional Review Board in advance of the research. Students were informed they were assisting with research that would be published by the authors in a book and in journals. Students were allowed to withdraw interviews they conducted from the study sample at the end of the class if they believed, for any reason, that publishing that information, even with identifying information withheld, would be problematic. Confidentiality and anonymity were guaranteed to all those interviewed over the course of the research.

The process of training the student interviewers was the same for all three samples. Students were first educated about the topic of men's and women's individual friendships and then about couple friendships. They were next trained how to conduct a qualitative interview through watching videotapes of the authors' interviews and through practicing interviews with other students using the semi-structured qualitative interview guide consisting of open-ended questions. Following their training, they conducted their first interview and then returned to discuss their experiences with the interview guide and to raise questions about the meaning of the questions and how to respond to questions raised by the participants they interviewed. They completed the remainder of the interviews with the opportunity each week to discuss what they were finding and to begin to interpret the data they were gathering. Students audiotaped the interview and then transcribed it to share with other students during class meetings. This process further helped to build an understanding of the questions and the possible ways of interpreting the questions to the interviewees during later interviews. This iterative process builds on the interviewers' understanding of the topic. Students discussed their findings and impressions each week. Those impressions are also helpful in gaining a better understanding of the data. We also shared our own interpretation of the data with the students to see if those interpretations were consistent with their impressions.

Students read each other's interviews and presented their findings to the class for feedback so that consensus about possible interpretation of what was being heard could be sought and so that students could learn from each other. Each student also wrote a paper (including a review of the relevant literature) analyzing the findings from the research conducted during the semester. The students interviewed both couples and individuals who were known to them, people they met through contacts with friends and family, and people they met in public locations (e.g., schools, shopping malls, religious organizations, or on public Web sites, including a neighborhood community Web site, i-neighbors.org). The interviews took place in a location most convenient for the participants (e.g., either in private homes or public places).

Asking open-ended questions in a qualitative interview is a form of naturalistic inquiry that is similar to the therapeutic interview in that emotionally laden material may emerge.[1] The open-ended questions form anchors that allow subjects to respond to broad topics. As little information was available on these relationships, we believed a mixed-methods approach was best to gain a beginning understanding of their complex nature.

Data from the written questionnaires were entered into a database; the qualitative interviews were coded independently and also entered into a database. For a few items, the questions were asked both on the questionnaire and during the interviews, though in slightly different ways. Grounded theory was used to develop themes to understand the nature of the responses.[2] By this is meant that we did not go into the research expecting to learn specific things. With the topic so wide open, we (Geoff and Kathy) had hunches but little else to go on. We independently coded for themes from the couples based, in part, on understanding gained from the students' work. We had close to 90% agreement on the codes and resolved differences in the coding through discussion where they appeared.

For the 2009 sample, one of the principal investigators (PIs) and a research assistant independently coded responses and then met to resolve differences. While not quite as high a level of agreement as with the PIs, there was still a significant rate of agreement, approximately 85%. For the 2010 qualitative interviews, the two authors again independently coded the responses and met to resolved differences. Agreement on coding was above 90%. This verification process and triangulation are common in this type of research. As this is the first research study on this topic, we consider these findings that will need further verification through more rigorous research approaches in the future.

The *first study*, conducted in 2008, was of 76 couples interviewed about their couples' friendships with other couples. As mentioned in Chapter 2, the sample was gathered by 17 graduate students, who were first trained as research inter- viewers by the first author and then asked to interview 5 couples either known or unknown to them using a 31-item paper-and-pencil questionnaire (quantitative) and a qualitative interview guide consisting of 15 open-ended questions about their friendships with couples. Most students interviewed people they knew or people whose names they received from other interviewees. They were asked to select couples who they believed would not be upset by being interviewed and whose couple relationship appeared to be stable. Written questionnaires were com- pleted separately by each member of the couple; interviews were then conducted jointly with both members of the couple present. These interviews could last up to an hour depending on how loquacious the couple was. Eighty-five interviews were completed in total. Nine interviews were dropped from the analysis, six of which were conducted with only one member of the couple. Three interviews with couples who self-described as gay or lesbian and involved in same-sex partner- ships or marriages were dropped as this book's focus is on heterosexual couples.

As mentioned in Chapter 2, when couples were interviewed together in 2008 we were unsure if they were being circumspect around each other. At the same time, couples proved helpful to each other with recall and impressions and tended to give a couple's view of their friendships. A year later, for the *second study,* we super- vised 122 interviews with individuals who were partners in couples without their partners *ever* being interviewed. We wondered if interviewing just one partner in the couple would give us different information about couple friendships. It did not provide us with substantial new information. Rather this information tended to reinforce broad themes that we had learned from the first interviews. We added a number of new questions, though, that further expanded our understanding of the topic. These questions included asking whether the study participant worried about how the spouse/partner would act around others, whether the participant looked forward to introducing the spouse/partner to others, whether the partici- pant or the spouse/partner would be happy not socializing, whether the spouse/ partner flirts when they are out, and if alcohol interferes with their socializing.

Essentially the same approach was used as in 2008. Twenty-one students each interviewed six individuals who were partners in couples that had lived together for at least 1 year and both were at least 21 years old. Four interviews with people who self-described as gay or lesbian and involved in same-sex partnerships or marriages were excluded from this analysis.

The *third study,* conducted in 2010, was of 58 divorced individuals and of an additional 47 couples. Nineteen students were each asked to interview three divorced people and three couples. For the divorced sample, we were interested in what the impact of divorce was on their couple friendships. For the couples, we were interested in further refining our understanding of the categories of

Table A.1   Demographics

Who Was Interviewed	Couple Together (N = 246)	One Member of Couple (N = 122)	Divorced (N = 58)	Total (N = 426)
Race/Ethnicity				
Caucasian Non-Hispanic	73.8%	75.2%	75.8%	74.4%
African American	20.9%	9.9%	10.3%	16.3%
Hispanic, Asian, and Others	5.3%	14.8%	13.8%	9.3%
Gender				
Female	123	62	38	52.4%
Male	123	60	20	47.6%
Age				
21–35	49.2%	50%	25%	43.6%
36–50	18.7%	20.4%	29%	22.4%
51–70	27.2%	26.2%	45%	29%
71–95	4.8%	3.3%	0%	3.8%
Current Marriage Status				
Married	75.8%	81.5%		77.9%
Partnered	24.2%	18.5%		22.1%
Years Married/Partnered Range	.25–65	1–54	1–26.5	
Mean Years Married/Partnered	14.15	12.8	10.25	12.4
Median Years Married/Partnered	6	6.5	10	7.5
Children	75%	54%	77.6%	69%
Religion				
Protestant	46.9%	38.5%	55.2%	45.6%
Catholic	21.4%	29.5%	10.3%	22.2%
Jewish	12.8%	12.3%	13.8%	12.8%
Atheist/Agnostic/None/Other	18.8%	18.8%	20.7%	19.1%
Type of Employment				
Blue Collar	17%	8.8%	15.5%	14.4%
White Collar	51.5%	60%	50%	53.7%
Professional	14.5%	10.4%	29.3%	15.3%
Student	3.7%	8%	3.4%	4.9%
Retired	10.8%	9.6%	0	9%
Unemployed	2.5%	3.2%	1.7 %	2.6%

(Continued)

Table A.1   Demographics (Continued)

Who Was Interviewed	Couple Together (N = 246)	One Member of Couple (N = 122)	Divorced (N = 58)	Total (N = 426)
Income Level				
Lower/Lower-Middle	14.3%	18.9%	15.8%	15.8%
Middle	49.6%	50%	61.4%	51.2%
Upper-Middle/Upper	36.1%	31.1%	22.8%	32.9%
Education Level				
High School	20.3%	12%	15.5%	17.3%
Some College	10.6%	7%	18.9%	10.7%
Completed College Degree	43.4%	41%	32.8%	41.3%
Post College	25.6%	40%	32.8%	30.7%

friendships we had developed (*Seeker, Keeper,* and *Nester*) as well as our under-standing of how couples interacted with their couple friends, that is, whether they engaged in more fun sharing activities or emotion sharing activities. The students went through a similar training and classroom experience as the previous classes. Some students interviewed more divorced people and others interviewed more couples. Again, a few interviews were excluded for reasons similar to those in the 2008 and 2009 studies.

After an analysis of key variables, and finding no significant differences between groups,[3] we combined the couples interviewed in 2008 and 2010. Table A.1 shows the demographic background of the participants in each of the studies: interviews conducted with both partners in the couple (2008 and 2010), interviews conducted with one partner in the couple (2009), and interviews conducted with divorced people (2010).

STUDENT INTERVIEWERS

The students, all getting their master of social work degree, ranged in age from their early 20s to their early 50s. They were a racially and ethnically diverse group and tended to interview people of their same ethnic and racial background. The majority were female.

2008 AND 2010 STUDY: COUPLES INTERVIEWS WITH MARRIED/PARTNERED

The 123 couples (246 participants) range in age from 21 to 95. The median age of the individual participants is 36. Thirteen (10.6%) of the 123 couples are interracial. Seventy-three percent reported this was their first marriage/partnership. The median number of years lived in their area was 10. The number of couples who the participants agreed were couple friends ranged from 1 to 30, with the median being 5.

SECOND STUDY: INDIVIDUAL INTERVIEWS
WITH MARRIED/PARTNERED

The second sample, 122 individuals (60 males and 62 females), range in age from 22 to 80 and their partners from 22 to 77. The median age of the individual participants is 34 and of the partner was 36 years old. Thirteen percent of the couples are interracial. Seventy-seven percent reported this was their first marriage/partnership. The participants and their partners have lived in their area a median of 12 years. The number of couple friends ranged from 0 (one person gave this response) to 22, with the median being 5.

THIRD STUDY: INDIVIDUAL INTERVIEWS WITH DIVORCED/SEPARATED

The 58 people (38 females and 20 males) in the divorced sample range in age from 22 to 67. The median age is 46 years old. Almost 14% were interracial marriages.[4] The median number of years living in the area is 15. The median number of couple friends in the last year of marriage was 2, with the range being 0 to 15.

By completion, interviews have been conducted with 123 heterosexual couples (246 individuals), 122 individuals who were members of couples, and 58 people who were divorced at one point. Though not shown in Table A.1, one-third of this group are currently remarried. These interviews provide insight into more than 300 couples. Given the complexity of understanding these relationships, we chose to focus on heterosexual partnerships and not gay and lesbian marriages/partnerships. When we present information about couples, we sometimes choose to present information gained from the 2008 and 2010 study of couples. Other times we choose to present information from the interviews with the individuals in 2009. Other times we use the findings from the participants who have been divorced. At no point do we present as a certainty findings that are contradictory between studies. For example, a finding may be significant in one study and be a trend in the next without reaching significance and still be reported. But if it is significant in one study and directly contradictory in the other (this rarely happened), we do not include those findings unless specifically explained.

When we use the term *findings* in the book we are referring to (1) statistically significance results ($p < .05$) based on analyzing data from the written questionnaires or (2) statistically significant results from the qualitative interviews based on coding participant responses and analyzing them by means of a chi-square test. For the data from the written questionnaires, we ran group comparisons (*t*-tests and ANOVAs), chi-square tests, and correlations. When we use the term *trends* in the book, we are referring to (1) results based on analyzing data from the written questionnaires that approached, but did not meet, statistically significance ($p < .10$) or (2) qualitative results that could be understood only in broad terms. Finally, we use the term *impressions* when what we offer is based on our sense of what we learned from the interviews we conducted, our knowledge of human behavior, and a reading of the literature.

AUTHORS' INTERVIEWS

We (Kathy and Geoff) conducted our own interviews with couples and individuals over the course of 3 years. The interviews from the three studies comprise one portion of the book, and the more than 20 couples we interviewed are used to highlight the complexity of couple relationships and couple friendships. The information from the three studies is used to draw broad conclusions about couple friendships. To some extent, our interviews put the meat on the bones of the topic. The three studies are a skeleton that we build on with our interviews with couples who are willing to talk about friendships. Our interviews are used to illustrate certain points and to bring the topic to life as only in-depth qualitative interviews can. We interviewed people we knew and people we did not know. A few couples heard us talking about our work on friendships, approached us about it, and agreed to be interviewed. In some cases we flew to other states to conduct interviews with couples who we thought would add to the racial and geographic diversity of the study.

LIMITATIONS

These convenience samples are both a strength and limitation of the study. It is difficult to know the nature of the couple friendships for those who either refused to be interviewed or were outside the interviewers' sphere of contact. Although the samples were not random, the relatively large number of interviewers resulted in a sample that was demographically diverse as well as nonclinical. The generalizability of the study's findings is limited by its use of couples who agreed to a personal request to be interviewed on this topic; the experiences and responses of these couples may not be representative of the larger population. When percentages of responses are provided, these percentages only apply to these samples. For example, knowing that x% of couples define couples friendships as very important does not indicate that couples in the United States would respond this way to this question; only *these* couples have responded this way.

We also wish we had gained greater diversity in the sample. This tends to be a sample of whites and African Americans. Recognizing that Latinos are now the largest minority group in the United States, we wish we had greater representation from them as well as from Pacific Rim nations. We analyzed the data that we have by race through three different approaches. The first is looking at each group separately. Because the number of groups other than white and African Americans was small, this did not prove effective. We also considered grouping whites as one group and all people of color as another group. But this distinction does not allow for the obvious racial differences within groups. Third, we only compared whites and African Americans. Racial differences become difficult to explore given the increasing number of people both of mixed-race origin and who have intermarried. Comparing a white person's response about the meaning of couple friendship when he is married to an African American with a white person's response when he is married to a Hispanic or a white becomes problematic. What if each of these couples has friends that are mixed race? We realized that we were chasing too many variables and would miss the broader picture concerning couples in general. We have written elsewhere about how race may affect the construction of friendships[5] for individuals. Here we include comments made by interviewees concerning how their race may affect their friendships with couples (e.g., Chapter 4), but we offer conclusions about race with caution given the dynamic nature of race in the United States. Geographic diversity was also considered. The majority of the couples interviewed were living on the East Coast at the time of the interviews, although some moved east only recently. We asked how long couples have lived in their area. We made attempts to broaden the sample and specifically interviewed couples from outside the East Coast. We do not know what geographic diversity may mean in relation to how a couple determines how to understand and manage their friendships. Again, we were wary of chasing too many variables but did determine that length of time in one area did not appear strongly correlated with other variables we were examining.

Despite these limitations, we believe this study is unique in that it represents an effort to begin exploration of an underresearched area using a mixed-methods design that allows us to hear the voices of the couples.

IMPLICATIONS FOR FUTURE RESEARCH

Our study findings reported throughout this book suggest numerous areas for future research. For our study we primarily interviewed couples together. As we mentioned in Chapter 2, this choice made it difficult to determine some gender differences. For example, do men and women have different preferences for fun sharing versus emotion sharing in couple friendships? Since this was a mixed-methods study (quantitative and qualitative), we developed additional questions after analyzing the first round of data. As a result, some of the most interesting questions that we developed later (whether couples identified themselves as *Seekers, Keepers,* or *Nesters*; whether they were fun sharing or emotion sharing) were asked of a portion of the sample. Replication of our study, particularly these latest findings, would help expand knowledge about couples' orientation to couple friendships, how couples relate to their couple friends, and how couple friendships affect their marriage. With two exceptions, the vast majority of our interviews explored couple friendships from the perspective of only one couple. One exception, found in Chapter 8, relates a joint interview of two couples who have been close friends for decades. The other exception is Chapter 9, in which we report on our interview of a group of seven couples. By interviewing the couples together, we were able to explore how couples affect, and are affected by, each other's marriages. Exploring the interactive process that occurs in couple friendships is another possible area for future research.

Steve Duck's work on romantic relationships between two people could also be used as a basis for a greater understanding of couple friendships. Attachment styles between people could be related to attachment styles between couples. Finally, the role that social networks play in helping couples form friendships could also be explored. Duck notes, "People are sensitive to the norms of society that dictate how relationships are 'done' or must be managed, particularly when under strain."[6] Research could focus on how society and the immediate social network influence how couple friendships should operate as well as how they utilize their network when they are in need of assistance.

Appendix B: Questions for Marriage Enrichment Groups

1. Couples who have trouble agreeing about how much time to spend together as a couple are also those whose marriage seems less happy. How should a couple negotiate spending time together? Are you satisfied with how you and your spouse balance time with each other, friends, family, work, and outside interests?

2. Must you as a couple be close friends with both members of the other couple?

3. Young couples are often friends with one person who then gets married (or partnered). What happens if you do not like the new partner of the old friend?

4. Sonia in Chapter 4 told us that she does not talk about her conversations with her friends to her husband. If he wants to know those friends, he has to get to know them himself. Other couples give each other a heads-up about the couple with whom they are about to socialize. Do you agree with Sonia's approach?

5. Can you think of an example when your friendship with another couple helped your marriage? For example, Bianca in Chapter 8 described how she wanted to be with couples as it gave her and Mick an identity as a couple that was distinct from her identity as his wife.

6. In Chapter 8 we present one picture of how two couples can sustain a life-long friendship. What would your vision of a close friendship with another couple look like?

7. In Chapter 9, a couples group is presented. Would you want to have a similar experience over the course of 25 years?

8. If you have children, did their entry into your family cause any changes to your couple friendships?

9. If you have grown children, did your couple friendships shift when they left the family home for college or work?

10. In Chapter 4, Will and Zoe describe keeping certain kinds of information that they decide not to share in "the vault." Does a couple need to agree in advance on what to share that may be highly personal when

they are out with another couple? Is any topic off limits? How does a couple decide what to share?

11. In Chapter 5, Oscar describes friends as better than family: "Friends are more important than relatives. It is a different life with friends than with relatives. I found you can disclose more innermost secrets with friends than with family. Our relationship with friends was very strong in our marriage. You travel with them, you don't travel with relatives." What is your experience with friends versus family?

12. *Seekers, Keepers,* and *Nesters* are three categories for considering couples' styles of orientation to making friends. Which of these best fits you as a couple? You as an individual? How do you negotiate if your styles are different?

13. When you are with your couple friends, are you more apt to be emotion sharing, fun sharing, or some mixture of both? What are the implications of your choice for your own marriage?

14. What is the best way to end a friendship with another couple if they say or do something that results in your wanting to end this relationship?

15. If a couple who are friends of yours divorces, and you would like to remain friends, what steps could you take? How would you like the divorcing couple (or one member of the couple) to communicate to you that they would like to maintain the relationship?

16. What should you do if one of your couple friends is flirting with you or your spouse?

17. *Two Plus Two* implies that a relationship is enhanced by friendship with another couple. Do you agree and, if so, why?

Appendix C: Couple's Quiz

Find out to what extent you agree with your partner about your friendships with other couples. This quiz is to be taken by both members of the couple. There are no right or wrong answers. Answer the questions separately and then discuss your responses to see where you agree and what issues may be worth further discussion.

1. We as a couple:
   a. look for ways to add to our couple friendships
   b. want to keep our numerous couples friends and might be open to meeting another couple
   c. prefer remaining with a few close couple friends
2. We as a couple:
   a. prefer socializing with other couples
   b. are content either being with other couples or alone with each other
   c. would prefer to be alone with each other
3. We as a couple:
   a. tend to be social extroverts
   b. are a combination of extrovert and introvert
   c. tend to be social introverts
4. Being with other couples helps to reaffirm and enrich our marriage/relationship:
   a. frequently
   b. some of the time
   c. rarely
5. Spending time just the two of us alone is:
   a. rarely something we choose
   b. sometimes our preference
   c. often our preference
6. When I think of my parents and their couple friends, I want:
   a. something very different for myself and my partner
   b. something very similar for myself and my partner
   c. to keep some things my parents did and do other things differently

7. Our family commitments make it difficult for us to make new couple friends:
   a. Agree
   b. Neither agree nor disagree
   c. Disagree
8. When we get together with our couple friends we primarily want to:
   a. enjoy ourselves, relax, have fun
   b. discuss what's going on in our lives and how we feel
   c. a mixture of a and b
9. We balance our time well between our individual friends, our family, our couple friends, and time for us as a couple.
   a. Agree
   b. Neither agree nor disagree
   c. Disagree

Endnotes

CHAPTER 1

1. Many studies have documented this. See, e.g., Berkman & Syme (1979) and Winefeld, Winefeld, & Tiggerman (1992).
2. Christiakis & Fowler (2007).
3. Waite & Gallagher (2000). p. 163.
4. Note, as reporter Tara Parker-Pope points out, that these benefits accrue to people in happy marriages; unhappy marriages hurt health. From her review of research, Parker-Pope (2010) reports that divorced people are worse off health-wise than never-marrieds. Being in a good marriage (or a significant partnership we surmise) also benefits health. Slatcher (2010a) describes the benefits of marriage further.
5. A great deal has been written about egalitarian marriages (e.g., Jacobson & Holtzworth-Munroe, 1986; Schwartz, 2002) and trust in partner relationships. Egalitarianism is often an explicit goal of marital therapy. Schwartz describes how couples want increased intimacy and may share tasks to achieve it. Underpinning egalitarianism is the need for trust between partners. Murray et al. (2009), for example, describe, in a literature review, how when there is equality between partners, the partners will be more optimistic about the partner's responsiveness to them. Trust also underpins friendships between platonic friends (Greif, 2009).
6. Birditt & Antonucci (2007).
7. Gottman & Gottman (2008).
8. Slatcher (2010b).
9. Pew Research Center (2010a).
10. Greif (2009). Bendtschneider and Duck (1993) conducted a study of 165 dating college students (99 women and 65 men, average age of 19). The students were given a questionnaire and asked questions about the differences between their individual and couple friends. These were individual, not couple-generated, responses. One interesting finding was that women found more satisfaction in their individual friendships than in their couple friendships and men found them equally satisfying. The couples tended to spend more time in friendships that originated from the male's group of friends than from the female's.
11. Greif (2009). Twenty-five percent of women and 40% of men said they either did not have enough friends or were unsure if they had enough friends.
12. Greif (2009).
13. Greif (2009).
14. Antonucci & Akiyama (1995); Fox, Gibbs, & Auerbach (1985).
15. Strough, Leszcynski, Neely, Flinn, & Margrett (2007).
16. Adams (1994).
17. Kramer (2002).
18. Ellison (1990).
19. Coleman, Ganong, & Rothrauff (2006).
20. Roberts (1994).

21. Griffin, Amodeo, Clay, Fassler, & Ellis (2006).

22. Nardi (2007).

23. Cohen (1992).

24. Allan, 1998, as cited in Rose (2007).

25. Krause & Borawski-Clark, 1995, as cited in Rose (2007).

26. Morello (2011).

27. Brown, Orbuch, & Bauermeister (2008).

28. Bratter & King (2008).

29. Milardo (1982).

30. Johnson & Leslie (1982).

31. Hibbler & Shinew (2002).

32. Lehmiller & Agnew (2007).

33. Agnew, Loving, & Drigotas (2001).

34. Agnew et al. (2001).

35. In 2007, according to the CDC, *National Marriage and Divorce Rate Trends*, 856,000 marriages ended in divorce or annulments while 2,197,000 marriages occurred.

36. Addo & Sassler (2010). Addo and Sassler, two professors of policy analysis and management, found a correlation between relationship quality and shared bank accounts in low-income families. They suggest, given their findings, that relation skills courses include information on budgeting and the meaning of banking accounts.

37. Allgood, Crane, & Agree (1997).

38. Kalmijn & Bernasco (2001).

39. Schwartz (2002).

40. Gottman (1994).

41. Aron, Aron, & Smillan (1992).

42. Stein, Bush, Ross, & Ward (1992).

43. Drawn from www.famous-couple.com.

44. *Time Magazine* lists these four along with others, including *The Great Gatsby, Anna Karenina*, and *Hamlet*. Easton Press gives a different top ten: *Pride and Prejudice, 20,000 Leagues Under the Sea, The Scarlett Letter, Dr. Jekyll and Mr. Hyde, Walden, Gulliver's Travels, Moby Dick, A Farewell to Arms, The Red Badge of Courage*, and *The Jungle Book*. It is safe to say that there is not much emphasis on couple friendship in these seminal works.

45. American Medical Association (n.d.).

46. American Medical Association (2008).

47. Women's International Center Web site. Retrieved 12/17/08.

48. Werner (2005).

49. See, e.g., U.S. Department of Labor (2009a).

50. McPherson, Smith-Lovin, & Brashears (2006).

51. Laurenceau, Barrett, & Pietromonaco (1998), p. 1238.

52. Allgood et al. (1997), p. 111.

53. Bost, Cox, Burchinal, & Payne (2002).

54. Agnew et al. (2001), p. 1044.

55. Agnew et al. (2001).

56. Please contact the authors for copies of the questionnaires and interview guides for the four studies that underpin the research.

CHAPTER 2

1. Marks (1986, 1989).
2. Marks (1989, p. 22).
3. Marks (1986, 1989).
4. Kearns & Leonard (2004); Milardo (1986).
5. Julien, Markman, Léveillé, Chartrand, & Bégin (1994).
6. Oliker (1989).
7. Oliker (1989); Proulx, Helms, & Payne (2004).
8. Stein et al. (1992).
9. Wright & Scanlon (1991).
10. Rose (2007).
11. Helms, Crouter, & McHale (2003); Rubin (1985).
12. Oliker (1989, p. 123).
13. Proulx et al. (2004, p. 401).
14. Oliker (1989); Rubin (1985).
15. Helms et al. (2003); Julien et al. (2000); Proulx, Helms, Milardo, & Payne (2009).
16. Helms et al. (2003).
17. Julien et al. (2000).
18. Marks (1986, 1989).
19. Bryant & Conger (1999); Cotton, Cunningham, & Antill (1993); Hansen, Fallon, & Novotny (1991); Widmer, Kellerhals, & Levy (2004).
20. Milardo & Helms-Erikson (2000).
21. Stein et al. (1992).
22. Agnew et al. (2001); Bryant & Conger (1999); Cotton et al. (1993); Hansen et al. (1991); Widmer et al. (2004).
23. To determine this, we asked the question, "How would your spouse/partner characterize your marriage/relationship? Very happy; Happy; Somewhat happy; or Not happy."
24. Aron, Aron, & Norman (2001).
25. Strong & Aron (2006).
26. Aron et al. (2001).
27. Aron, Norman, Aron, McKenna, & Heyman (2000); Strong & Aron (2006).
28. Slatcher (2007, 2010b).
29. Larson, Mannell, & Zuzanek (1986).
30. Milardo & Helms-Erikson (2000, p. 39).
31. Those that believe couple friendships are very important are most likely to say they want more couple friends, to say they frequently seek them out, and are least likely to have between only 0 and 2 couple friends. We asked during the final round of qualitative interviews how important couple friendships were and whether the couple saw themselves as *Seekers, Keepers,* or *Nesters.* Too few people identified themselves as *Nesters* and *Seekers* in the sample to test significance, but none of the 6 *Nester* couples thought couple friendships were very important as compared with 6 of the 7 *Seeker* couples and 18 of 27 *Keeper* couples.
32. Slatcher (2007, 2010b).
33. The majority of these pairings involved friends of the same gender. Couples in our study rarely reported independent socializing with the person of opposite gender from one of their couple friends.

CHAPTER 3

1. Pew Research Center (2010b).
2. To participate in the study, you had to have been living together for at least a year and be at least 21 years old.
3. As noted in Chapter 1, Morello (2011) notes from U.S. Census data that recent marriages are occurring at a later age and are less likely to end in divorce.
4. Sherman, de Vries, & Lansford (2000).
5. Johnson & Leslie (1982); Milardo, Johnson, & Huston (1983).
6. Burger & Milardo (1995).
7. Agnew et al. (2001).
8. Kearns & Leonard (2004).
9. Hansen et al. (1991).
10. Kalmijn & Bernasco (2001).
11. Allgood et al. (1997).
12. Kalmijn & Bernasco (2001).
13. Hibbler & Shinew (2002).
14. Lehmiller & Agnew (2007).
15. Kalimijn & Bernasco (2001).
16. Matthews (1988).
17. Bost et al. (2002).
18. Marks (1989).
19. If we are doing a formal interview, as we did with Jenny, we present them with a consent form first.

CHAPTER 4

1. U.S. Department of Labor (2009b).
2. U.S. Department of Labor (2008).
3. Fry & Cohn (2010).
4. Fry & Cohn (2010).
5. Blieszner & Roberto (2004).
6. We compared the oldest couples with a total age of 101 or more years with the youngest couples with a total age of 42 to 60 years and middle-age couples with a total age of 61 to 100 years: 31% of the oldest couples, 20% of the youngest couples, and 16% of the middle-age couples had 10 or more couple friends. The differences were not statistically significant but may be suggestive of a trend. One statistically significant finding that mirrors this is that couples who are partnered or married for over 10 years are most likely to find couple friendships to be very important, those married 1 to 3 years are the next most likely to find couple friendships very important, and those married between 3.25 and 9.5 years are least likely to find couple friendships very important. While age is related to finding couple friendships important, there may be a period where having children and being partnered for a number of years is linked to less of a belief in the importance of couple friendships.
7. Bryant & Conger (1999).
8. Cotton et al. (1993).
9. Widmer et al. (2004).
10. Hansen et al. (1991).

11. Bulanda (2007); Gorchoff et al. (2008); Umberson, Williams, Powers, Chen, & Campbell (2005).
12. Gorchoff et al. (2008).
13. Chito Childs (2005).
14. Bratter & King (2008).

CHAPTER 5

1. Pew Research Center (2010b).
2. Pew Research Center (2010b).
3. Fry & Cohn (2010).
4. Fry & Cohn (2010).
5. Lieber & Sandefur (2002), using data from the Wisconsin Longitudinal Study.
6. Adams (1994).
7. Liang et al. (2002).
8. Kramer (2002).
9. Fox et al. (1985).
10. Biesanz, West, & Millevoi (2007).
11. Antonucci & Akiyama (1995).
12. Zalesin (2010).
13. See Chapter 2 for a discussion of Slatcher's (2010b) research.
14. See Slatcher's work.
15. Greif (2009).

CHAPTER 6

1. Jeske (1997), p. 58.
2. Jeske, p. 71.
3. Greif (2009).
4. Greif & Sharpe (2010). This was true for 65% of the women and 50% of the men.
5. Greif (2009).
6. Greif (2009).
7. Greif (2009).
8. Matthews (1986), p. 74.
9. Matthews (1986), p. 74.
10. Enright & Rawlinson (1991), p. 321.
11. The numbers who said they were very picky and their spouse was very picky were small; this showed a trend that was not statistically significant.
12. We also considered the meaning of enemies. Enemies, according to *Webster's* definition, imply hatred and the wish to harm another. Note that this is the exact opposite of Aristotle's view where a friend means caring for the friend for the friend's sake. Whereas little has been written about couple friendships, nothing has been written about couple enemies. Plug in the search word *enemies* into psychinfo.com, the best academic search engine for this type of research, and "international conflict" pops up with an occasional mention of bullying. Our guess is that friends who turn into enemies are more common with individual friendships although it certainly has happened with couples.

13. Younger couples were more likely to agree with the question, "Some couples have the experience of liking one member of the couple and not the other. Has this happened to you?" This indicates to us that they may be less willing to put up with the behavior of another member of a couple.

14. Further, two-thirds of those who said they had never experienced disliking a member of the other couple said they had never been dumped and never have dumped another couple. By comparison, slightly less than half of those who said they had experienced disliking a member of another couple also said they experienced dropping or being dropped by another couple. It may be that this first group, again, do not have friendships on their radar and do not know if they have been dumped or not (or if they have dumped another couple).

15. Galanes (2011).

16. Marks (1986, 1989).

CHAPTER 7

1. In previous centuries marriages ended differently. In the 1800s and earlier, death was more likely to end a marriage. Consider the vagaries of war, illness, factory work, field work, and child birth. If someone was unhappy with their spouse, they were unlikely to live with him or her into old age. Divorce did not begin to outstrip death as a reason for a person to become single until the early 1960s (with the exception of the periods immediately following the World Wars).

2. U.S. Census Bureau (2011), p. 840.

3. Morello (2011).

4. When looking at individuals who comprise the couples we interviewed together and the members of couples we interviewed separately without ever interviewing their partner, roughly one-sixth were married at least once before. One-fifth of the remarried group were raising at least one stepchild. These partners look similar to those who are in their first marriage or partnership in terms of race and religion. They are less likely to have children than those married or partnered for the first time.

5. Gigy & Kelly (1992).

6. Parker-Pope (2008).

7. Del Rosso (2011).

8. Kearns & Leonard (2004).

9. Wang & Amato (2000), p. 657.

10. Rands (1988).

11. Lebow (2008).

12. The other responses for the divorced sample were 48% said couple friendships were somewhat important and 35% said they were slightly or not important. With the married/partnered sample, 35% said they were somewhat important and 22% said they were slightly or not important. We did not ask them how important friendships were to them as individuals.

13. Johnson & Leslie (1982). See Kalmijn & van Groeneu (2005) for more on the dyadic withdrawal hypothesis.

14. See, e.g., Felmlee (2001), whose study is described later in this chapter.

15. Those who most strongly believe in the importance of socializing were also more likely to say that friendships were very important.

16. Less than 1 in 10 said their spouse/partner flirted, 1 in 25 said their spouse/partner competed with them, and 1 in 17 said alcohol got in the way when they socialized.
17. Felmlee (2001).
18. It does not matter whether they have remarried; the number of friends is essentially the same.
19. See, e.g., Greif (2009).
20. See, e.g., Johnson & Leslie (1982).

CHAPTER 8

1. All four reviewed a draft of this chapter.
2. See, e.g., Milardo (1982).
3. Julien et al. (1994); Milardo (1986).
4. Slatcher (2010b) found that as couples shared more, they became closer.

CHAPTER 9

1 We discussed this prior relationship with the group before conducting the formal group interview.
2. Given the number of couples and their appearing only in this chapter, we chose to not give them names, as we believed that might be confusing.
3. The method of tracking individual group members in a couples psychotherapy group (which this group is not) can be found in Laurie Abraham's fascinating book, *The Husbands and Wives Club: A Year in the Life of a Couples Therapy Group* (New York: Touchstone Books, 2010) in which she observes the work of psychologist Judith Coche. Coche also has written a book for professionals, titled *Couples Group Psychotherapy* (New York: Routledge, 2010).
4. See, e.g., Bowling, Hill, & Jencius (2005). See also the entire October 2004 issue of *Family Relations,* which describes many programs related to marriage enrichment and education, including government programs.

CHAPTER 10

1. See Chapter 2 for information on Marks's model of balancing competing interests in marriage. For therapists working with couples around the issue of time management, see Fraenkel and Wilson (2000).
2. Marks (1986, 1989).
3. Larson et al. (1986).
4. Slatcher (2007; 2010b). As mentioned in Chapter 2, the subjects in Slatcher's research were college students who were dating each other.

APPENDIX A

1. Padgett (2008).
2. Charmaz (2006).
3. We thank Dr. Philip Osteen for this statistical expertise and consultancy on this and other related matters.

4. We did not separately analyze interracial couples because of their small numbers and because many different races comprise these couples.
5. Greif & Sharpe (2010).
6. Duck (2011), p. 16.

References

Abraham, L. (2010). *The Husbands and Wives Club: A year in the life of a couples therapy group*. New York: Touchstone Books.

Adams, R. G. (1994). Older men's friendship patterns. In E. H. Thompson (Ed.), *Older men's lives* (pp. 159–177). Thousand Oaks, CA: Sage.

Addo, F. R., & Sassler, S. (2010). Financial arrangements and relationship quality in low-income couples. *Family Relations, 59,* 408–423.

Agnew, C. R., Loving, T. J., & Drigotas, S. M. (2001). Substituting the forest for the trees: Social networks and the prediction of romantic relationship state and fate. *Journal of Personality and Social Psychology, 81,* 1042–1057.

Allgood, S., M., Crane, D. R., & Agee, L. (1997). Social support: Distinguishing clinical and volunteer couples. *American Journal of Family Therapy, 25,* 111–119.

American Medical Association, (n.d.). *Women in medicine: An AMA timeline.* Chicago: Author.

American Medical Association. (2008). *Physician characteristics and distribution in the U.S.* Chicago: Author.

Antonucci, T. C., & Akiyama, H. (1995). Convoys of social relations: Family and friendships within a lifespan context. In R. Blieszner & V. H. Bedford (Eds.), *Aging and the family: Theory and research* (pp. 355–371). Westport, CT: Praeger.

Aron, A., Aron, E. N., & Norman, C. C. (2001). Self-expansion model of motivation and cognition in close relationships and beyond. In G. J. O. Fletcher & M. Clark (Eds.), *Blackwell handbook of social psychology: Interpersonal processes* (pp. 478–501). Malden, MA: Blackwell.

Aron, A., Aron, E. N., & Smillan, D. (1992). Inclusion of other in the self and the structure of interpersonal closeness. *Journal of Personality and Social Psychology, 60,* 596–612.

Aron, A., Norman, C. C., Aron, E. N., McKenna, C., & Heyman, R. E. (2000). Couples' shared participation in novel and arousing activities and experienced relationship quality. *Journal of Personality and Social Psychology, 78*(2), 273–284.

Bendtschneider, L., & Duck, S. (1993). What's yours is mine and what's mine is yours: Couple friends. In P. J. Kalbfleisch (Ed.), *Interpersonal communication: Evolving interpersonal relationships* (pp. 169–186). Hillsdale, NJ: Erlbaum.

Berkman, L. F., & Syme, S. L. (1979). Social networks, host resistance, and mortality: A nine-year follow-up study of Alameda County residents. *American Journal of Epidemiology, 109,* 186–204.

Biesanz, J. C., West, S. G., & Millevoi, A. (2007). What do you learn about someone over time? The relationship between length of acquaintance and consensus and self-other agreement in judgments of personality. *Journal of Personality and Social Psychology, 92,* 119–135.

Birditt, K. S., & Antonucci, T. C. (2007). Relationship quality profiles and well-being among married adults. *Journal of Family Psychology, 21,* 595–604.

Blieszner, R., & Roberto, K. A. (2004). Friendship across the life span: Reciprocity in individual and relationship development. In F. R. Lang & K. L. Fingerman (Eds.), *Growing together: Personal relationships across the lifespan* (pp. 159–182). Cambridge, UK: Cambridge University Press.

Bost, K. K., Cox, M. J., Burchinal, M. R., & Payne, C. (2002). Structural and supportive changes in couples' family and friendship networks across the transition to parenthood. *Journal of Marriage and Family, 64,* 517–531.

Bowling, T. R., Hill, C. M., & Jencius, M. (2005). An overview of marriage enrichment. *The Family Journal, 13,* 87–94.

Bratter, J. L., & King, R. B. (2008). "But will it last?" Marital instability among interracial and same-race couples. *Family Relations, 57,* 160–171.

Brown, E., Orbuch, T. L., & Bauermeister, J. A. (2008). Religiosity and marital stability among black American and white American couples. *Family Relations, 57,* 186–197.

Bryant, C. M., & Conger, R. D. (1999). Marital success and domains of social support in long-term relationships: Does the influence of network members ever end? *Journal of Marriage and the Family, 61,* 437–450.

Bulanda, J. (2007). *Marital quality in later life.* Paper presented at the American Sociological Association annual meeting, New York.

Burger, E., & Milardo, R. M. (1995). Marital interdependence and social networks. *Journal of Social and Personal Relationships, 12,* 403–415.

Charmaz, K. (2006). *Constructing grounded theory: A practical guide through qualitative analysis.* Thousand Oaks, CA: Sage.

Chito Childs, E. (2005). *Navigating interracial borders: Black-white couples and their social worlds.* Piscataway, NJ: Rutgers University Press.

Christiakis, N. A., & Fowler, J. H. (2007). The spread of obesity in a large social network over 32 years. *New England Journal of Medicine, 357,* 370–379.

Cohen, T. (1992). Men's families, men's friends: A structural analysis of constraints on men's social ties. In P. M. Nardi (Ed.), *Men's friendships* (pp. 115–131). Newbury Park, CA: Sage.

Coleman, M., Ganong, L. H., & Rothrauff, T. C. (2006). Racial and ethnic similarities and differences in beliefs about intergenerational assistance to older adults after divorce and remarriage. *Family Relations, 55,* 576–587.

Cotton, S., Cunningham, J. D., & Antill, J. K. (1993). Network structure, network support and the marital satisfaction of husbands and wives. *Australian Journal of Psychology, 45*(3), 176–181.

Del Rosso, L. (2011, January 23). Saying "I don't" to release the anger. *New York Times,* Style Section, p. 5.

Duck, S. (2011). *Rethinking relationships.* Thousand Oaks, CA: Sage.

Ellison, C. G. (1990). Family ties, friendships, and subjective well-being among black Americans. *Journal of Marriage and Family, 52,* 298–310.

Enright, D. J., & Rawlinson, D. (1991). *Oxford book of friendships.* New York: Oxford University Press.

Felmlee, D. H. (2001). No couple is an island: A social network perspective on dyadic stability. *Social Forces, 79,* 1259–1287.

Fox, M., Gibbs, M., & Auerbach, D. (1985). Age and gender dimensions of friendship. *Psychology of Women Quarterly, 9,* 489–501.

Fraenkel, P., & Wilson, S. (2000). Clocks, calendars, and couples: Time and the rhythms of relationships. In P. Papp (Ed.), *Couples on the fault line: New directions for therapists* (pp. 63–103). New York: Guilford Press.

Fry, R., & Cohn, D. (2010). *The new economics of marriage: The rise of wives.* Retrieved August 10, 2011. http://pewresearch.org/pubs/1466/economics-marriage-rise-of-wives.

Galanes, P. (2011, June 5). How to be a foul-weather friend. *New York Times,* p. C10.

Gigy, L., & Kelly, J. B. (1992). Reasons for divorce: Perceptions of divorcing men and women. *Journal of Divorce & Remarriage, 18,* 169–187.

Gorchoff, S. M., John, O. P., & Helson, R. (2008). Contextualizing change in marital satisfaction during middle age: An 18-year longitudinal study. *Psychological Science, 19*(11), 1994–2000.

Gottman, J. M. (1994). *Why marriages succeed or fail.* New York: Simon & Schuster.

Gottman, J. M., & Gottman, J. S. (2008). Gottman method couple therapy. In A. S. Gurman (ed.). *Clinical handbook of couple therapy* (4th ed., pp. 138–164). New York: Guilford Press.

Greif, G. L. (2009). *Buddy system: Understanding male friendships.* New York: Oxford University Press.

Greif, G. L., & Sharpe, T. (2010). The friendships of women: Are there differences between African Americans and whites? *Journal of Human Behavior in the Social Environment, 20,* 791–807.

Griffin, M. L., Amodeo, M., Clay, C., Fassler I., & Ellis, M. (2006). Racial differences in social support: Kin versus friends. *American Journal of Orthopsychiatry, 76,* 374–380.

Hansen, F. J., Fallon, A. E., & Novotny, S. L. (1991). The relationship between social network structure and marital satisfaction in distressed and nondistressed couples: A pilot study. *Family Therapy, 18,* 102–114.

Helms, H. M., Crouter, A. C., & McHale, S. M. (2003). Marital quality and spouses' marriage work with close friends and each other. *Journal of Marriage and Family, 65,* 963–977.

Hibbler, D. K., & Shinew, K. J. (2002). Interracial couples' experience of leisure: A social network approach. *Journal of Leisure Research, 34,* 135–156.

Jacobson, N. S., & Holtzworth-Munroe, A. (1986). Marital therapy: A social learning-cognitive perspective. In N. S. Jacobson & A. S. Gurman (Eds.), *Clinical handbook of marital therapy* (pp. 29–70). New York: Guilford Press.

Jeske, D. (1997). Friendship, virtue, and impartiality. *Philosophy and Phenomenological Research, 57,* 51–72.

Johnson, M. P., & Leslie, L. (1982). Couple involvement and network structure: A test of the dyadic withdrawal hypothesis. *Social Psychological Quarterly, 45,* 34–43.

Julien, D., Markman, H. J., Léveillé, S., Chartrand, E., & Bégin, J. (1994). Networks' support and interference with regard to marriage: Disclosures of marital problems to confidents. *Journal of Family Psychology, 8*(1), 16–31.

Julien, D., Tremblay, N., Belanger, I., Dube, M., Bégin, J., & Bouthiller, D. (2000). Interaction structure of husbands' and wives' disclosure of marital conflict to their respective best friend. *Journal of Family Psychology, 14,* 286–303.

Kalmijn, M., & Bernasco, W. (2001). Joint and separated lifestyles in couple relationships. *Journal of Marriage and Family, 63,* 639–654.

Kalmijn, M., & von Groeneu, M. B. (2005). Differential effects of divorce on social integration. *Journal of Social and Personal Relationships, 22,* 455–476.

Kearns, J. N., & Leonard, K. E. (2004). Social networks: Structural interdependence, and marital quality over the transition to marriage: A prospective study. *Journal of Family Psychology, 18,* 383–395.

Kramer, B. (2002). Men caregivers: An overview. In B. J. Kramer & E. H. Thompson (Eds.), *Men as caregivers: Theory, research, and service implications* (pp. 3–19). New York: Springer.

Krause, N., & Borawski-Clark, E. (1995). Social class differences in social support among older adults. *The Gerontologist, 35,* 498–508.

Larson, R., Mannell, R., & Zuzanek, J. (1986). Daily well-being of older adults with friends and family. *Psychology and Aging, 1,* 117–126.

Laurenceau, J.-P., Barrett, L. F., & Pietromonaco, P. R. (1998). Intimacy as an interpersonal process: The importance of self-disclosure, partner disclosure, and perceived partner responsiveness in interpersonal exchanges. *Journal of Personality and Social Psychology, 74,* 1238–1251.

Lebow, J. (2008). Separation and divorce issues in couple therapy. In A. S. Gurman (Ed.), *Clinical handbook of couple therapy* (4th ed., pp. 459–477). New York: Guilford Press.

Lehmiller, J. J., & Agnew, C. R. (2007). Perceived marginalization and the prediction of romantic relationship stability. *Journal of Marriage and Family, 69,* 1036–1049.

Liang, B., Tracy, A., Taylor, C. A., Williams, L. M., Jordan, J. V., & Miller, J. B. (2002). The relational health indices: A study of women's relationships. *Psychology of Women Quarterly, 26,* 25–35.

Lieber, C. A., & Sandefur, G. D. (2002). Gender differences in the exchange of social support with friends, neighbors, and co-workers at midlife. *Social Science Research, 31,* 364–391.

Marks, S. R. (1986). *Three corners: Exploring marriage and the self.* Lexington, MA: Lexington Books.

Marks, S. R. (1989). Toward a systems theory of marital quality. *Journal of Marriage and Family, 51,* 15–26.

Matthews, A. M. (1988). *Why did I marry you, anyway? Good sense and good humor in the first year … and after.* Boston: Houghton Mifflin.

Matthews, S. H. (1986). *Friendships through the life course: Oral biographies in old age.* Beverly Hills, CA: Sage.

McPherson, M., Smith-Lovin, L., & Brashears, M. E. (2006). Social isolation in America: Changes in core discussion networks over two decades. *American Sociological Review, 71,* 353–375.

Milardo, R. M. (1982). Friendship networks in developing relationships: Converging and diverging social environments. *Social Psychological Quarterly, 45,* 162–172.

Milardo, R. M. (1986). Personal choice and social constraint in close relationships: Applications of network analysis. In V. J. Derlega & B. A. Winstead (Eds.), *Friendship and social interaction* (pp. 145–166). New York: Springer.

Milardo, R. M., & Helms-Erikson, H. (2000). Network overlap and third-party influence in close relationships. In C. Hendrick & S. S. Hendrick (Eds.), *Close relationships: A sourcebook* (pp. 33–46). Thousand Oaks, CA: Sage.

Milardo, R. M., Johnson, M. P., & Huston, T. L. (1983). Developing close relationships: Changing patterns of interaction between pair members and social networks. *Journal of Personality and Social Psychology, 44,* 964–976.

Morello, C. (2011, May 18). Number of long-lasting marriages in the U.S. has risen, Census Bureau reports. *Washington Post.* Retrieved from http://www.washington-post.com/local/number-of-long-lasting-marriages-in-us-has-risen-census-bureau-reports/2011/05/18/AFO8dW6G_story.html

Murray, S. L., Aloni, M., Holmes, J. G., Derrick, J. L., Stinson, D. A., & Leder, S. (2009). Fostering partner dependence as trust insurance: The implicit contingencies of the exchange script in close relationships. *Journal of Personality and Social Psychology, 96,* 324–348.

Nardi, P. M. (2007). Friendship, sex, and masculinity. In M. Kimmel (Ed.), *The sexual self: The construction of sexual scripts* (pp. 49–57). Nashville, TN: Vanderbilt University Press.

Oliker, S. J. (1989). *Best friends and marriage: Exchange among women.* Los Angeles: University of California Press.

Padgett, D. K. (2008). *Qualitative methods in social work research* (2nd ed.). Thousand Oaks, CA: Sage.

Parker-Pope, T. (2008, October 27). Love, sex, and the changing landscape of infidelity. *New York Times,* p. D1. Retrieved January 17, 2011, from http://www.nytimes.com/2008/10/28/health/28well.html

Parker-Pope, T. (2010, April 18). Is marriage good? *New York Times Magazine,* pp. 46–51.

Pew Research Center. (2010a). *The decline of marriage and rise of new families*. Retrieved July 28, 2011, from http://pewsocialtrends.org/2010/11/18/the-decline-of-marriage-and-rise-of-new-families/

Pew Research Center. (2010b). *Millennials: A portrait of generation next. Confident. Connected. Open to change*. Retrieved July 28, 2011, from www.pewresearch.org/millennials

Proulx, C. M., Helms, H. M., Milardo, R. M., & Payne, C. C. (2009). Relational support from friends and wives' family relationships: The role of husbands' interference. *Journal of Social and Personal Relationships, 26*(2/3), 195–210.

Proulx, C. M., Helms, H. M., & Payne, C. C. (2004). Wives' domain-specific "marriage work" with friends and spouses: Links to marital quality. *Family Relations, 53*, 393–404.

Rands, M. (1988). Changes in social networks following marital separation and divorce. In R. Milardo (Ed.), *Families and social networks* (pp. 127–145.) Newbury Park, CA: Sage.

Roberts, G. W. (1994). Brother to brother: African American models of relating among men. *Journal of Black Studies, 24*, 379–390.

Rose, S. M. (2007). Enjoying the returns: Women's friendships after 50. In V. Muhlbauer & J. C. Chrisler (Eds.), *Women over 50: Psychological perspectives* (pp. 112–130). New York: Springer.

Rubin, L. B. (1985). *Just friends: The role of friendship in our lives*. New York: Harper & Row.

Schwartz, P. (2002). Maintaining relationships in the millennium. In J. H. Harvey & A. Wenzel (Eds.), *A clinician's guide to maintaining and enhancing close relationships* (pp. 303–319). Mahwah, NJ: Erlbaum.

Sherman, A. M., de Vries, B., & Lansford, J. E. (2000). Friendship in childhood and adulthood: Lessons across the life span. *International Journal of Aging and Human Development, 51*, 31–51.

Slatcher, R. B. (2008). Party of four: Creating closeness between couples (Doctoral dissertation, University of Texas at Austin, 2007). *Dissertation Abstracts International: Section B: The Sciences and Engineering, 68*(9-B), 6393.

Slatcher, R. B. (2010a). Marital functioning and physical health: Implications for social and personality psychology. *Social and Personality Psychology Compass, 3*, 1–15.

Slatcher, R. B. (2010b). When Harry and Sally met Dick and Jane: Creating closeness between couples. *Personal Relationships, 17*, 279–297.

Stein, C. H., Bush, E. G., Ross, R. R., & Ward, M. (1992). Mine, yours and ours: A configural analysis of the networks of married couples in relation to marital satisfaction and individual well-being. *Journal of Social and Personal Relationships, 9*, 265–283.

Strong, G., & Aron, A. (2006). The effect of shared participation in novel and challenging activities on experienced relationship quality: Is it mediated by high positive affect? In K. D. Vols & E. J. Finkel (Eds.), *Self and relationships: Connecting intrapersonal and interpersonal processes* (pp. 342–359). New York: Guilford Press.

Strough, J., Leszcynski, J., Neely, T. L., Flinn, J. A., & Margrett, J. (2007). From adolescence to later adulthood: Femininity, masculinity, and androgyny in six age categories. *Sex Roles, 57*, 385–396.

Umberson, D., Williams, K., Powers, D. A., Chen, M. D., & Campbell, A. M. (2005). As good as it gets? A life course perspective on marital quality. *Social Forces, 84*, 493–511.

U.S. Census Bureau. (2011). *Statistical Abstract of the United States: 2011*. Table 1335. Washington, DC: Government Printing Office.

U.S. Department of Labor. (2008, December). *Women in the labor force: A databook* (Rep. No. 1011). Washington, DC: U.S. Bureau of Labor Statistics.

U.S. Department of Labor. (2009a, July). *Highlights of women's earnings in 2008* (Rep. 1017). Washington, DC: U.S. Bureau of Labor Statistics.

U.S. Department of Labor. (2009b, November). *Quick stats on women workers, 2009. Employment and earnings, 2009 annual averages and the Monthly Labor Review.* Washington, DC: U.S. Bureau of Labor Statistics.

Waite, L., & Gallagher, M. (2000). *The case for marriage: Why married people are happier, healthier, and better off financially.* New York: Doubleday.

Wang, H., & Amato, P. R. (2000). Predictors of divorce adjustment: Stressors, resources, and definitions. *Journal of Marriage and the Family, 62,* 655–668.

Werner, W. (2004, May). Where have the women attorneys gone? *Law Practice Today.* Retrieved August 19, 2011. http://apps.americanbar.org/lpm/lpt/articles/mgt05041.html.

Widmer, E. D., Kellerhals, J., & Levy, R. (2004). Types of conjugal networks, conjugal conflict and conjugal quality. *European Sociological Review, 20*(1), 63–77.

Winefeld, H. R., Winefeld, A. H., & Tiggerman, M. (1992). Social support and psychological well-being in young adults: The multi-dimensional support scale. *Journal of Personality Assessment, 58,* 198–210.

Wright, P. H., & Scanlon, M. B. (1991). Gender role orientations and friendships: Some attenuation but gender differences abound. *Sex Roles, 24*(9), 551–566.

Zalesin, J. (2010, June 1). Senior years really are golden: Happiness increases after age 50, Gallup poll finds. *New York Daily News,* p. 2.

Acknowledgments

We have many people to thank for their assistance with this book. Stacy Timlin, MSW, played a key role for 2 years in getting data into Excel and analyzing it at all hours of the day and night. Her conscientious work has made the research process much easier. Elise Bowman, our RA, has also been helpful with data entry and reference checking since 2010. Our GRA, Hae Jung Kim, helped organize data from the original interviews. Carol Sandler did a wonderful job with editing at the late stages of the project and with developing the book's title. Student interviewers in the Master's Program at the University of Maryland School of Social Work are numerous and helped with not only finding and interviewing couples and individuals but also with offering their perspectives through written and oral contributions. They are (starting with the 2008 group): Nancy Borger, Kate Cernak, Monique Couteau, Jeremy Darden, Paige Goldstein, Lindsey Goslee, Peggy Guzman, Shannon Harris Robertson, Nicole Hatch, Dolly Moore, Sara Moothart, Marsha Ross, Kimkia Smith, Erin Tiberio, Claire Wexler, Litsa Williams, and Phyllis Yates-Manigault; (2009 group): Regis Aguglia, Jani Benitez, Aimee Block, Shawn Burke, Florangel Cuesta, Rebecca Dodge-Katz, Matt Dorsey, Nancy Feig, Jennifer Glendening, Katia Hernandez, Marita Hipolito, Carrie Leach, Judith Leitch, Adele McRae, Meghan Neville, Jill Pieri, Lindsay Reep, Kinda Serrano-Creese, Tiffany Spaulding, Samantha Watts, and Laura Weideman; and (2010 group): Christine Anchan, Jonathan Boltz, Kelly Davis, Justin Decker, Lisa Diker, Natalie Elliott, Courtney Ellwood, Ishshah Escabi Cruz, Kelly Garafola, Whitney Gordon, Ivy Gross, Courtney Haile, Ben Kaufman, Icia Ragsdale, Nicole Romans, Kara Smith, Marissa Sussman, Joanna Turner, and Rob Zelikoff.

At Routledge, George Zimmar, our editor, showed interest in the project from the beginning and was wonderfully open about the book's direction. Also at Routledge, Marta Moldvai and Linda Leggio cheerfully guided us through the process. We also wish to thank the many couples whom we interviewed and who gave so kindly of themselves and of their time.

Finally, we wish to thank the two people who make us members of happy couples—Maureen Lefton-Greif and David Deal.

Author Index

A

Abraham, Laurie, 201n(9)3
Addo, F. R., 196n(1)36
Agnew, Christopher R., 9, 19, 45
Amato, Paul, 124
Aristotle, 105, 108–109, 119, 154, 199n(6)12
Aron, Arthur, 29

B

Barrett, Lisa, 18
Bendtschneider, L., 195n(1)5
Bowling, T. R., 201n(9)4
Bratter, Jenifer L., 79

C

Coche, Judith, 201n(9)3

D

Del Rosso, Lisa, 124
Drigotas, S. M., 45
Duck, Steve, 189, 195n(1)5

F

Felmlee, Diane, 135–136

G

Galanes, Philip, 119
Gallagher, Maggie, 3
Gorchoff, Sara M., 68
Gottman, John M., 3, 10
Greif, G. L., 195n(1)5

H

Hansen, Finy Josephine, 67
Helms, H. M., 27
Helms-Erikson, H., 30

Hill, C. M., 201n(9)4
Holtzworth-Munroe, A., 195n(1)5

J

Jacobs, Richard, 122–123, 143
Jacobson, N. S., 195n(1)5
Jencius, M., 201n(9)4
Jeske, Diane, 108–109, 111, 115, 118
Julien, Danielle, 28

K

Kant, Immanuel, 108–109, 112
Kearns, Jill, 124
King, Rosalind B., 79
Kramer, Betty, 88

L

Larson, R., 30
Laurenceau, Jean-Philippe, 18
Lebow, Jay, 125, 127
Lehmiller, Justin, 9
Leonard, Kenneth, 124
Liebler, Carolyn, 87, 105
Loving, T. J., 45

M

Mannell, R., 30
Marks, Stephen, 25–26, 28, 29, 57, 64, 119, 174, 177, 201n(10)1
Matthews, Sarah, 46, 110
Milardo, R. M., 30, 45
Morello, C., 198n(3)3
Murray, S. L., 195n(1)5

O

Oliker, Stacey, 27
Osteen, Philip, 201n(A)3

Subject Index

A

African Americans, friendships, 7
Age
    and compatibility, 88
    and couple friendships, 6–7, 37, 66,
        198n(4)6
    and decreasing competition, 147
    and friendships, 6–7, 105, 146
    and increased happiness, 88–89
    and men's friendships, 6–7, 37, 88
    and tolerance, 88, 101, 104, 118
    and women's friendships, 6–7, 37, 88
Alcohol, and socializing, 38, 132, 140,
    201n(7)16
All in the Family, 14
Alternative companionship theory, 136
Altruism, 163

B

Baby Boomer generation, 68–69, 85
Bank accounts, shared, 10, 196n(1)36
Betrayal, by friends, 109, 110
Bob and Ted and Carol and Alice, 15
Breakups; *See* Divorce/Breakups
Butch Cassidy and the Sundance Kid, 15

C

Childless couples
    middle years, 73–78
    view of couple friendships, 37, 47–48
Children
    and couple friendships, 37, 47–48, 70, 87,
        115–116, 162
    divorce and, 44–45, 125
    and middle-aged couple friendships, 70
    and new couple friendships, 47–48
    and older couples, 87
Churches, couple groups, 159–170
Class; *See* Socioeconomic class
Cohabitation; *See* Partnerships
Commitment

    and friendship, 108–109
    and marriage, 7–8, 46
    and partnerships, 46
Communication
    and couple friendships, 46, 178
    electronic, 43–44
    and marriage, 10
Competition
    between couples, 91–92
    decreasing with age, 147
Competition hypothesis, 45
Confidentiality, couples groups, 164
Confrontations, 112–113
Cosby Show, The, 13, 14
Couple friendships
    as a buffer, 123
    affection and, 117
    and age, 6–7, 37, 66, 198n(4)6
    benefits of, 19, 177
    boundaries, 40, 57–58
    cautions, 179
    change in economic status, 62
    changing couple dynamics, 171–173
    child-centered, 37, 70, 115–116, 162
    childless couples, 37, 47–48
    common interests/views, 154, 161–162
    and communication, 46, 178
    comparisons between couples, 175
    and competition, 91–92
    confrontations, 112–113
    dating as couples, 148
    death of male friends, 98, 102, 103–104
    divorce and; *See* Divorce/Breakups
    and electronic communication, 43–44
    elitist/picky attitude toward, 81–83
    emotion sharing; *See* Emotion sharing
        couples
    empty nesters, 68–69, 80–83, 162
    end to, 111–112; *See also* Dumped/being
        dumped
    equality in, 81, 90
    and family, 11–12
    first time marriage/partnership, 37
    fluidity, 39–40, 197n(2)33